D0759626

LIBRARIES

DIVIDEND POLICY

Financial Management Association Survey and Synthesis Series

The Search for Value: Measuring the Company's Cost of Capital
Michael C. Ehrhardt

Lease or Buy? Principles for Sound Decision Making
James S. Schallheim

Derivatives: A Comprehensive Resource for Options, Futures, Interest Rate Swaps, and Mortgage Securities
Fred D. Arditti

Managing Pension Plans: A Comprehensive Guide to Improving Plan Performance
Dennis E. Logue and Jack S. Rader

Efficient Asset Management: A Practical Guide to Stock Portfolio Optimization and Asset Allocation
Richard O. Michaud

Real Options: Managing Strategic Investment in an Uncertain World
Martha Amram and Nalin Kulatilaka

Beyond Greed and Fear: Understanding Behavioral Finance and the Psychology of Investing
Hersh Shefrin

Dividend Policy: Its Impact on Firm Value
Ronald C. Lease, Kose John, Avner Kalay,
Uri Loewenstein, and Oded H. Sarig

DIVIDEND POLICY

Its Impact on Firm Value

Ronald C. Lease
Kose John
Avner Kalay
Uri Loewenstein
Oded H. Sarig

Harvard Business School Press
Boston, Massachusetts

Copyright 2000 President and Fellows of Harvard College
All rights reserved
Printed in the United States of America

03 02 01 00 99   5 4 3 2 1

Credits: Credits appear on pages 207 and 208, which constitute an extension
of the copyright page.

Library of Congress Cataloging-in-Publication Data

Dividend policy: its impact on firm value / Ronald C. Lease . . . [et al.].
     p.   cm. — (Financial Management Association survey and
  synthesis series)
   Includes index.
   ISBN 0-87584-497-9 (alk. paper)
   1. Dividends.   2. Corporations—Valuation.   I. Lease, Ronald C.
II. Series.
  HG4028.D5D579 1999
  658.15'5—dc21   99-28695
                                                  CIP

The paper used in this publication meets the requirements of the American
National Standard for Permanence of Paper for Publications and Documents
in Libraries and Archives Z39.48-1992.

Text design by Wilson Graphics & Design (Kenneth J. Wilson)

Contents

Preface

The two main categories of decisions that corporate financial managers make are investment and financing decisions. Investment decisions determine the size and composition of the left-hand side of the firm's balance sheet, or the asset section. Financing decisions determine the structure of the right-hand side of the firm's balance sheet, or the liabilities and equity sections.

Financing decisions also involve an important secondary type of decision—the dividend decision. The dividend decision, determined by a firm's dividend policy, affects the level of equity retained in the firm. If dividends paid are not replaced dollar for dollar by new equity, the dividend decision also influences the financial structure of the firm, at least temporarily.

For the most part, financial managers pay careful attention to their choice of a dividend policy for their firm. This level of concern relates to managers' belief that dividend policy influences significantly the value of their firm and, in turn, the wealth of their shareholders. However, some managers, and an even higher percentage of economics/ finance academics, question the value added of a carefully chosen dividend policy. Some go so far as to suggest that dividend policy is irrelevant. In this context, irrelevance implies that no matter how much care is taken in establishing a dividend policy, the action has no beneficial impact on the wealth of shareholders. The purpose of this book is to review the theory and empirical evidence regarding the impact of dividend policy on shareholder wealth.

In Chapter 1 we introduce and underscore the importance of the topic of dividend policy. We present a brief history of the evolution of dividends, provide economywide statistics on dividends relative to profits and capital investments, highlight the importance of dividends as a component of investor total returns, summarize the "mechanics" of dividends, and discuss what has become known as the "dividend puzzle."

In Chapter 2 we develop the basic stock valuation equation as a function of a future dividend stream. This equation illustrates the relationship of dividends to share price.

In Chapter 3 we present the results of the classic Miller and Modigliani study and demonstrate that, under the conditions of perfect capital markets (e.g., no differential taxes) dividend policy is irrelevant. We show irrelevance under the conditions of both certainty and uncertainty. Under certainty, future operating cash flows and investment opportunities are known with perfect certainty. Under uncertainty, future cash flows and investments are unknown, although the market has formed expectations about their levels and distribution. The conclusion is that a purely residual policy—paying whatever is left from operating cash flows after capital expenditures—has the same impact on shareholders' wealth as does a managed policy. Accordingly, and under these conditions, owners' wealth cannot be enhanced by manipulating the dividend stream to achieve a desired pattern.

In Chapters 4–7 we relax the conditions of perfect capital markets. We address the question of whether the presence of market imperfections (e.g., transaction and flotation costs, irrational investor behavior, taxes, conflicts of interest between managers and other stakeholders, and the differences in information held between managers and other interested parties) can reverse the conclusion drawn that under perfect capital markets dividend policy is irrelevant. After decades of research, the complications of market imperfections still plague us. The answers regarding which, if any, market imperfections make the dividend policy decision relevant, are still controversial.

In Chapter 8 we explore whether managers do manage their firms' dividend payments and, if so, how they go about making dividend decisions. John Lintner's classic study provides the backbone of this discussion.

In Chapter 9 we examine the evidence on dividend policies in countries other than the United States. The conclusions drawn suggest similarities in dividend policies and the impact on share price across countries.

In Chapter 10 we examine common stock repurchases as an alternative to paying cash dividends. Evidence is presented on the relative importance of these two methods of distributing cash to shareholders, along with the pros and cons for each technique.

In Chapter 11 we present our interpretation of how managers should incorporate market imperfections in designing dividend policies. We give advice for making dividend decisions. Since dividend relevance depends on market imperfections, managers must assess the impact of these imperfections on their firm, and its shareholders, for insights into how to tailor dividend policy.

Because of the enormous volume of research that forms the basis of this book, and because we do not wish to burden the reader with excessive footnotes, we cite all of our references to the finance and economics literature by author(s) and year in the text. We provide full citations in the Reference section at the end of the book.

We have attempted to provide a comprehensive integration of both the theoretical and empirical research on dividend policy, but we realize that we have not cited some of the published research because we had to be somewhat selective. To the authors whose work we have omitted, we apologize in advance.

Acknowledgments

We wish to thank Marjorie Williams and, especially, Kirsten Sandberg at the Harvard Business School Press for their patience in working with us during this project. Similarly, we appreciated working with Mike Long, Phil Cooley, Ken Eades, and Art Keown, editors of the *Survey and Synthesis Series* sponsored by the Financial Management Association during the protracted development of this book. Special thanks are extended to Mike, who supplied many useful ideas on the original design and coverage of this book, and to Ken, who assisted us greatly in refining the final version of the book, especially the concluding chapter on management implications. Among our respective colleagues, with whom we discussed our ideas for this book and who have provided us with important suggestions, we especially wish to thank Jim Schallheim of the University of Utah. Thanks to Keith Jacob, who read the manuscript and identified several problem areas. Finally, we owe a great debt to Judy Lease, who cheerfully edited the many drafts of the entire manuscript and secured permissions for copywritten quotes, figures, and tables.

This book is dedicated to our respective wives: Judy, Teresa, Sarina, Liz, and Yael.

DIVIDEND POLICY

Chapter *1*

Introduction

A starting assumption in much of the academic finance literature is that managers work to maximize the wealth of the firm's
shareholders.[1] Shareholders, the owners of the firm, elect the board of
directors that, in turn, hires, promotes, compensates, and fires managers. Through this board linkage, managers, at least in theory, work
on behalf of the shareholders.

In the process of maximizing the wealth of shareholders, managers
must constantly be concerned with how their decisions influence the
price of their firms' shares. Share price is the critical determinant of
shareholder wealth.

The specific focus of this book is how, if at all, managers' dividend
policy decisions affect common stock share prices and, therefore, the
wealth of shareholders. By *dividend policy*, we mean the payout policy
that management follows in determining the size and pattern of cash
distributions to shareholders over time.

This first chapter sets the stage for our inquiry into the relevance of
dividend policy by

- emphasizing the importance of dividend policy decisions,
- presenting a brief history of the evolution of dividends,
- providing important summary statistics that document the magnitude of dividend payments in the aggregate economy, and
- highlighting the "dividend puzzle" that has fascinated academics
  and troubled financial practitioners for over three decades.

---

[1] The mangerial objective of maximizing shareholder wealth is assumed in the first three
chapters of this book. For an overview of this objective, as well as additional references,
see Ross, Westerfield, and Jaffe (1999), p. 14. We allow for the possibility that managers
do not follow this objective when we introduce market imperfections, particularly in
Chapter 6 on agency costs.

In Chapter 2 we develop an intuitive basis for how shares are priced in the marketplace. We show that share price is simply the present value of expected future cash flows generated by a firm after deduction of its capital expenditures. This "excess cash" is not required by the firm for its operations or to fund future growth and, accordingly, should be distributed to shareholders. In Chapter 3, and under the conditions of perfect capital markets, we illustrate how dividend payments designed to achieve a specific dividend payout pattern that exceed the excess cash generated by the firm will *not* increase shareholder wealth.[2] In other words, the specific dividend policy that a firm adopts is irrelevant under perfect conditions! This conclusion is one of the most important developments in modern finance.

However, beginning in Chapter 4 and thereafter, our major emphasis is the systematic examination of "real-world" capital market conditions, including market imperfections, or frictions, such as taxes, to demonstrate how dividend policy influences shareholder wealth in a more realistic and complex environment.[3] Along the way we show how financial managers actually make their dividend decisions, how dividend policies vary around the world, and how share repurchases compare as an alternative payout mechanism to dividends. Finally, incorporating all the complexities of the marketplace, we attempt to prescribe how managers should set the dividend policy for their firm.

1.1 Does Anyone Really Pay Attention to Dividends? (*Or, Why Should I Care?*)

As authors of a book about dividends, we feel obliged to provide some motivation for you to continue reading this book. We are, after all, professors—and perhaps too preoccupied with "ivory tower" academic issues that are of little interest to practicing financial managers or investors. To provide a glimpse of what the real world thinks about the importance of dividends and dividend policy, we have drawn the following excerpts from the popular financial press.

- Income managers are worst-off in the hunt for new investments. Since early 1995, the dividend yield [dividends per share divided by

---

[2] Perfect capital markets are defined formally in Chapter 3. However, for the present think of these "perfect" markets as being free of taxes, transactions costs, and other distasteful factors, which we define as market imperfections, or frictions.

[3] We use the terms *imperfections* and *frictions* interchangeably.

share price] on the Standard & Poor's 500-stock index has plunged to 1.6% from 2.9%, as companies buy back stock rather than boosting dividends. To be sure, investors themselves favor capital appreciation rather than income, thanks in part to capital-gains tax cuts in the new tax laws. But strategists and investors argue a sizable number of investors still hunt—in vain—for yield. "Individual investors, with high net worth, or people who are coming close to retirement, want something in their portfolios that will give them yield or income," says Greg Smith, chief investment strategist at Prudential Securities. "They've been part of a wonderful three years in the stock market, but it's left them asset rich and cash poor." (*Wall Street Journal*, October 22, 1997, p. C1)

- Corporate managers around the world are clearly attuned to the tax consequences of repurchases as compared with dividends. Consider the case of Reuters Holdings, the London-based media giant, which suspended its move to effectively buy back 5% of its shares in October 1996, after the British government announced it would toughen tax laws on such deals. . . . Instead of using the special dividend structure, . . . "Reuters might consider doubling up its regular dividend." (*Wall Street Journal*, October 9, 1996, p. A18)

- Dividend changes historically are a lagging indication of corporate profitability and at the same time a sign that corporate boards have confidence in the future. Because dividend reductions are seen as a very bad sign, companies hate to raise payouts to an unsustainable level. (*New York Times*, January 3, 1997, Section D, p. 4)

- One big disadvantage of larger dividends is that they erode a company's cash cushion for recessions. All of the Big Three auto makers quickly burned through their cash reserves during the last recession five years ago, and they have been determined not to repeat the experience. Larger dividends and lower cash reserves also mean slightly less assurance to bondholders that a company will be able to repay them in hard times. As a result, companies with generous dividends tend to have slightly lower credit ratings, which raise their borrowing costs. (*New York Times*, May 17, 1996, Section D, p.1)

- Changes in dividend policy tend to coincide with the release of other important news concerning the company. Some firms, like Microsoft, pay no dividend because they can generate higher returns for shareholders investing their profits back in the company. Interestingly, there is evidence that investors typically underestimate the full importance of fluctuating dividends. In a number of recent studies, economists were not surprised to find that the share prices of firms that cut dividends underperformed firms that increased dividends in the 12-month period preceding the announcement of the cut. (*Detroit News*, August 4, 1996, p. F2)

- Elisabeth Goth, a dissident member of the family that controls Dow Jones & Co., raises questions about its dividend policy, contends Dow Jones has increased its dividends at the expense of reinvesting its earnings to fuel future growth. (*Wall Street Journal*, March 13, 1997, p. B15)

- Meanwhile, shareholders who enjoyed stock run-ups and rising dividends in the 1980s, are unhappy that Bell CEOs want to curb dividend growth and use profits to improve their networks and diversify at home and abroad. (*Business Week*, October 5, 1993, p. 123)

- Financial theory says that share splits, buybacks, and dividend cuts should not affect share prices, but they do because investors believe that managers are trying to convey information with these actions. . . . [A] dividend cut suggests that insiders expect profits to languish for years. These moves have gained their signaling power partly because investors do not trust managers to tell them the truth. (*Economist*, August 15, 1992, p. 14)

- According to Peter Blanton, a vice-president in Salomon Brothers' equity syndicates group, investors seeking to identify companies that are determined to raise shareholder value should look for classic, maturing businesses that are producing large profits. In addition, investors should watch out for large stock-repurchase plans, substantial dividend increases, and special situations that might spur management to boost the stock. (*Fortune*, February 20, 1995, p. 111)

- To capitalize on corporate America's success, investors should eschew stocks with rich current yields in favor of stocks with a decent yield that is likely to rise. Although many dividend stars of the past—drug and tobacco companies—have been devastated by price wars and regulatory threats, some companies with abysmal dividend records are now beginning to treat shareholders lavishly. (*Fortune*, August 22, 1994, p. 27)

These excerpts from the popular financial press illustrate that firms' dividend policies indeed have real-world relevance. Accordingly, we believe that the contents of this book will be of interest to financial practitioners, finance students, and finance and economics academics alike.

1.2 A Short History of Dividend Policy

Before beginning our quest to determine the impact of dividend policy on shareholder wealth, let's review the origin and evolution of corporate dividends. By understanding this evolutionary process, you can gain insights into the dividend decisions that managers make today.

Frankfurter and Wood (1997) provide an excellent comprehensive survey of the history of corporate dividend policy since the inception of shareholder-held corporations.[4] These authors note that early in the sixteenth century captains of sailing ships in Great Britain and Holland began selling to investors claims to the financial payoffs of the voyages. At the conclusion of the voyages, proceeds from the sale of the cargo and shipping assets, if any, were divided among the participants proportionate to ownership in the enterprise. These distributions were, in fact, payments that effectively liquidated the venture, or *liquidating dividends*. By this practice, claimholders avoided complex accounting practices, such as accrual accounting procedures. In addition, the liquidation of ventures minimized potentially fraudulent bookkeeping practices. By the end of the century, these claims on voyage outcomes began trading in the open market. These claims to outcomes were later replaced by share ownership.

Even before the development of modern capital market theory, along with the statistical measurement of the impact of diversification on portfolio risk, investors in these sailing ventures regularly purchased shares from more than one captain to diversify the inherent risk in these endeavors. Also, as in the modern corporation, investors provided capital for these ventures, while the captains offered their specialized skills—for instance, seafaring and management skills.

However, as time passed owners began to realize that the complete liquidation of assets at the end of each voyage was inefficient; start-up and liquidation costs for new ventures were significant. A track record of success for a captain, and increasing confidence by shareholders in the accountability of the management of the firm, gave way to a system of partial liquidation at the termination of specific ventures—dividends in the range of 20 percent of the profits but not liquidating dividends.

The concept of firms as "going concerns" without a finite life corresponding to the length of a "voyage" persisted and produced the first dividend payment regulation. Corporate charters included limitations

---

[4] This section draws heavily from the thorough review provided by Frankfurter and Wood.

of dividends to payments from profits only. By 1700, the British Parliament had passed two standards that regulated dividend payments: the *profit rule* and the *capital impairment rule*. The profit rule was intended to protect creditors from de facto liquidations of the firm to the benefit of shareholders. The capital impairment rule, which restricted transfers from retained earnings to dividends, was adopted to provide for the firm's continuing existence.

The success of the stock ownership structure of shipping companies spread to numerous new industries in the latter part of the seventeenth century—for example, mining, banking, retailing, and utilities.

The first U.S. enterprise with characteristics that are recognized in the modern corporation was chartered in Philadelphia in 1768. This firm had the catchy name of The Philadelphia Contributionship for the Insuring of Houses from Loss by Fire.[5] Dividend policies began to follow. For instance, in 1781, the charter of the Bank of North America specified that the board of directors "pay generous dividends" regularly out of profits. The 1790 charter of the Bank of the United States specified the payment of semiannual dividends.

The first dividend statute in the United States was enacted in New York in 1825 and was quickly emulated by other states. This new law made it illegal to pay dividends except from profits. An insolvency rule, first adopted in Massachusetts in 1830, prohibited dividends if the firm was insolvent and/or the payment of the dividend would create insolvency. Again, this regulation was quickly adopted by other states. Following the Civil War, the majority of northern manufacturing firms paid regular dividends in the range of 8 percent of profits. The general lack of financial information resulted in investors trying to establish firm value by analyzing the firm's dividend track record. The general increases in dividend payments were reflected in rising share prices. After 1920, U.S. firms for the first time began to "smooth" dividend payments, that is, create a relatively stable dividend payment stream less volatile than earnings. During the 1920s, average payout ratios grew to about 70 percent of profits.

Following the market crash in 1929, General Motors declared that all earnings would be paid out as dividends during "tough" economic periods. Large corporations distributed in excess of 80 percent of their earnings in the 1930s to restore investors' faith in the stock market. During World War II, dividends were paid with Liberty Bonds to help finance government debt for the war effort.

---

[5] We can only speculate on what the ticker symbol might be today for a firm with such an ungainly name!

In the years following World War II, corporate dividend policy remained relatively unchanged, and payout levels have stayed fairly constant. By 1960, the payout level for all corporations was slightly in excess of 60 percent. Management continued to smooth dividends and, indeed, does so to this day.

1.2.1 Summary of the Evolution of Dividends

The history of dividends began with the payout of liquidating dividends when sailing ventures were terminated upon completion and the profits and proceeds from asset sales were distributed to claimholders. However, due to inefficiencies induced by total liquidation, dividends began being paid from profits. Earnings were retained to finance new investments, and dividend payments became only small partial, or symbolic, liquidations.[6]

Frankfurter and Wood (1997) conclude their study on the evolution of dividends with the following observation:

> Our conclusion, based on this study, is that dividend-payment patterns (or what is often referred to as "dividend policy") of firms are a cultural phenomenon, influenced by customs, beliefs, regulations, public opinion, perceptions and hysteria, general economic conditions and several other factors, all in perpetual change, impacting different firms differently. *Accordingly, it cannot be modeled mathematically and uniformly for all firms at all times* [emphasis added]. (p. 31)

Note especially the last sentence in the quote from Frankfurter and Wood's article. In this book we document the success, or lack thereof, of researchers' attempts to model dividend behavior mathematically and relate dividend policy to share-price levels.

1.3 Profits, Dividends, and Capital Expenditures

Table 1.1 shows the annual time series in billions of dollars of after-tax profits, dividends, payout rates (dividends divided by after-tax profits), capital expenditures for plant and equipment, and the ratio of dividends to capital expenditures for U.S. companies since 1950.[7] Note

---

[6] Anytime a firm pays out cash as a dividend, or repurchases common stock, the firm has been reduced in size, or in a real sense partially liquidated.

[7] These data are taken from various issues of the *Federal Reserve Bulletin*. The figures are not adjusted for inflation.

Table 1.1 Profits, Dividends, and Investment ($ billions)

Year	After-Tax Profits (dollars)	Dividends (dollars)	Dividend Payout (percentage)	New Plant and Equipment (dollars)	Dividends to Investment (percentage)
1950	$ 22.80	$ 9.20	40%	$ 20.60	45%
1951	19.70	9.00	46	25.60	35
1952	17.20	9.00	52	26.50	34
1953	18.10	9.20	51	28.30	33
1954	16.80	9.80	58	26.80	37
1955	23.00	11.20	49	28.70	39
1956	23.50	12.10	51	35.08	34
1957	26.00	11.70	45	36.96	32
1958	22.30	11.60	52	30.53	38
1959	28.50	12.60	44	32.54	39
1960	26.70	13.40	50	35.68	38
1961	27.20	13.80	51	34.37	40
1962	31.20	15.20	49	37.31	41
1963	33.10	16.50	50	40.77	40
1964	38.40	17.80	46	46.97	38
1965	46.50	19.80	43	54.42	36
1966	49.90	20.80	42	63.51	33
1967	46.60	21.40	46	65.47	33
1968	46.20	21.90	47	67.76	32
1969	43.80	22.60	52	75.56	30
1970	37.00	22.90	62	79.71	29
1971	44.30	23.00	52	81.21	28
1972	54.60	24.60	45	88.44	28
1973	67.10	27.80	41	99.74	28

Source: Various Issues of *The Federal Reserve Bulletin:* Corporate Profits and Their Distribution, Section 1.48. The Fed obtains these statistics from the U.S. Department of Commerce, *Survey of Current Business.*

that, in 1997, U.S. firms paid out just over $275 billion in cash dividends, representing 56 percent of reported after-tax profits.

Over the forty-eight-year period covered in Table 1.1, after-tax profits grew at a compound annual rate of 6.6 percent, dividends grew at 7.3 percent, and plant and equipment expenditures grew at 7.9 percent. The average payout rate over this period was 52 percent. By

Table 1.1 (cont.)

Year	After-Tax Profits (dollars)	Dividends (dollars)	Dividend Payout (percentage)	New Plant and Equipment (dollars)	Dividends to Investment (percentage)
1974	$ 74.50	$ 31.00	42%	$ 112.40	28%
1975	70.60	31.90	45	112.78	28
1976	92.20	37.50	41	120.15	31
1977	104.50	42.10	40	135.72	31
1978	140.30	44.60	32	153.82	29
1979	165.10	52.70	32	270.46	19
1980	149.80	58.60	39	295.63	20
1981	140.00	66.50	48	321.49	21
1982	104.80	69.20	66	282.71	24
1983	130.40	71.50	55	304.78	23
1984	146.10	79.00	54	254.44	31
1985	127.80	83.20	65	387.13	21
1986	115.30	91.30	79	379.47	24
1987	148.40	98.20	66	389.67	25
1988	180.50	110.00	61	455.49	24
1989	172.60	123.50	72	507.40	24
1990	227.10	153.50	68	534.76	29
1991	234.10	160.00	68	528.39	30
1992	256.20	171.10	67	546.60	31
1993	300.50	197.30	66	586.73	34
1994	348.50	216.20	62	638.37	34
1995	424.60	205.30	48	a	a
1996	454.10	261.90	58	a	a
1997	488.30	275.10	56	a	a

[a] The Fed changed the definition of new investment in 1995. Thus subsequent figures are not comparable.

decade, the payout rate was 49 percent in the 1950s, 48 percent in the 1960s, 43 percent in the 1970s, 60 percent in the 1980s, and 62 percent for the first eight years in the 1990s.

Clearly, dividend payments are significant relative to corporate earnings and investment. Figures 1.1 and 1.2 show the pattern of dividends versus after-tax profits and investments, respectively.

Figure 1.1 Dividends versus After-Tax Profits

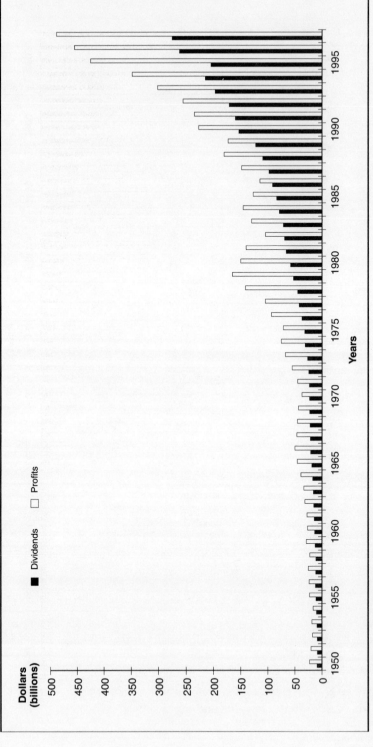

Source: Federal Reserve Bulletin, various issues.

Figure 1.2 Dividends versus New Investments

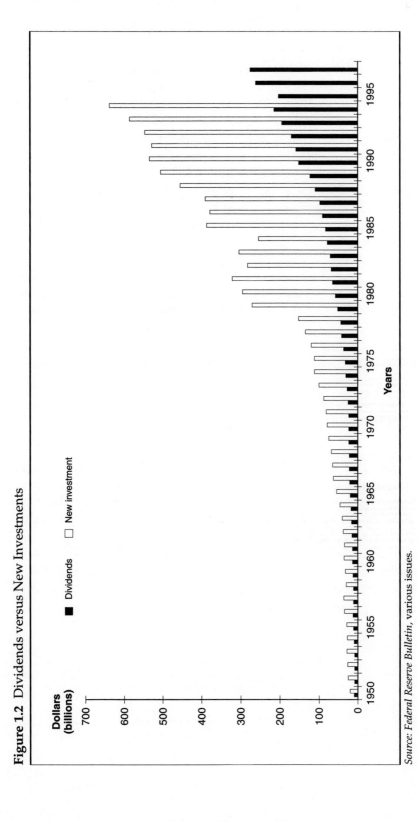

Source: Federal Reserve Bulletin, various issues.

The visual evidence suggests that managers, at least in aggregate, appear to continue to smooth dividend payments relative to earnings and capital expenditures. In other words, the aggregate data suggest that managers are "managing" dividends and that dividends are less volatile than earnings. To test this impression, we calculated the standard deviations of the annual time series of the data. The standard deviation was $72 billion for dividends, compared to $119 billion and $190 billion for profits and investment, respectively. These statistics confirm the graphic impression of lower volatility of dividends versus earnings and investments.[8] We examine the dividend patterns of individual companies in Chapter 8.

We call management's attempt to achieve a specific pattern of dividend payments a *managed dividend policy*. Alternatively, we call a management policy of simply paying out the amount "left over" after the deduction of capital expenditures from internally generated cash flows a *residual dividend policy*. In this book we frequently use these designations to differentiate these generic dividend policies. The significance of this distinction between a managed and a residual dividend policy will become obvious later.

1.4 Dividend Returns versus Total Common Stock Returns

Dividend returns also have been a significant component of total common stock returns, or dividends plus capital gains. Since 1950, total stock returns on the S&P 500 have averaged 14.14 percent without the reinvestment of dividends. Dividend returns have been 4.11 percent, or 29.07 percent of the total returns.[9] Figure 1.3 shows the annual relationship of dividend returns to total returns since 1950. Clearly, dividend returns are an important component of returns to investors. The evidence also indicates that, while total returns have been erratic from year-to-year, dividend returns have been quite stable.

---

[8] However, perhaps a more appropriate comparison of the "relative" volatility of these variables is the coefficient of variation, or the standard deviation divided by the mean of each time series. Here we find that earnings have a lower coefficient of variation (1.02) than dividends (1.10). Therefore, in terms of measuring absolute volatility, or standard deviation, dividends are lower, but in terms of relative volatility, the coefficient of variation, earnings are lower. The lower mean for dividends more than offsets the lower standard deviation and reverses the ranking.

[9] Ibbotson and Associates (1998).

Figure 1.3 Dividend and Total Returns

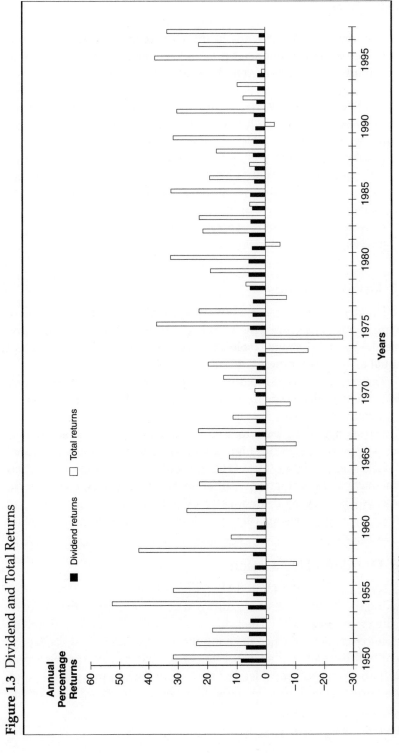

Source: Ibbotson and Associates (1998).

The "power" of dividends in influencing investment returns has not been lost on the financial press. Consider the following excerpt from an article that appeared in the *Wall Street Journal:*[10]

> Dividends get very little respect these days, and no wonder. For the past couple of years, they have accounted for only about 10% of stock-market investors' total returns. Capital gains are sexier, and get better tax treatment to boot.
>
> But over the long haul, it's a different story. In the 100-year history of the Dow Jones Industrial Average, dividends have directly accounted for about 40% of investors' returns. Throw in the gains from reinvesting the dividends, and you are talking about roughly half of investors' total returns.

1.5 Dividend Yields

Dividend yields, or annual dividends divided by share price, vary greatly across firms, even the very large firms that comprise the Dow Jones Industrial Average. Table 1.2 illustrates the dividend yields and annual dividends for these thirty companies.

The overall average yield of the Dow as of January 15, 1999, was 1.80 percent, with a range from 3.88 percent for J. P. Morgan to 0.39 percent for Wal-Mart. This average yield of the Dow is very low, historically speaking. Going back to 1905, the average yield of the Dow has been 4.30 percent. A record high yield was 16.60 percent in May 1932.

Given these data, you might naturally ask: Why do individual firms have such dramatically different dividend yields, and why do these yields vary so dramatically over time? These questions are among the many questions about dividends that this book addresses.

1.6 Dividend Declaration

Most firms in the United States pay dividends quarterly. After making the dividend decision during a board meeting, a firm's board of directors releases information on the size of the dividend on the *announcement date*. Further, the announcement states that the cash payment will be made to "shareholders of record" as of a specific *record date*. However, because of delays in the share transfer process, the stock goes "ex-dividend" two business days before the record date, or the

---

[10] Dorfman (1996).

Table 1.2 Dow Jones Industrial Index Firms: Dividend Yields and Annual Dividends

Firm Name	January 1999 Yield (percentage)	Annual Dividend (dollars)
J. P. Morgan	3.88%	$3.96
Philip Morris	3.32	1.76
Chevron	3.05	2.44
Minnesota Mining	3.05	2.20
Caterpillar	2.57	1.20
DuPont	2.55	1.40
Eastman Kodak	2.50	1.76
General Motors	2.47	2.00
Goodyear	2.42	1.20
Exxon	2.35	1.64
International Paper	2.27	1.00
Sears, Roebuck	2.13	0.92
Union Carbide	2.06	0.90
Alcoa	1.83	1.50
Boeing	1.67	0.56
AT&T	1.61	1.32
Merck	1.48	2.16
AlliedSignal	1.46	0.60
General Electric	1.44	1.40
Procter & Gamble	1.34	1.14
United Technology	1.33	1.44
Johnson & Johnson	1.28	1.00
CitiGroup	1.14	0.72
American Express	0.94	0.90
Coca-Cola	0.94	0.60
Hewlett-Packard	0.91	0.64
Walt Disney	0.58	0.21
IBM	0.49	0.88
McDonald's	0.47	0.36
Wal-Mart	0.39	0.31

Source: Data from *Wall Street Journal*, January 15, 1999.

ex-dividend date. After the stock goes ex-dividend, the shares trade *without* the rights to the *forthcoming* quarterly dividend. The dividend checks are mailed to shareholders of record on the *payment date,* which is about two weeks after the record date. Figure 1.4 shows the time line of the period from the board meeting through the mailing of the dividend checks.

1.7 The Dividend Puzzle

Based on the preceding discussion of the magnitude of dividend payments relative to after-tax earnings and investments—and the importance of dividends as a component of total stock returns—the following quote by Black (1976) may seem paradoxical:

> Why do corporations pay dividends? Why do investors pay attention to dividends?
>
> Perhaps the answers to these questions are obvious. Perhaps dividends represent the return to the investor who put his money at risk in the corporation. Perhaps corporations pay dividends to reward existing shareholders, and to encourage others to buy new issues of common stock at high prices. Perhaps investors pay attention to dividends because only through dividends or the prospect of dividends do they receive a return on their investment or the chance to sell their shares at a higher price in the future.
>
> Or perhaps the answers are not so obvious. Perhaps a corporation that pays no dividends is demonstrating confidence that it has

Figure 1.4 Dividend Time Line

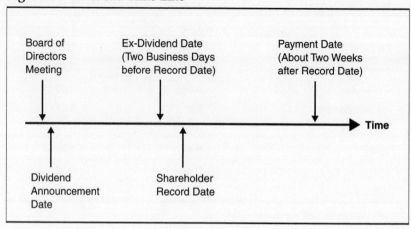

attractive investment opportunities that might be missed if it paid dividends. If it makes these investments, it may increase the value of the shares by more than the amount of the lost dividends. If that happens, its shareholders may be doubly better off. They end up with capital appreciation greater than the dividends they missed out on, and they find they are taxed at lower effective rates on capital appreciation than on dividends.

In fact, I claim that the answers to these questions are not obvious at all. The harder we look at the dividend picture, the more it seems like a puzzle, with pieces that just don't fit together. (p. 5)

Although Professor Black's observations were made two decades ago, financial economists still are wrestling with the "dividend puzzle."

1.8 Where We Are Headed

We designed this book to shed as much light as possible on the dividend puzzle outlined by Professor Black. To accomplish this task, in this book we

- minimize the use of mathematics,

- develop an intuitive basis for share valuation,

- illustrate the irrelevance of dividend policy in share valuation under the conditions of perfect capital markets,

- review and integrate both the theoretical and empirical literature on dividend policy, incorporating the various market imperfections, or frictions, such as taxes,

- describe how managers go about making the dividend policy decision,

- discuss dividend policies around the world,

- contrast dividend payout to stock repurchases,

- inject relevant real-world anecdotes taken from the financial press, annual reports, and other sources, and

- outline our recommendations on how firms should incorporate the market imperfections most relevant to them in setting dividend policy.

Now, let's begin our journey—toward an understanding of *Dividend Policy: Its Impact on Firm Value.*

Chapter **2**

Stock Valuation

The value of any asset, real or financial, is a function of the size, timing, and risk of the cash flows that accrue to the owner of the asset.[1,2] For the owner of a share of common stock, the expected cash flows are the selling price of the stock plus any distributions the shareholder receives from the firm while owning the stock.

Firms distribute cash to shareholders in two primary ways:

- cash dividends and
- stock repurchases.[3,4]

Historically, however, the most significant method for distributing cash from the firm to shareholders is via cash dividends.

In Appendix 2A we develop the valuation model for a share of common stock as a function of future dividends. All that is required to follow the derivation of share value is high school algebra plus an introductory knowledge of present value, or the time value of money.[5] To understand the valuation process and gain insight into how a firm's

---

[1] Real assets, tangible and intangible, are listed on the left-hand side of the firm's balance sheet. Financial assets, such as bonds and stocks, are listed on the right-hand side of the balance sheet.

[2] The motivation for any investment is to provide for future consumption. Cash flows from investments are a source of funds for this consumption and hence the source of value of the investment. Providing an estate for family members or a charity is considered a form of consumption.

[3] Inside shareholders (e.g., managers and board members) may receive cash in other ways, such as a variety of compensation plans.

[4] In a share repurchase, the firm buys back shares from shareholders. From the shareholders' perspective, selling the shares back to the corporation is equivalent to selling the shares to any other investor. We discuss stock repurchases in Chapter 9.

[5] Any introductory finance textbook provides the basics for present value calculations. For instance, see Ross, Westerfield, and Jaffe (1999).

19

dividend policy may affect its share price, we encourage you to work through Appendix 2A, unless you already are familiar with this valuation process.[6] However, for those who prefer to avoid the mathematics, we present the following intuitive explanation of stock valuation.

2.1 Capital Gains versus Dividends

Assume that you are considering buying a share of stock. How much are you willing to pay? The price you pay must be justified by the size, timing, and risk of the future cash flows you expect to receive, or

- dividends plus
- the selling price at the end of your investment horizon, however long.

But how is this future selling price determined? This selling price, less the price you originally pay for the stock, determines the capital gain you expect to earn on your investment.

Assuming that future buyers of your share are rational, these individuals are willing to pay your selling price only because they expect future dividends plus a selling price that justifies this price. Thus this original share of stock can pass through an infinite series of owners to an infinite time horizon.

2.1.1 Stylized Examples of the Impact of Investment Horizon

To try to visualize the process of share valuation, assume that a start-up firm will sell 100 percent ownership for $100 and, for simplicity, this ownership is represented by one share of stock. Further, assume that this firm has a finite life of four years and then will be liquidated with all proceeds going to the final owner. To simplify further, assume that the future cash flows are risk free, and that all investors require an expected rate of return of 10 percent per year on their investments, the risk-free rate at the time. Since the investment is risk free, the future cash flows are known with certainty, as if all investors had a "crystal ball." Based on this perfect foresight, the following dividend and pricing schedule is available.

---

[6] If you happen to be a finance student, your professors likely will hold you responsible for the mathematical derivations contained in the appendices at the end of this and the following chapters. To be forewarned is to be forearmed!

Time Period	Today, or the Start of the Firm's Life	End of Year 1	End of Year 2	End of Year 3	End of Year 4—Firm Is Liquidated
Share Price (dollars)	100.00	105.00	110.00	115.00	0
Dividend Paid (dollars)	0	5.00	5.50	6.00	126.50 (liquidation dividend)

2.1.1.1 *The Case of Four One-Year Owners*

If this single share representing 100 percent ownership is held by a series of one-year owners, each receives the required 10 percent return. The first buyer sells in one year, receiving a $5.00 dividend plus a $105 selling price. The $5.00 dividend plus $5.00 capital gain ($105.00 – $100.00) represents a 10 percent return on the $100 investment ($10.00/$100.00). The second buyer in one year pays $105.00 and one year later receives a $5.50 dividend plus a $5.00 capital gain, again a 10 percent return ($10.50/$105.00). Similarly, considering the dividends plus capital gains each year, this 10 percent return is earned by the third and fourth one-year owners. Alternatively, the price of the stock at the end of each year is set to provide the necessary 10 percent return over the coming year.

Note that over all four years of the life of this hypothetical company, the price received by the seller is the price paid by the next buyer. For instance, the price of $105.00 received by the first seller is paid by the first buyer. Therefore, when buyers and sellers are aggregated, all the transaction prices wash, except the price paid to the firm to originate the business by the first investor. The capital gains realized by each seller are the result of the dividend growth of the company (i.e., capital gains are caused by expected future dividend growth). The only real cash flows and source of value comes in the form of the dividends paid by the company.

2.1.1.2 *The Case of One Four-Year Owner*

The series of one-year transactions in the preceding example of four one-year owners nets out to the same share price as when one owner holds the stock for four years. Let's consider the case of one owner over the four-year firm life.

The buy-and-hold investor pays $100 and receives dividend flows of $5.00, $5.50, and $6.00 in years 1–3 and the liquidation dividend of $126.50 at the end of year 4. The present value of this dividend stream requiring a 10 percent return is $100, the original price of the stock. This price is independent of the share prices at the end of years 1, 2, 3, and 4. The $100 value today is the result of the dividend flows over the life of the firm, including, of course, the liquidation value of the share.

How is the price of $105 at the end of year 1 determined? That price is simply the present value at 10 percent of the dividends to be received at the end of years 2, 3, and 4. The price at the end of year 2 is the present value of the year 3 and year 4 dividends and, finally, the price of $115 at the end of year 3 is the present value of the liquidating dividend of $126.50 at the end of year 4.

2.1.1.3 *Summary*

The point of these examples is that the stock price at any specific time is determined by the expected future dividends at that time. Therefore, in the valuation of a share of common stock, the future prices of the stock are irrelevant; the determinants of share price at any time are a function of the future dividends and the required rate of return on the stock. This required rate of return is a function of the risk that future dividends will be paid.

Therefore the value of a share of stock is just the present value of the future dividend stream until the firm is liquidated. If the firm is liquidated in year N, the following equation can be used to value a share of stock as of today, or year 0:

$$p_0 = \sum_{t=1}^{N} \frac{d_t}{(1 + r)^t} \, ,$$

where

p_0 = the present value of the future dividends or the price of the share today;

t = the time of the dividend (i.e., $t = 1$ to $t = N$);

Σ = the summation of all future dividends from 1 to N;

N = the time of the last dividend received, or at firm liquidation;

d_t = the per share dividend at time period t; and

r = the required rate of return, given the risk of this dividend stream.

If the life of the firm is considered perpetual, an infinity symbol can be used instead of N in the preceding equation.

To summarize, let's step back and examine the real source of cash flows to a share of common stock. Fundamentally, a share of stock represents a claim to the cash flows earned by the corporation.[7] The only way an owner of common stock receives cash from the corporation is via cash dividends or a stock repurchase. The share price, current or future, must reflect this source of value.

2.2 Common Stock Valuation Example

In the preceding examples, the opening share price and the values of future share prices and dividends were given. However, let's use the same logic to value a share of stock in a more realistic setting. Assume that you don't know the share price. Perhaps the stock you are valuing is not traded publicly. Therefore you cannot open the *Wall Street Journal* to determine what the market believes the stock to be worth. Alternatively, you may want to develop an independent valuation of a stock and compare it with the listed market value to assess whether the firm is overvalued or undervalued.

Assume that you have carefully studied the firm you are valuing. Based on your analysis, you have made an *estimate* of the future dividend stream and an appropriate risk-adjusted discount rate. These estimates are shown in the following table.

End of Year	0	1	2	3	4	5	6
Expected Dividend (dollars)	—	1.50	1.75	2.00	2.25	2.50	2.62
Required Return, r (percentage)	15	15	15	15	15	15	15

After the year 5 dividend of $2.50, you estimate that the dividends will grow at a constant rate of 5 percent to infinity. In other words, the $2.62 figure shown under year 6 in the table is just 5 percent larger than the year 5 dividend of $2.50. The year 7 dividend would be 5 percent larger than the year 6 dividend, and so on.

What is your estimate of the share price today? For the moment, concentrate on finding the present value, PV_0, of the first five years of expected dividends, or

---

[7] A shareholder may receive cash during a corporate liquidation. However, this liquidation value is just another form of dividend, a liquidating dividend in this case.

$$PV_0 = \frac{\$1.50}{(1.15)^1} + \frac{\$1.75}{(1.15)^2} + \frac{\$2.00}{(1.15)^3} + \frac{\$2.25}{(1.15)^4} + \frac{\$2.50}{(1.15)^5}$$

$$= \$1.30 + \$1.32 + \$1.32 + \$1.29 + \$1.24$$

$$= \$6.47.$$

However, we have omitted a significant component of the share value: the value of the cash flows beyond year 5. From present value mathematics we know that the present value of a cash flow to be received in one year and growing at a constant rate to infinity is

$$PV_0 = \frac{CF_1}{(r - g)},$$

where

PV_0 = the present value of the future cash flow;
CF_1 = cash flow at the end of period 1;
r = the required rate of return; and
g = the growth rate per period of CF_1 to infinity.

This equation is often called the *constant growth model*.

In our share valuation example, imagine that we are transported forward in time until the end of year 5. We can rewrite the preceding equation as

$$p = \frac{d_6}{(r - g)},$$

where we have substituted d_6 for CF_6.

In other words, the share value at the *end of year 5*, p_5, is just the present value of the cash flows beyond year 5 . This value is the present value of next year's dividend, d_6, and subsequent dividends, d_7, d_8, and so on, which are assumed to grow at rate g to infinity. Using this equation and adding the present value of the first five years of dividend payments gives us the following equation for finding the present value of the stock today, or year 0:

$$p_0 = \sum_{t=1}^{5} \frac{d_t}{(1.15)^t} + \frac{p_5}{(1.15)^5}$$

$$= \sum_{t=1}^{5} \frac{d_t}{(1.15)^t} + \frac{d_6/(r - g)}{(1.15)^5}.$$

The first term on the right-hand side of the equation is the present value of the first five years of dividends; the second term is the present value of the year 5 share price, p_5. Recall that r is 15 percent and g is 5 percent.

Earlier we calculated the present value of the first five years of dividends at $6.47. The present value of p_5 is

$$\$13.03 \ = \ \frac{(\$2.62)/(0.15 \ - \ 0.05)}{(1.15)^5} \ .$$

The total share price today, then, is

$$\begin{aligned} p \ &= \ \$6.47 \ + \ \$13.03 \\ &= \ \$19.50. \end{aligned}$$

Therefore you estimate the value of the stock as $19.50 for a required rate of return of 15 percent and your estimate of the future dividends of the stock.

This example provides you with an intuitive method of share-price valuation. An important point to remember is that the share is valued as the present value of future dividend cash flows.

2.3 Dividend Policy and Share Price

Given the share-price valuation model just developed, consider whether the specific dividend policy that a firm adopts can influence shareholder wealth. Recall from Chapter 1 that by *dividend policy* we mean the practice that management follows in making dividend payout decisions or, in other words, the size and pattern of cash distributions over time to shareholders.

In Chapter 3 we demonstrate that, under perfect capital market conditions and if managers make optimal capital investment decisions, the specific dividend policy adopted by the firm is *irrelevant* to shareholders. In other words, one dividend policy is as good as any other dividend policy.

Appendix 2A

Common Stock Valuation Model

*I*f you're considering the purchase of a share of common stock and expect to hold it one year before selling it ex-dividend at price p_1, how much would you be willing to pay today, or p_0?[8] If you estimate the stock is in a risk class requiring r as an expected return, you would be willing to pay

$$p_0 = \frac{d_1}{(1 + r)^1} + \frac{p_1}{(1 + r)^1} \, , \qquad (2A.1)$$

where d_1 and p_1 are the expected year-end dividend and share price, respectively.

But why would the individual who purchases your share be willing to pay p_1 at the end of year 1? Unless you believe in the "bigger fool" theory, that buyer at the end of year 1 must believe that future cash flows justify the price p_1.[9] If that buyer also plans to hold the stock one year, receiving d_2 before selling the share for p_2, his or her expectation must be such that

$$p_1 = \frac{d_2}{(1 + r)^1} + \frac{p_2}{(1 + r)^1} \, . \qquad (2A.2)$$

Substituting Equation (2A.2) into Equation (2A.1) yields

$$p_0 = \frac{d_1}{(1 + r)^1} + \frac{d_2/(1 + r)^1 + p_2/(1 + r)^1}{(1 + r)^1} \, , \qquad (2A.3)$$

or

---

[8] Again, p_0 represents the price at time 0, or today. Selling the stock ex-dividend at the end of year 1 means that you will receive the year 1 dividend, d_1, *and* the selling price, p_1.

[9] By *bigger fool*, we mean that the buyer at $t = 1$ will be willing to buy the share from the prior owner without considering the economic fundamentals. The prior owner also ignored future cash flows at the time of purchase.

$$p_0 = \frac{d_1}{(1 + r)^1} + \frac{d_2}{(1 + r)^2} + \frac{p_2}{(1 + r)^2} \cdot \qquad (2A.4)$$

Following the same rationale, we ask how price p_2 is established and develop an expression similar to Equation (2A.2) in terms of d_3 and p_3. Substituting the p_2 value into Equation (2A.4) gives

$$p_0 = \frac{d_1}{(1 + r)^1} + \frac{d_2}{(1 + r)^2} + \frac{d_3}{(1 + r)^3} + \frac{p_3}{(1 + r)^3} \cdot \qquad (2A.5)$$

Repeating this process for $p_3, p_4, \ldots, p_N$, yields

$$p_0 = \frac{d_1}{(1 + r)^1} + \frac{d_2}{(1 + r)^2} + \cdots + \frac{d_N}{(1 + r)^N} + \frac{p_N}{(1 + r)^N} \cdot \qquad (2A.6)$$

As N approaches infinity, $N \to \infty$, the final term approaches zero because the denominator becomes infinitely large. Accordingly, we can summarize the expression as

$$p_0 = \sum_{t=1}^{\infty} \frac{d_t}{(1 + r)^t}, \qquad (2A.7)$$

which indicates that the price today, p_0, is a discounted value of all future dividends. Thus, even though no specific owner has the intention of holding the stock until infinity, the share price is determined by discounting this infinite future cash flow stream at the required rate of return. No future share price appears on the right-hand side of Equation (2A.7) since all future share prices are simply the value of expected dividends to be received beyond the time the share is being valued.

On reflection, this valuation process should make economic sense. Asset values are based on cash flows, and expected cash dividends are the primary conduit for cash to flow from the corporation to the investor.[10] Note that we have said nothing about the pattern or size of the dividend stream. Elements in this stream of cash flows may have any pattern and, in fact, may be zero.[11]

---

[10] In perfect capital markets, corporate share repurchases are a perfect substitute for cash dividends. We define perfect capital markets in Chapter 3. Further, corporate liquidation is another alternative, albeit unique, to cash dividends.

[11] This cash flow pattern is in sharp contrast to the promised cash payments for bonds where the interest and principal payments contractually are determined in advance at the time the bonds are issued.

Chapter **3**

Dividend Policy and Owners' Wealth

Given the share-price valuation process that we developed in Chapter 2, we now turn to the question of whether the specific dividend policy that a firm adopts can influence shareholder wealth. Again, recall from Chapter 1 that by *dividend policy* we mean the practice that management follows in making dividend payout decisions or, in other words, the size and pattern of cash distributions over time to shareholders.

3.1 What We Really Mean by Dividend Policy

In Chapter 1 we defined *excess cash* as a firm's internally generated cash flow less any desirable capital expenditure opportunities that are available. Project desirability is measured by net present value, NPV.[1] A project with a positive NPV is desirable and should be accepted to maximize the wealth of the owners. Conversely, a project with a negative NPV should be rejected. Following this acceptance/rejection criterion for investment projects is called *following the NPV Rule*.

If a firm follows the NPV Rule and distributes whatever is left from its internally generated cash flow, the firm is defined as following a *residual dividend policy*. The amount of the dividend is simply the cash

---

[1] NPV is simply the present value of a project's cash inflows minus the present value of the project's outflows. All cash flows are discounted at their required rate of return. In a positive NPV project, the present values of inflows exceed the present value of the outflows. Accordingly, the project "earns" more than the required rate of return. Accepting positive NPV projects will enhance shareholders' wealth; the projects are expected to earn a rate of return greater than the required rate, often referred to as the firm's *cost of capital*. Alternatively, projects with negative NPVs should be rejected; these projects earn less than the required rate of return and acceptance will decrease shareholder wealth.

left after the firm makes desirable investments. Obviously, with internally generated cash flows having inherent variability and desirable investment projects becoming available in an unpredictable fashion over time, the amount of the residual dividend is likely to be highly variably and often zero.[2]

Alternatively, managers may pay out more than this residual amount. In these cases, we say that the firm is following a *managed dividend policy*. If managers believe that a managed dividend policy is important to their investors and share price valuation can be positively influenced by the firm's dividend policy, they will adopt such a managed policy.

3.1.1 Stylized Examples of Residual and Managed Dividend Policies

Assume that a firm has forecast internal cash flows and capital expenditures for five years according to the data in the following table. Using these data, we illustrate the residual dividend policy and one of many possible managed dividend policies. Note that under both policies we assume that the desirable investment opportunities are taken and that the NPV Rule is followed.

Time	Year 1 (dollars)	Year 2 (dollars)	Year 3 (dollars)	Year 4 (dollars)	Year 5 (dollars)
Internal Cash Flows	100	95	120	115	130
Desirable Investment Opportunities	85	105	95	120	100
Residual Dividend Policy	15	0	25	0	30
Managed Dividend Policy	15	20	25	30	35
Managed Minus Residual Dividend	0	20	0	30	5

Under the residual dividend policy (row 3) any dividend paid is simply the difference between internal cash flows and investment opportunities taken. In years when internal cash flow exceeds the level of desirable capital expenditures, the residual is paid out as a dividend. In

---

[2] Firms should always pay out at least the residual dividend. Why? Remember, the residual dividend is the difference between the internally generated cash flows and cash flows needed to take all positive NPV projects. If the residual dividend is not paid out, the firm is implicitly making an investment in negative NPV projects—all the positive NPV projects have been taken. Any action that increases the cash balance of a firm is an investment decision and should be subject to an NPV analysis.

years when capital expenditures exceed internal cash flow, years 2 and 4, the firm pays zero dividends. Indeed, in these two years the firm must raise external capital to fund the shortfall in order to undertake all desirable projects.

Note the high variability of the dividends paid under a residual dividend policy. Under this policy, it would be difficult for a shareholder to predict future dividends. What would you predict for the level of the year 6 dividend?

Under the managed dividend policy (row 4 of the table), managers are managing the dividend level and growth; dividends are growing in even increments and are predictable. Shareholders would have much more confidence in predicting the dividend in year 6 ($40) than would shareholders under a residual policy.

However, where does the funding come from to finance the extra dividends under the managed dividend policy? Row 5 of the table shows the difference between the managed and residual dividends. In years 2, 4, and 5 the managed dividend exceeds the level of excess cash generated in that year. Money for this extra dividend has to come from somewhere; it must come from raising the needed funds externally to pay the managed part of the dividend.

3.2 Dividend Policy and the Miller/Modigliani Conclusion

In 1961, two future Nobel laureates in economics, Merton Miller and Franco Modigliani (M&M), published a seminal academic paper illustrating that, under certain simplifying assumptions, a managed dividend policy is irrelevant.[3] In other words, managing a dividend payment in excess of the residual dividend cannot increase shareholder wealth—all dividend policies are equivalent; no particular dividend policy can increase (or decrease) shareholders' wealth over an alternative dividend policy. This conclusion was greeted with dismay, contempt, or amusement by most financial practitioners as well as many academics.[4] The conventional wisdom at the time maintained that a managed dividend policy had a significantly positive impact on share prices and shareholder wealth.

---

[3] The seminal publication we reference here, along with their other path-breaking research in economics and finance, earned both Professors Miller and Modigliani the Nobel Prize in economics (1990 and 1988, respectively).

[4] The conclusions of M&M were greeted with a variety of strong emotional reactions, ranging from ridicule to admiration. However, over the years their analysis has stood the test of time, given the assumptions that gave rise to their conclusions.

Miller and Modigliani approached the question of the relevance of dividend policy using for the first time the tools of the economist. To avoid commingling too many complicating issues at one time, M&M framed their analysis in the context of a *perfect capital market* (PCM) with rational investors.

In Appendix 3A, we formally define PCM and rational investors. For a simplified list of PCM conditions, think of markets with all information freely available to all, no taxes, no transaction costs, and no conflicts of interest between managers and holders of securities. Rational investors simply prefer more wealth to less wealth.

In the appendix we provide the essence of the M&M derivation that illustrates the irrelevance of a managed dividend policy in cases of future certainty and uncertainty. Here we provide the intuition for the M&M conclusion.

3.2.1 The M&M Intuition

If the firm decides to pay a dividend over and above the residual dividend—let's call it the managed portion of the total dividend paid—it must raise an amount equal to the managed portion of the dividend in the capital market. Remember, all the firm has available from internal sources is the internal cash flow less capital expenditures, or the excess cash flow.

For a moment, let's assume that this extra financing must be repaid during the next time period. Further, let's assume that this financing requires a rate of return of *r*, or effectively the interest rate.

What will be the repayment consequences of this incremental financing next period? The incremental repayment in one time period will equal the amount raised for the managed portion of the dividend plus the required rate of return on this financing. Therefore next period's excess cash for the residual dividend will be reduced by this principal plus interest. Thus what the shareholders gain in extra dividends (the managed portion of the dividend) in this period, they give up in the next period plus interest at rate *r*.

You get it now, or you get it later! In present value terms, what is gained in extra dividend today is offset exactly by future dividends lost, which, in turn, are worth the extra dividend today.

Given the linkage of market value to dividends, an extra dollar of dividends paid out today over and above the excess cash flow available for the residual dividend will result in a loss of market value of *exactly* $1 since this price decline represents the present value of future dividends sacrificed. With PCM, which includes no differential taxes, this offsetting price decline implies dividend policy irrelevance. The extra dollar in dividends is exactly offset by the loss of capital gains of $1.

For instance, when the residual dividend is $0 but management decides to pay a managed dividend of $2 per share, management must raise $2 per share in the market at the rate of, say, 10 percent. The shareholders receive a dividend check for $2 per share owned. Simultaneously, the market recognizes that the firm has increased its liabilities by the managed dividend, which decreases the firm's ability to pay dividends next period by $2 plus interest per share, or a total of $2.20 per share.

What will happen to the share price? Since share price is the present value of future dividends—and next period's dividend will drop by $2 plus interest—the present value of this reduction per share is

$$\frac{\$2(1\ +\ r)}{(1\ +\ r)} \quad \text{or} \quad \frac{\$2(1.10)}{(1.10)} = \$2.$$

Hence the share price will drop by $2. The extra dividend is exactly offset by a loss of market value.[5]

What happens if the share price drops by less than $2 or more than $2? In these cases, an arbitrage opportunity exists in the market.[6] Savvy market participants will enter into transactions and earn higher than justified rates of return.

3.2.1.1 *What if the share price drops by less than the extra dividend paid?*

Say that the firm pays a managed dividend of $2 per share but that the stock price predictably drops by only $1. What actions can investors take to capitalize on this price behavior?

Let's say that the stock is selling for $100 when the firm declares a managed dividend of $2. The stock should drop to $98 on the ex-dividend date, but it only drops to $99.[7] How could you profit? You could buy the stock after the dividend announcement but before the

---

[5] Even if the $2 of additional financing is never repaid, our conclusion does not change. The firm will still have to pay financing costs annually of $2(r). The present value of this as a perpetuity is $2(r)/(r)$, or $2.

[6] In an arbitrage situation, the exact same good sells for two different prices. Traders can buy low and sell high and earn excess returns in the process. The buying and selling pressure will return the two goods to the same price.

[7] See Chapter 1 to review the dividend payment process and the definition of the ex-dividend date.

ex-dividend date for $100. You collect the $2 extra dividend and on the ex-dividend date sell the share for $99. You have inflows of $101 ($2 + $99) and outflows of $100, or a $1 profit per share times the number of shares you purchased, an arbitrage profit of $1 per share.

3.2.1.2 *What if the share price drops by more than the extra dividend paid?*

Say that the stock is selling for $100 when the firm announces a managed dividend of $2 and predictably drops to $97 on the ex-dividend day. How could you profit? If you own the share when the dividend is declared, you sell it for $100 just before the ex-dividend day. You do not receive the dividend. On the ex-dividend day you buy it back for $97. You had an inflow of $100, "lost" the dividend of $2, and repurchased the share for $97. You owned the share before and after the ex-dividend day and pocketed a $1 arbitrage profit ($100 – $2 – $97).

But what if you do not own the stock when the dividend is announced? In this case, you can sell the stock short just before the ex-dividend day and receive the $100.[8] On the ex-dividend day, you would buy back the share for $97 and close out your short position. You again have earned a $1 arbitrage profit per share ($100 – $2 – $97).

3.3 The Dividend Policy Controversy

Even to this day the M&M dividend policy irrelevance conclusion is not accepted by all academics or financial managers. Some strongly believe that a managed dividend policy can have a positive impact on owners' wealth or that share price will not drop by the full amount of the incremental dividend paid. However, if dividend policy is important to shareholders, some of M&M's assumptions must be in error. The assumptions that are suspect are the PCM assumptions; they must be at the root of our undoing *if* dividend policy counts.

Once we leave the idealized world of perfect capital markets and look at real world market imperfections, or frictions, the conclusion that dividend policy is irrelevant becomes much more debatable. Differential tax rates, security issue or flotation costs, brokerage fees, conflicts of interest between managers and shareholders, and differences

---

[8] In the short-selling process, you "borrow" the share from your broker, who "borrows" it from another investor, and sells it to yet another investor. However, since two investors now own the share and the corporation will pay only one dividend per share, you are responsible for paying the dividend to the second investor. Hence you buy the stock back, return it to your broker, and close out your short position.

in information between insiders and outsiders provide significant hurdles for drawing convincing conclusions regarding the impact of dividend policy on share price.

Let's now proceed to examine real-world phenomena. Will the departure from the perfect capital markets environment cause us to alter our basic conclusion that dividend policy is irrelevant? We do not pretend that the PCM assumptions are realistic. However, to destroy the irrelevance arguments, real-world market frictions and investor preferences will have to affect valuation *systematically* for dividend policy to become a relevant decision variable.

Appendix 3A

Dividend Policy and Owners' Wealth

In this appendix we deal with the question of how dividend policy affects owners' wealth or, in other words, the impact of dividend policy on share price. To appreciate fully the magnitude of this question, we must go back more than three decades.

3A.1 Miller and Modigliani

In the early 1960s, two future Nobel laureates, Merton Miller and Franco Modigliani (M&M) (1961), approached the question of the relevance of dividend policy, using for the first time the tools of the economist. To avoid commingling too many complicating issues at one time, M&M framed their analysis in a perfect capital market (PCM) context with rational investors.[9]

3A.1.1 *Perfect Capital Markets (PCM)*

Under PCM, the following conditions are assumed.

- Information is costless and available to everyone equally.[10]

- No distorting taxes exist.[11]

- Flotation and transaction costs are nonexistent.

- No contracting or agency costs exist.[12]

---

[9] Strictly speaking, the M&M analysis does not require that *all* investors be rational. Rational investors prefer more wealth to less wealth. Under PCM, rational investors are indifferent to whether a specific increase in their wealth comes in the form of a dividend or an identical increment to the value of their shares (i.e., capital gains). However, even the existence of just one rational investor, assuming that this investor has no wealth constraints, will satisfy the required conditions. Implicit in the M&M analysis is the absence of arbitrage opportunities (i.e., two identical assets such as shares of stock in two firms with the *same* risks and future cash flows cannot sell at two different prices). With PCM, rational investors would purchase the lower priced asset and sell the higher priced asset until equilibrium was reached (i.e., the prices of the assets were equal).

[10] This assumption implies that *all* individuals are symmetrically informed or that they all have free access to the same information.

[11] For example, taxes that discriminate between capital gains and ordinary income.

[12] Contracting or agency costs refer to the costs of managing conflicts of interest that may arise between classes of holders of securities or between management and holders of securities.

• No investor or firm individually exerts enough power in the markets to influence the price of a security.[13]

Miller and Modigliani's controversial (putting it mildly!) conclusion indicated that, given a firm's optimal investment policy, *the firm's choice of dividend policy is irrelevant;* that is, dividend policy has no impact on shareholders' wealth. In other words, all dividend policies are equivalent; no particular dividend policy can increase (or decrease) shareholders' wealth over an alternative dividend policy.

Their conclusion was contrary to the conventional wisdom that dividends were vastly preferred by shareholders, by some unspecified multiple, to retained earnings.[14] According to this traditional position, the more generous the dividend policy, the higher will be owners' wealth, all other things being equal. However, M&M proved that with PCM this conclusion is erroneous; with PCM owners' wealth is independent of firms' dividend policies.

In addition to assuming PCM and rational investors, as a first pass we also assume certainty with regard to our forecast of the firm's cash flows.[15] In other words, all aspects of the firm's future, including investment opportunities, are known with certainty. PCM and perfect certainty assist us in developing economic intuition on the issue of dividend policy without the serious complications of market imperfections, such as taxes. Later in this appendix, we introduce uncertainty with respect to the firm's future operating cash flows and investment opportunities. In Chapters 4–7, we relax the PCM assumptions to examine whether market frictions affect dividend policy relevance.

3A.2 Dividend Policy under PCM and Certainty

Imagine that we establish a brand new firm that is entirely equity financed. Although an all-equity capital structure is not necessary to make our point, this capital structure assumption simplifies development of our case. The all-equity capital structure allows us to avoid evaluating the *joint* impact of dividend policy and financial leverage policy on a firm's value. To simplify the algebra, we assume that dividends, operating cash flows, investment outlays, and new (equity) financing all occur at the *start* of each period.

---

[13] Therefore all participants are price takers.

[14] See, for example, Graham, Dodd, and Cottle (1961).

[15] From here on, when we refer to PCM conditions, we implicitly include the assumption of investor rationality.

The total market value of our all-equity firm at $t = 0$ is

$$S_0 = \sum_{t=0}^{T} \frac{D_t}{(1 + i)^t} ,$$ (3A.1)

where

S_0 = the market value of *all* common stock outstanding at $t = 0$;
D_t = total dividends paid at the start of time t on shares outstanding at $t = 0$;
i = the market rate of interest on all securities in all periods;[16] and
T = some future date when the firm is liquidated.

Note that Equation (3A.1) is just the aggregated firm version (the price per share times the number of shares outstanding) of the individual share-price version, p_0, shown in Equation (2A.7).

Recall from your introductory accounting and finance courses that the total sources of funds for a firm must equal the total uses of funds. This equality of sources and uses holds for each time period as well as over time. In equation form,

Sources = Uses

$$CF_t + F_t = D_t + I_t + (1 + i)F_{t-1} .$$ (3A.2)

where

CF_t = operating cash flows received by the firm at the start of time t, which depend only on previous investments plus any cash flows upon firm liquidation;
F_t = new equity funds raised at the start of time t; and
I_t = investment in all assets (including increases in the cash level) undertaken at time t.

Sources at time t consist of the cash flows from operation, CF_t, plus external equity funds raised, F_t. Three possible uses of funds exist at

---

[16] We easily could allow i, the interest rate, to vary by time period. Note, in the certainty case, the rate of return on *all* assets in any period is *equal*. This return equality is driven by the economic fact that yield differences are a product of variations in the risk or uncertainty of the cash flows generated by the underlying asset. Here we have assumed no uncertainty.

time t: dividends paid out, D_t, investments made, I_t, and the repayment of prior period financing, F_{t-1}, plus interest on those funds at the rate i.[17]
Rearranging Equation (3A.2), we obtain

$$D_t = CF_t + F_t - I_t - (1 + i)F_{t-1}. \tag{3A.3}$$

Substituting D_t from Equation (3A.3) into Equation (3A.1), we have

$$S_0 = CF_0 + F_0 - I_0 - (1 + i)F_{-1} + \frac{CF_1 + F_1 - I_1 - (1 + i)F_0}{(1 + i)^1} + \sum_{t=2}^{T} \cdots$$

Since we started our hypothetical firm at $t = 0$, CF_0 and F_{-1} are both zero. We have no operating cash flows at the start of the life of our new firm, and we have no prior period financing to repay. Thus we have

$$S_0 = F_0 - I_0 + \frac{CF_1 + F_1 - I_1 - (1 + i)F_0}{(1 + i)^1} + \sum_{t=2}^{T} \cdots$$

Note that F_0 and $-(1 + i)F_0/(1 + i)^1$ cancel. Similarly, $F_1/(1 + i)^1$ cancels with the third term, or $-(1 + i)F_1/(1 + i)^2$. Continuing, we arrive at

$$S_0 = \sum_{t=0}^{T} \frac{(CF_t - I_t)}{(1 + i)^t}. \tag{3A.4}$$

Equation (3A.4) expresses the current value of the all-equity firm as the present value of $(CF_t - I_t)$ for all periods t. The difference between operating cash flows, CF_t, and investments, I_t, is the "residual" or excess cash available for shareholders, or the cash flow from operations less the investments in all positive NPV projects identified for the period. This quantity is called *free cash flow* in the finance literature. Equation (3A.4) therefore means that the value of a firm's securities is the present value of the free cash flow it is expected to generate. Free cash flow also is available to pay out as a *residual dividend*, or the dividend left over from operating cash flows for shareholders after the investment decision. If the quantity $(CF_t - I_t)$ is negative, which means that positive NPV project investment outlays exceed operating cash flows,

---

[17] For convenience, we assume that the prior period's financing, F_{t-1}, is repaid at the end of $t - 1$, or at the start of period t. At the start of t, new financing, F_t, replaces the old financing. Incremental financing also may be obtained. Any refinancing assumption will serve just as well.

the firm must make up the negative shortfall by raising funds in the external capital markets—in this case, equity funds. Any other action would violate the NPV Rule.

Note that D_t does not appear in Equation (3A.4). Operating cash flows are simply a function of investment decisions in prior years, that is, prior investments made in projects that had expected positive NPVs. Since neither the CF_ts or the I_ts are a function of dividend policy under the NPV Rule, dividend policy is irrelevant. *Dividend policy irrelevance* means that paying out a dividend that exceeds $(CF_t - I_t)$ does *not* increase owners' wealth; it merely requires that the firm sell equity to finance the optimal investment plan. This conclusion holds in spite of the fact that the value of the firm is solely a function of future residual dividends and the market rate of interest.

If the residual amount $(CF_t - I_t)$ is not paid out to shareholders but retained by the firm, the firm implicitly has increased I_t since sources must equal uses. However, I_t already includes *all* wealth-increasing projects because the firm follows the NPV Rule. Therefore retention of all or part of $(CF_t - I_t)$ implies that the firm is investing in zero or negative NPV projects. Investment in negative NPV projects is suboptimal since it will decrease shareholders' wealth by causing the share price to decline.[18]

However, this conclusion may seem paradoxical. Dividends count (see Equation 3A.1) but dividend policy does not count (see Equation 3A.4). What kind of financial alchemy can produce this result?

A brief example may clarify the concept. The firm receives operating cash flows, CF_t, in any period t. The firm makes the decision to invest in all positive NPV projects, I_t, in that same period. If the firm makes a decision to pay out dividends in excess of $(CF_t - I_t)$, the firm must raise an incremental amount ΔF_t in the market to fund the *incremental* dividend, ΔD_t, over and above the *residual* dividend available. You can verify this assertion by reexamining Equation (3A.3), or

$$D_t = CF_t + F_t - I_t - (1 + i)F_{t-1} .$$

If the firm decides to pay an additional ΔD_t, it must raise an equal amount of additional ΔF_t in the equity market, or

$$D_t + \Delta D_t = CF_t + F_t + \Delta F_t - I_t - (1 + i)F_t . \qquad (3A.5)$$

---

[18] If the additional investment is in NPV = 0 projects, the value of the firm is unaffected.

Note that ΔD_t must equal ΔF_t, since sources must continue to equal uses.

Now, if the firm decides to increase the residual dividend with external financing, what will be the repayment consequences of this incremental financing during the next period? The incremental repayment will equal $(1 + i)\Delta F_t$, or the extra financing plus interest. Therefore next period's dividend will be reduced by $(1 + i)\Delta F_t$. In our example, where we retire incremental financing at the end of each period, we have

$$\Delta D_t = \Delta F_t = \frac{(1 + i) \, \Delta F_t}{(1 + i)} , \qquad (3A.6)$$

where ΔD_t is the incremental dividend paid in t, ΔF_t is the incremental financing raised in t to pay the extra dividend, and the final term is the present value of the incremental financing repaid one period away.[19] Thus what the shareholders gain in extra dividends in period t, they give up in the next period, $t + 1$, plus interest.

You get it now, or you get it later! In present value terms, what is gained in extra ΔD_t today is offset exactly by future dividends lost which, in turn, are worth ΔD_t today.

Given the linkage of market value to dividends, an extra dollar of dividends paid out today—over and above the residual, $(CF_t - I_t)$—will result in a loss of market value of *exactly* \$1 because this price decline represents the present value of future dividends sacrificed. With PCM, which includes no differential taxes, this offsetting price decline implies dividend policy irrelevance.

For instance, say that management decides to increase the dividend over the residual dividend by \$1 today. Therefore $\Delta D = \$1$. The shareholder receives a check for an additional dollar. Simultaneously, the market recognizes that the firm has raised an additional dollar of external financing, which must be repaid next period plus interest at i. This decision decreases the firm's ability to pay dividends next period by $\$1(1 + i)$. What will happen to the share price? Since share price is the present value of future dividends—and next period's

---

[19] If the firm refuses to cut the dividend next period by $(1 + i)\,\Delta F_t$, it will have to raise this additional amount in the market at $t + 1$. Then, in period $t + 2$ the firm will owe $-(1 + i)^2\,\Delta F_t$, and so on. Eventually, the "piper" will have to be paid, however. What is the present value of ultimate repayment postponed for n periods or $-(1 + i)^n\,\Delta F_t$? It will be $-(1 + i)^n\,\Delta F_t/(1 + i)^n$, which also equals the extra dividend in t.

dividend will drop by $1(1 + i)$—the present value of this reduction is $1(1 + i)/(1 + i)$, or $1. Hence the share price will drop $1. The extra dollar in dividend is exactly offset by a loss of $1 in market value.[20]

3A.3 Dividend Policy under PCM and Uncertainty

In the preceding analysis, we assumed complete certainty concerning all the firm's future cash flows. This assumption implies that the market has complete knowledge of the future capital investment outlays, I_t, operating cash flows, CF_t, and dividends, D_t. Thus, in perfect capital markets with certainty, all stock in all firms is priced to yield an identical (risk free) rate of return, which we have denoted i.

However, what happens to the conclusion of dividend policy irrelevance when we recognize that the investment, earnings, and dividend streams are uncertain? Distributions of possible future cash flows replace certain amounts. Under uncertainty, will the value of the firm still be independent of its dividend policy?[21] The answer is yes! The irrelevance proposition holds.

A frequently heard argument attacking the irrelevance proposition is that more certainty is attached to dividend payments received now versus dividend retention for reinvestment in projects whose future returns are uncertain. This argument has been labeled *the bird in the hand principle*. (You remember the old saying, "a bird in the hand is worth two in the bush"?) The implications of this logic imply that a firm with the higher dividend payment (or a firm with a more stable dividend payment) will be valued more highly.[22]

The logic of this argument can be refuted rather quickly if we recall the assumptions and the basic decision process. Remember, the investment decision is given; therefore the firm should follow the NPV Rule and take all positive NPV projects. Although the future investment opportunities and project returns are uncertain, investors have formulated expectations about future cash flows. Whether the firm retains funds to finance this investment program or whether it distributes the money in dividends and raises the necessary investment dollars in the capital market is irrelevant. The value of the firm remains unchanged

---

[20] Even if the $1 of additional financing is never repaid, our conclusion does not change. The firm will still have to pay financing costs annually of $1($i$). The present value of this as a perpetuity is $1($i$)/($i$), or $1.

[21] We can also view this question as whether the discount rate applied to the stream of dividends is affected by the choice of dividend policy.

[22] For instance, see Gordon (1959).

since in either case the *uncertainty regarding the future* is unaffected. In one case, the current shareholders bear the project uncertainty; in the other case, the new equity holders share in the uncertainty. It does not make sense to believe that one group (current shareholders or new shareholders) is willing to pay more for the claim on future operating cash flows and/or investments than the other. Using this logic, we see that dividend policy is irrelevant under uncertainty. We simply substitute the required rate of return on equity, r, for the risk free rate, i, in the preceding equations.

3A.4 Summary of Dividend Policy under PCM

Under PCM, and given the cash flows available from operations, CF_t, the investment plans, I_t, and the need to refund past financing, the dividend policy decision can be simply a *residual decision*.[23] To pay dividends in excess of this residual amount (see Equation 3A.5), suggests that dividends are an active management decision variable. We have shown that this managed component of the dividend payment is irrelevant in the valuation process so long as the firm maintains an optimal investment plan. Share price will fall by the amount of the excess dividend paid.

---

[23] Again, this policy, which is *no better or no worse* than any other policy, implies paying out what (if anything) is left over, or $(CF_t - I_t)$.

Chapter 4

An Introduction to Imperfect Capital Markets

To this point our discussion of dividend policy has been framed in the context of perfect capital markets (PCM) and investor rationality. We specified the terms of these conditions in Chapter 3. We established that the dividend policy decision is irrelevant, with or without perfect certainty, in the sense that a managed dividend policy does not add to shareholder wealth relative to a strictly residual dividend policy.[1]

Of course, real-world financial markets do not come close to satisfying the strict conditions of PCM. Transactions can be expensive to execute (e.g., individuals and firms incur costs in buying and selling shares of stock), distorting taxes do exist, conflicts of interest can occur among the firm's stakeholders, and information is not freely available—interested parties have different sets of information.[2] Further, investors may be systematically irrational. Therefore, in the *absence* of PCM and/or investor rationality, we can no longer dismiss the possibility that a managed dividend policy may have an impact on shareholder wealth.

In the sections that follow, we discuss three market imperfections, or frictions, that have been identified in the literature as potentially making the dividend decision relevant: transaction costs, flotation

---

[1] Recall from Chapter 1 that a "managed" dividend policy is where managers attempt to achieve a specific pattern of dividend payments that they believe will maximize shareholder wealth. A "residual" dividend policy is where managers simply pay out the "residual" amount after capital expenditures have been deducted from operating cash flows—managers pay out the "free cash flow."

[2] Stakeholders include all economic agents that have an interest in the firm's affairs, that is, shareholders, bondholders, managers and other nonmanagerial employees, suppliers, customers, and the like.

costs, and irrational investor behavior. These frictions have not received a great deal of attention in the theoretical and empirical finance literature. In addition, we consider them to be relatively minor in the total scheme of imperfections, and label them the *little three* frictions. Because of their prominence in the finance literature, and their potential impact on the dividend irrelevance proposition, the *big three* frictions—taxes, agency costs, and asymmetric information—receive expanded treatment in separate chapters that follow.

4.1 Homemade Dividends and Costless Financing

The essence of the M&M argument under PCM is that investors can *undo* any dividend decision a firm's managers make. If an investor desires to receive from a corporation cash flows that exceeds the dividend payment chosen by the corporation's management, the investor can create *homemade* dividends by selling shares of stock to achieve the desired cash flow level. As we demonstrated in Chapter 3, this reduction in the shareholder's ownership stake in the firm from the stock sale exactly matches the decline in share value the investor would experience *if* the firm paid the desired dividend. Consequently, regardless of whether the firm pays the desired dividend or the investor creates a homemade dividend via selling stock, the investor is equally well off. Cash flow needs are equally satisfied and the investor's remaining shares have the same value.

Alternatively, if the investor receives dividend cash flows that exceed his or her consumption needs, the investor can still "neutralize" the firm's dividend decision. The investor simply reverses the flow of unwanted dividends with an equal outflow to purchase additional shares. With this transaction, the investor's investment position in the firm is unchanged from the dollar value of the holdings absent the dividend payment.

Accordingly, investors can counteract any dividend action a firm takes with respect to a dividend check that is "too small" or "too large." If investors can offset any dividend action by corporations costlessly, then the firm's dividend policy is irrelevant from the standpoint of transactions costs. Managers are providing a service by their dividend actions that shareholders can achieve on their own.

From the firm's standpoint, if the dividend payment under the desired dividend policy exceeds the operating cash flow less positive NPV investment expenditures, the firm makes up the financing shortfall by selling new shares in the marketplace. Under PCM selling shares is costless, so whether the firm finances new investments from internally or externally generated funds is immaterial. Hence, from both the investors' and the firm's perspectives, a managed dividend policy is no different from a residual policy.

4.2 Transaction Costs

Obviously, the conclusion that shareholders and managers are indifferent to dividend policy, since any dividend decision can be undone, is correct only if investors can achieve their desired cash flows and ownership positions without costs. However, in the real world these transactions entail expenses in the form of brokerage fees, bid–ask spreads, inconvenience, and so on. Since it is costly for shareholders to achieve their desired cash flows by selling shares while receiving dividends is not, paying routine dividends that satisfy the investors' cash flow needs may be an efficient way to distribute funds to shareholders. If so, a managed dividend policy sensitive to the consumption needs of the firm's shareholders may be valued in the marketplace and result in a higher share price than the price awarded the same shares under a residual dividend policy.

A wide variety of investors, forming potential *dividend consumption clientele* groups, may exist in the marketplace. Each of these groups may have a unique set of cash flow preferences. On the one hand, high income investors may prefer to invest in firms that pay a minimum, or residual dividend, to avoid the inconvenience and transaction costs associated with reinvesting dividend receipts for which they have no immediate use. On the other hand, retired individuals may prefer a high and stable dividend stream as a means of financing their daily consumption and therefore may prefer firms with high dividend payout ratios. For these investors large dividend receipts save the transaction costs and inconvenience associated with generating cash flows by routine liquidation of share holdings (which effectively create homemade dividends). Moreover, these investors prefer a stable dividend policy (i.e., a *managed* policy) to an unmanaged policy (i.e., a *residual* policy) with its inherent instability.

4.2.1 Qualifications on the Impact of Transaction Costs

Although a managed dividend policy may save costs that shareholders incur, these savings do not necessarily mean that such a policy enhances share value. In a market that is perfect except for transaction costs, competition among corporations to pay dividends to a specific dividend consumption clientele that wishes to cut transaction costs may drive the value of this service to zero, since the marginal cost of providing this service (by paying dividends) is zero. When a match exists between the dividend policies of corporations and the cash needs of investors, individual firms cannot benefit by tailoring their dividend policies to particular clienteles. One clientele is just as good as another if, in equilibrium, all clienteles are served.[3] In such a perfectly matched situation, the specific dividend policy adopted by a firm does not affect share value.

In addition, and more important, several other market imperfections, such as taxation, agency costs, and information asymmetries, may exist and dominate the transaction–cost effects of dividends. Because of their importance and the substantial body of research that has focused on them, we discuss them in detail in Chapters 5–7.

4.3 Flotation Costs

While transaction costs incurred by investors who seek dividends to generate needed cash flows justify high and stable dividend payments, other transaction costs suggest that lowering dividend payouts is optimal. Specifically, firms pay hefty costs upon floating securities. Smith (1977) estimates that total flotation costs for underwritten equity offerings average 6.17 percent of the issue and are substantially higher for small offerings. Security issuance also may entail additional costs. If management's information indicates that the market undervalues the firm, selling the undervalued securities will cost the existing shareholders the difference between the securities' intrinsic (true) value and the selling price the firm receives. Whereas firms that issue securities incur flotation costs, firms that finance cash needs by avoiding or lowering dividend payments do not incur such expenses. Consequently, firms that need funds (e.g., finance attractive investment opportunities) may find it optimal to follow a residual policy.[4]

---

[3] By *equilibrium*, we mean that demand equals supply; no pressure exists for prices to change. The observation on the alignment of the dividend policies and dividend clienteles originally was made in Miller and Modigliani's (1961) seminal article on dividend policy.

[4] A residual dividend might not be optimal in a given period if the firm expects capital expenditure requirements to exceed operating cash flows in future periods. Under these conditions, a firm might pay out less than the residual dividend in order to retain funds for future investment opportunities and minimize the flotation expenses associated with equity sales.

4.4 Behavioral Explanations for Dividend Policy Relevance

To this point we have assumed that investors are "rational," preferring more wealth to less wealth. However, some argue that investors prefer a managed dividend policy to provide discipline in their investment and consumption decisions.[5] The starting point for this argument is the notion that individuals are both farsighted "planners" and myopic "doers." Accordingly, investors formulate logical long-term investment plans but have problems sticking with their plans in the short term. For such investors capital gains and dividends are not perfect substitutes, even if the present value of the eventual cash received is equal. Financing daily expenses from a stable dividend stream may be psychologically more conducive to following self-imposed plans. The implication is that the *form* of the cash flow received by individual investors is more important than the *substance* of the cash flow.

An example illustrates the central idea in this behavioral literature to which many of us can relate. Many individuals have difficulty in sticking to a diet when they have a specific weight-loss objective. Based on medical evidence, they know that this objective is in their long-term best interest. Accordingly, these individuals wish to avoid excessive eating but have trouble avoiding the temptation—they lack self-control. Obviously, if they had sufficient willpower, they could attain their goal without assistance. Lacking self-control, they may join a weight-monitoring program in which they buy a supply of diet meals and subject themselves to public ridicule if they do not follow the plan and lose weight on a schedule. Thus individuals have imposed the discipline on themselves to achieve their objectives. The proliferation of weight-monitoring organizations suggests that a strong demand exists for this type of external discipline.

How does this diet example relate to the issue of dividend policy? Most investors have long-term investment goals. By adjusting their consumption to the level of dividends received, investors substitute the discipline of the firm's dividend policy for the self-control they may lack if they have to routinely sell shares of stock to finance consumption: When financing consumption by selling shares, investors might sell more than the needed number of shares and "overconsume" in the short run. Therefore investors can avoid the necessity of repeatedly

---

[5] The following discussion draws heavily from the ideas contained in Thaler and Shefrin (1981) and Shefrin and Statman (1984).

deciding how much to consume by consuming only from the dividend stream of their portfolio (and other periodic income).

A similar form of dividend discipline is often imposed on not-for-profit organizations and other endowed institutions. These institutions' charters often restrict spending to the period's income, where *income* is often defined to include interest and dividends but not receipts from liquidated stock holdings. Such institutions may prefer holding dividend paying stocks over holding stocks where the dividend stream is to be self-generated by routinely selling shares.

Does investor preference for discipline via dividends leave its mark on share prices? Given the range of dividend policies observed, assembling multiple portfolios with any desired dividend yield, or payout, is relatively easy. Consequently, an individual firm is unlikely to be able to influence its value by adopting a specific dividend policy: It is too easy for an investor to duplicate a firm's specific dividend stream to justify a price premium for that firm. Thus, while the aggregate dividend stream of the corporate sector may be important to investors, no individual firm's dividend decision affects its share price.

4.5 Conclusions

Market frictions are the key to the relevance of dividend policy. If these imperfections are insignificant, or offsetting, the conclusion that dividend policy is irrelevant under PCM may continue to hold. We provided a summary of three of these frictions—transaction costs, flotation costs, and irrational investor behavior—in this chapter. However, in the total scheme of imperfections, we label these three the "minor" frictions. With respect to their potential impact on how dividend policy relates to firm value, the big three imperfections—taxes, conflicts of interest among managers and security holders, and differential information among market participants—seem to us to loom larger. Because of the vast amount of research on these three frictions, both the theoretical and empirical, we devote a separate chapter to each. Indeed, our discussion of these three major imperfections forms the backbone of this book. In total the discussion of frictions provides the foundation for recommendations designed to assist managers in tailoring their firm-specific dividend policies to the imperfections that are most relevant to their unique circumstances.

Chapter **5**

Dividends and Taxes

As discussed in Chapters 1 and 2, the market value of any asset (e.g., a share of common stock) is equal to the cash flows expected to be received by the owner of the asset. More specifically, market value is determined by discounted expected *after-tax* cash flows. Consequently, any differential tax treatment of capital gains relative to dividends might influence investors' after-tax returns and, in turn, affect their demand for dividends. Accordingly, taxes may affect the dividend payment decisions by managers who desire to maximize market value, thereby influencing the supply of dividends. As a result, financial economists have hypothesized that taxes might have important effects on *both* personal investment decisions and corporate dividend decisions.

This chapter presents the tax-related theoretical issues and available empirical evidence as they impact dividend policy. Here we cover the potential effects of the U.S. tax code and defer discussion of the international aspects of taxation. Even after several decades of research, many questions about how taxes influence the demand for and supply of dividends remain unanswered. With imperfect markets, our theory tells us that taxes should matter. The empirical evidence, however, is still inconclusive.

5.1 The Tax Environment

Current Internal Revenue Service (IRS) regulations tax dividends at a higher rate than long-term capital gains for individual investors.[1]

---

[1] The maximum tax rate on realized long-term capital gains, profits from selling capital assets held for more than eighteen months, is 20 percent for individuals. If the realized gain is short term (i.e., the asset is held for less than eighteen months), the gain is taxed as ordinary income. Taxes are not due until the asset is sold (i.e., unrealized gains are not

While historically this differential tax advantage of capital gain versus dividend income has existed, capital gains still had a tax advantage even during periods when the tax rate on realized capital gains equaled the tax rate on dividends. Because unrealized capital gains were not taxed until the asset was sold, investors could affect the timing and amount of their tax payments by choosing when and what securities to trade. Rational investors, for example, could selectively liquidate parts of their portfolios to minimize their tax liability (i.e., sell securities with no capital gains or with losses). In fact, unrealized capital gains can be deferred forever.[2]

How large is the economic value of being able to defer tax payment to the future? Postponing the payment of taxes can reduce the effective tax rate substantially. Consider the effects of deferring capital gains for twenty years. For simplicity, let's assume perfect certainty, an annual interest rate of 10 percent, and a capital gains tax of 20 percent. If an investor has $100 in currently unrealized long-term capital gains on a security and sells the shares, or if capital gains taxes are not deferrable, the investor will pay taxes of $20. However, if the investor can defer this same gain for twenty years, the taxes owed have a present value of $2.97, an 85 percent savings! In other words, the effective tax rate is lowered to 2.97 percent.

Deferring capital gains for long periods implies long-term investments. Does this strategy affect the liquidity of investors' portfolios? Does it force them to defer consumption to the future? Not necessarily. First, investors can borrow against their portfolios to finance current consumption. Second, they can liquidate unappreciated or losing parts of their portfolios and avoid taxes. Finally, they can create capital losses by short selling securities similar to those held. Exercising the losing part of this position will help provide funds for current consumption.[3]

---

taxed). The top individual tax rate on ordinary income, including dividends, is 39.6 percent. The top corporate tax rate on ordinary income is 35 percent. However, for corporations 70 percent of dividend income received from other corporations is exempt from taxation.

[2] Constantinides (1983, 1984) modeled this deferral feature of the tax code and labeled it the "tax-timing option." Financial theory tells us that investors should be willing to pay for this option. The market value of this option captures the tax advantage of long-term capital gains.

[3] However, the IRS imposes some limitations on such strategies. For a strategy to be feasible, the financial instruments should be sufficiently different so that the strategy involves business risk. Buying IBM long and selling it short, for example, is not a feasible strategy.

In the presence of a preferential tax treatment of capital gains, rational investors should have a tax-related dividend aversion.[4] Other things being equal, investors should prefer low dividend-yield stocks.[5] When stock prices are in equilibrium (i.e., supply and demand are in balance and no pressures exists for prices to change), dividend aversion requires larger *pre-tax* risk-adjusted returns for stocks with larger dividend yields. Tests of this hypothesis—a tax-induced positive relationship (correlation) between dividend yield and risk-adjusted returns—can be divided into two categories: (1) tests used to examine the relationship between dividend yield and risk-adjusted return; and (2) tests used to examine the behavior of share prices around the ex-dividend period.

5.2 Dividend Yields and Risk-Adjusted Returns

5.2.1 The Theory

The tests that examine the relationship between dividend yield and risk-adjusted returns were motivated by a model developed by Brennan (1970). Brennan's version of the capital asset pricing model (CAPM) states that a security's pre-tax excess return is linearly and positively related to its systematic risk and to its dividend yield.[6] A higher pre-tax return compensates investors for the tax disadvantage of dividends. The model implies that higher dividend yield stocks will have lower prices, all else being equal. The Brennan model can be written as

$$E(r_{it} - r_{ft}) = a_1 + a_2\,\beta_{it} + a_3(d_{it} - r_{ft}),$$

where r_{it} is the rate of return on stock i during period t, β_{it} is its systematic risk for period t, d_{it} is the dividend yield on stock i, and r_{ft} is the

---

[4] Not all investors have a tax-related dividend aversion. Short-term capital gains are taxed as ordinary income, and some investors are tax exempt. Corporations pay a lower tax rate on the dividends they receive. Furthermore, Miller and Scholes (1978) suggest a scheme whereby investors can convert dividend income to tax-deferred capital gains. If their strategy could be followed costlessly, investors should not have a dividend aversion. However, their method is costly, and the evidence indicates that investors seldom use it (see Peterson, Peterson, and Ang, 1985).

[5] Faced with investors' dividend aversion, corporations should avoid paying dividends to the extent possible. Why do firms keep paying dividends? See Chapters 6 and 7 for discussions of possible motivations for corporate dividend payments even when dividends have tax disadvantages.

[6] We assume that you are familiar with the CAPM and the concept of systematic, or non-diversifiable, risk, commonly measured by "beta." You can review these concepts, if necessary, in Chapter 10 of Ross, Westerfield, and Jaffe (1996).

riskless rate of interest during period t. If a_3 is significantly positive, the results are interpreted as evidence of a tax disadvantage of dividends. In other words, investors demand higher pre-tax risk-adjusted returns on stocks yielding higher dividends to compensate for the tax disadvantages of these returns.

5.2.2 The Evidence

The two most influential empirical tests of the Brennan model—those of Black and Scholes (1974) and Litzenberger and Ramaswamy (1979)—present seemingly conflicting results.[7] Black and Scholes (B&S) found no evidence of a tax effect; Litzenberger and Ramaswamy (L&R) concluded that returns are positively related to dividend yield. The current confusion regarding these studies can best be illustrated with the following quotation:[8]

> It is surprising that the results of such uniformly high-quality research can be so contradictory. One can only hope that the ambiguities will be cleared up in the future. (p. 499)

5.2.2.1 *The Black-Scholes Experiment*

Black and Scholes constructed portfolios of stocks and examined the effect of dividend yield on their risk-adjusted expected returns. They used a "long-run" estimate of dividend yield—the preceding year's dividends divided by the end-of-year share price. They classified a stock with a large estimated dividend yield as having a high yield throughout the next year. Using sophisticated methodology, B&S found no difference between the pre-tax risk-adjusted return of high-yield and low-yield stocks. They also found no difference in the after-tax risk-adjusted returns of those stocks. Based on this evidence, they advised investors to ignore dividends when forming their portfolios.

5.2.2.2 *The Litzenberger and Ramaswamy Experiment*

The results of the L&R test of Brennan's model are dramatically different from those of the B&S experiment. The former classified a stock as having a positive dividend yield only during its ex-dividend

---

[7] Among other studies testing the Brennan model are Blume (1980), Gordon and Bradford (1980), Morgan (1982), Poterba and Summers (1984, 1985), and Rosenberg and Marathe (1979).

[8] Ross, Westerfield, and Jaffe (1996, 1999).

months. Thus a stock that pays its owners quarterly dividends is defined as having a positive dividend yield at the ex-dividend month and as having a zero dividend yield during the other two months.

The L&R test involves three steps. First, the systematic risk of each stock, or its beta, is estimated for each of the test months, using the market model regression.[9] For the same months, L&R provided an estimate of the expected dividend yield for each stock in the sample. The second step contains a cross-sectional regression of excess stock return on the estimates of the corresponding beta and short-run (that month) expected dividend yield for each month between 1936 and 1977. The third step computes the statistical significance of the regression's coefficients. The L&R test documented a significantly positive dividend yield coefficient. Litzenberger and Ramaswamy interpreted their finding as support for Brennan's pre-tax CAPM; that is, they interpreted the positive dividend yield coefficient as evidence of a dividend tax effect.

5.2.2.3 *B&S versus L&R*

In their test, B&S failed to find any difference in the long-run risk-adjusted pre-tax returns of stocks that yielded high and low dividends. In other words, investors do not gain a larger long-run (e.g., annual) risk-adjusted pre-tax returns on higher yield stocks (i.e., no cross-sectional risk-adjusted pre-tax return variations). In what seemed like a contrast, L&R found that stocks provide higher pre-tax risk-adjusted returns during the ex-dividend months than they do in other months (i.e., they found time series pre-tax risk-adjusted return variations). However, L&R's results do not conflict with B&S's *if* they present evidence of time series return variation only. Later in this chapter we review evidence that illuminates this issue.

5.2.2.4 *The Miller and Scholes Critique*

Miller and Scholes (1982) raised objections to L&R's interpretation of their results. Miller and Scholes argued that the L&R results can reflect only information effects. They pointed out a possible information

---

[9] The market model regression is estimated as

$$R_{ij} - R_{fj} = a_{ij} + \beta_{ij}(R_{mj} - R_{fj}) + \varepsilon_{ij}, \quad j = t - 60, \ldots, t - 1,$$

where R_{mj} is the return on the market portfolio during period j, R_{ij} is the rate of return on stock i during period j, β_{ij} is the estimated beta for stock i for period j, R_{fj} is the riskless rate of interest during period t, and ε_{ij} is the error term. For more details, see Chapter 11 in Ross, Westerfield, and Jaffe (1996).

induced bias in the L&R test of Brennan's model. The L&R method ignored announcements of dividend omissions, since omissions are not reported on the Center for Research in Security Prices (CRSP) tapes from which they obtained their data. An omission following a positive expected dividend is an announcement of a dividend reduction, which the market perceives as bad news. Ignoring omissions, L&R's method relates the resulting negative excess return (by assuming that it is not an ex-dividend month) to a zero expected dividend. This technical association can create a positive cross-sectional relationship between L&R's estimate of expected dividend yield and measured stock returns.

Litzenberger and Ramaswamy (1982) addressed this criticism by using alternative measures of expected short-term dividend yields that they based only on past information. In these tests, they assumed that stocks had positive expected dividends only during their ex-dividend months. These experiments resulted in statistically significant and positive dividend yield coefficients.

More recently, Kalay and Michaely (1993) (K&M) performed a modified L&R experiment, using weekly returns. They limited the sample to cases in which the dividend is announced during the week preceding the ex-dividend week (96.6 percent of the sample), excluding weeks containing dividend omissions. They still found a significantly positive dividend yield coefficient. Interestingly, this coefficient is almost identical to the one reported by L&R (obtained using monthly returns). Accordingly, the empirical evidence is inconsistent with the M&S conjecture that a positive dividend yield coefficient is the result of information induced biases.

Later we present an additional analysis of the relationships between dividend yields and pre-tax risk-adjusted returns. However, we first examine the other category of tests regarding the interaction of dividends and risk-adjusted returns, the ex-dividend day studies.

5.3 The Ex-Dividend Day Studies

5.3.1 The Theory

Studying the ex-dividend period is important because a direct comparison can be made between the market valuation of a dollar of dividend to the valuation of a dollar of realized capital gains. Recall from Chapter 1 that three important dates exist in every dividend period: the announcement day, the ex-dividend day, and the payment day.

On the announcement day the firm declares the dividend per share to be paid on the payment date to its shareholders of record on the last cum (with)-dividend day. The ex-dividend day is about two weeks after the announcement day and about two weeks before the payment day. Thus a stock purchased on the day before the ex-dividend day, the last cum-dividend day, includes a claim to the dividend declared (to be paid two weeks later). If the stock is purchased on the ex-dividend day, the buyer will not receive the dividend on the payment day. The ex-dividend price therefore should be lower than the cum-dividend price to reflect the lost dividend.

The theoretical analysis of share price behavior around the ex-dividend day compares the expected price drop to the dividend per share.[10] In perfect markets, assuming certainty, the share-price drop should equal the dividend per share. Any other share-price behavior provides arbitrage opportunities. A smaller (larger) price drop provides arbitrage profits for buying (selling short) on the cum-dividend day and selling (covering) on the ex-dividend day. A similar conclusion can be drawn under uncertainty if we assume that any excessive ex-dividend period risk is not reflected in the share price (i.e., the risk is not priced). This occurs if the risk is diversifiable and/or investors are indifferent to risk.[11]

Now, let's assume that the required rate of return for the ex-dividend period is no different from that for any other day. Since investors are interested in after-tax returns, differential taxation of realized capital gains and dividend income should affect the analysis. Elton and Gruber (1970) specified the conditions for "no profit" opportunities around the ex-dividend day in the presence of tax differentials.

---

[10] Earlier works on this issue were Campbell and Breanek (1955) and Barker (1959).

[11] Uncertainty affects the behavior of ex-dividend day traders. They can base an estimate of the expected ex-dividend day price drop on past ex-dividend days. In general, financial economists expect these estimates to be unbiased (i.e., on average, correct). Nevertheless, taking a position (long or short) to exploit profit opportunities around the ex-dividend day involves risk. Thus a difference between the expected ex-dividend day price drop and the dividend per share can provide profits but not riskless arbitrage opportunities. Indeed empirically, the period is a time of excessive volatility (see Lakonishok and Vermaelen 1986). The possible effects of risk on ex-dividend day trading are pointed out in Kalay (1984) and modeled in Heath and Jarrow (1988) and in Michaely and Vila (1995). If unusually large nondiversifiable risk exists during the ex-dividend period, the ex-dividend day price drop should be smaller than the dividend per share, giving shareholders their larger required rate of return. However, numerous ex-dividend events exist in any given calendar year, presenting substantial diversification possibilities. Investors also can hedge part of the risk by using options. Because of the risk reduction technology and the short time interval between closing on cum-dividend day and the opening on the ex-dividend day, the ex-dividend price drop should be "almost equal" to the dividend per share.

Equating the after-tax returns from capital gains to the after-tax returns from dividends results in

$$(1 - t_g)[E(P_a) - P_b] = (1 - t_d)D$$

and

$$\frac{E(P_a) - P_b}{D} = \frac{(1 - t_d)}{(1 - t_g)},$$

where t_g is the realized capital gains tax; t_d is the tax on ordinary income, or dividends; D is the dividend per share; P_b is the last cum-dividend share price (before); and $E(P_a)$ is the expected ex-dividend share price (after) for $t_g > t_d$. A larger tax on dividend income (i.e., $t_d > t_g$) results in an ex-dividend price drop smaller than the dividend per share. In such an economy the investors' marginal tax rates can be inferred from the relative price drop on the ex-dividend day.[12]

Elton and Gruber present empirical evidence showing that the ex-dividend price drop is smaller than the dividend per share. Taken at face value, this evidence is consistent with the hypothesis that investors have a tax-induced preference for capital gains. The story, however, is not that simple. Short-term capital gains are taxed as ordinary income. Thus, as Kalay (1982a) pointed out, an ex-dividend day share price drop smaller than the dividend per share provides profit opportunities for the short-term trader. Take a simple example. Let's say that the cum-dividend share price is $50, the dividend per share is $2, and the expected ex-dividend day price drop is 70 percent of the dividend per share, or $1.40. A short-term investor can buy the stock cum-dividend and sell it on the morning of the ex-dividend day. He or she would have a capital loss of $1.40 but would gain $2 in cash dividends. In other words, the expected pre-tax gain is $0.60 per share. If we assume a 50 percent tax bracket, the investor's net gain is $0.30 per share. This net gain is a daily percentage excess return of 0.6% which corresponds to an annual excess return of 788%!

Kalay (1982a) argues that without transaction costs, elimination of profit opportunities implies an expected ex-dividend price drop equal

---

[12] Prior to the Tax Reform Act of 1986, long-term capital gains were taxed at 40 percent of the personal individual tax rate. Therefore the marginal relative and absolute tax rates could have been calculated.

to the dividend per share.[13] Of course, limitations exist on the amount of short-term capital losses individuals can write off to offset dividend income (about $3,000 a year). Nevertheless, dealers are not subject to such limitations. Accordingly, they would eliminate any difference between the expected ex-dividend day price drop and the dividend per share.

Must the expected ex-dividend day price drop and the dividend per share be equal? Not necessarily. Consider the case of corporations investing in other corporations. As shareholders in other firms, corporations are taxed on only 70 percent of the cash dividends they receive. Realized capital gains are taxed at the corporate income tax rate. Thus for a corporation an expected ex-dividend day price drop that equals the dividend per share still provides profit opportunities. Let's return to the preceding example and assume now that the share price drops by $2. The firm pays tax, but on only 30 percent of the $2 dividend per share it receives, while it can deduct the full $2 capital loss. If we assume a 35 percent corporate tax rate, the per share after-tax dividend it receives is $1.79, whereas its per share after-tax capital loss is only $1.30. The net gain therefore is $0.49, or a return on investment of about 1 percent per day, which is equivalent to a 3,415 percent annual return!

Such a corporate practice is common and is called *dividend capture*. Firms trade around the ex-dividend day to take advantage of their favorable tax status. Dividend capture programs became so wide spread in the United States that the government imposed limitations on their use.[14] Since 1984, a corporation has had to own the stock for at least forty-five days to qualify for the 70 percent exclusion on its dividend income. What relationship between the dividend per share and the expected price drop would amount to "no profit" opportunities around the ex-dividend day for a corporate investor? The ex-dividend day price drop should exceed the dividend per share, so, in our example, a $2 dividend should correspond to a $2.72 expected share-price drop.

---

[13] This statement assumes that the required rate of return during the cum–ex-dividend period is arbitrarily close to zero and thus can be ignored. Also ignored are the trivial effects of the delayed payments of dividends. The actual payments are received about two weeks following the ex-dividend day; hence the realized capital losses should be compared to the present value of the dividends. The appropriate discount rate, in this case, is the risk-free rate, since we know of no default on a promised dividend. The potential effects of such modification are indeed trivial. A $2.00 dividend, for example, has a present value of about $1.998.

[14] Karpoff and Walking (1988) found evidence of price effects of short-term trading around the ex-dividend days of high-yield stocks. The volume of short-term trading seems negatively correlated to the level of transaction costs.

What is the equilibrium ex-dividend day price drop? Interestingly, in the absence of transaction costs, no equilibrium exists. The differential tax treatment of major economic players creates a large variety of relative valuation of dividends and capital gains. Any relative valuation of these cash flows in the market results in profit opportunities for some groups. On the one hand, if the ex-dividend day share-price drop equals the dividend per share, corporations can profit from dividend capture activity. On the other hand, if the ex-dividend day share-price drop is larger than the dividend per share, long-term investors would profit from timing their trades (selling before the ex-dividend date). Moreover, short-term traders would profit from shorting the stock cum-dividend and covering their positions on the ex-dividend day.[15]

Interestingly, transaction costs enable the existence of an ex-dividend day equilibrium. They provide a variety of relationships between the expected share-price drop and the dividend per share that are consistent with no profit opportunities. The only requirement is that the potential profits stemming from the different relative valuations be smaller than the costs of a round-trip transaction. Consequently, as Kalay points out, the marginal tax rates of the marginal investors cannot be inferred from the relative ex-dividend day price drop. Further, the relative ex-dividend price drop can be anywhere within the bounds where no profit opportunities exist.

5.3.2 The Evidence

The early studies of the ex-dividend day behavior of share prices document a price drop significantly smaller than the dividend per share.[16] Some subsequent empirical results support these findings.[17] Although we have no theory to link the relative ex-dividend day price drop to taxes, the evidence is consistent with the hypothesis that a dollar of capital gains is worth more than a dollar of dividends. However, further investigations of this behavior cast serious doubt on this explanation.

Indeed, the more empirical evidence on ex-dividend day behavior of share prices we obtain, the harder it becomes to interpret. Eades, Hess, and Kim (1984), for example, found positive excess returns be-

---

[15] See Dammon and Green (1987), and Dybvig and Ross (1986).

[16] See Campbell and Breanek (1955), Durand and May (1960), and Elton and Gruber (1970).

[17] See Kalay (1982a), Lakonishock and Vermaelen (1983), and Eades, Hess, and Kim (1984).

fore and including the ex-dividend day and abnormally negative returns following the ex-dividend day. In fact, the abnormal returns on the ex-dividend day were smaller than the excess return on the last cum-dividend day.

We reproduced Table 5 from Eades, Hess, and Kim as our Table 5.1. It shows that the cumulative excess return from day –5 to (and including) day 0 (the ex-dividend day) is 0.43 percent, whereas the ex-dividend day excess return is only 0.142 percent. The cumulative negative excess return from day +1 to day +5 is –0.24 percent. How can the theory explain the relatively large and systematic price changes before and following the ex-dividend day? What is the reason for a cumulative excess return of 0.288 percent during the five days preceding the ex-dividend day? Why can't professional investors with trivial transaction costs time their trades to exploit this phenomenon?

To help quantify the relationship between the excess return and the relative ex-dividend day share-price drop, note that the mean quarterly dividend yield is about 1 percent. For such an average stock, a relative ex-dividend day price drop of 0.85 (a price drop equal to 85 percent of the dividend per share) results in a 0.15 excess return. A strategy of owning the stock from day –5 to day 0 gives an excess return of 0.43 percent (equivalent to a relative price drop of 0.57). If you own a portfolio of stocks between day –5 and day +5, you will obtain an excess return of 0.24 percent (equivalent to a relative price drop of 0.76). Is this consistent with no profit opportunities around the ex-dividend day?

Corporate dividend capture activity cannot explain the unusual behavior of share prices during the ex-dividend period. Corporate tax preferences for dividends should lead to a negative (with dividend) ex-dividend day return. However, the evidence indicates that dividend capturing provides excess returns.

The results of additional Eades, Hess, and Kim's tests are even more puzzling. Table 7 of their article describes the behavior of share prices around the ex-dividend day of stock dividends and of nontaxable cash dividends. Interestingly, a similar pattern emerges. A strategy of buying stocks five days before the ex-dividend day and selling them on day +5, yields an excess return of 1.061 percent. A strategy of buying stocks on day –5 of nontaxable dividend and selling them on day +1 yields an excess return of 0.52 percent. Selling these stocks short on day 0 and covering on day +5 yields almost identical returns. Taxes have nothing to do with this share-price behavior. This evidence suggests that taxes are not a likely explanation of the ex-dividend day empirical regularities.

Table 5.1 Excess Returns before and Including the Ex-Dividend Day

Tests of the null hypothesis of zero excess returns for the ex-dividend period with a sample of all taxable distributions by N.Y.S.E. common stocks. Average daily excess and standardized daily excess returns of equally weighted ex-dividend day portfolios for each day in the ex-dividend period for the period July 2, 1962, to December 31, 1980. The number of ex-dividend day portfolios is 4,471, the number of trading days is 4,640, and the average number of stocks in each ex-dividend day portfolio is 18.6.

Trading Day Relative to Ex-Day	Average Percentage Excess Return[a]	Average Standardized Excess Return[b]	t-Statistic	Significance Level	Posterior Odds Ratios[c]	
					Uniform	Normal
−5	0.067	0.0631	4.218	<10⁻⁴	0.0073	0.0005
−4	0.046	0.0621	4.155	<10⁻⁴	0.0095	0.0006
−3	0.061	0.0832	5.561	<10⁻⁴	<10⁻⁴	<10⁻⁴
−2	0.066	0.0892	5.968	<10⁻⁴	<10⁻⁴	<10⁻⁴
−1	0.188	0.2340	15.647	<10⁻⁴	<10⁻⁴	<10⁻⁴
Ex-dividend day (0)	0.142	0.1756	11.741	<10⁻⁴	<10⁻⁴	<10⁻⁴
+1	−0.053	−0.0651	−4.355	<10⁻⁴	0.0041	0.0003
+2	−0.058	−0.0734	−4.911	<10⁻⁴	0.0003	<10⁻⁴
+3	−0.036	−0.0405	−2.707	0.0068	1.366	0.0824
+4	−0.046	−0.0627	−4.195	<10⁻⁴	0.0080	0.0005
+5	−0.043	−0.0553	−3.700	0.0002	0.0569	0.0037

Source: Eades, Hess, and Kim (1984), p. 20.

[a] Excess return equals the difference between the ex-dividend day portfolio return on day t and RP_t (the mean portfolio return for day t estimated during the sixty-day period surrounding the ex-dividend day).

[b] Standardized excess return equals the excess return for the ex-dividend day portfolio divided by the ex-dividend day portfolio standard deviation estimated during the sixty-day period surrounding the ex-dividend day (thirty days on each side of the ex-dividend day).

[c] Both cases assume that the null hypothesis of no tax premium is true with probability .5. The prior beliefs about the alternative hypotheses are represented as a .5 probability that (1) the mean ex-dividend day SER is between −1 and +1 with uniform probability, and (2) the mean SER is distributed as normal with a mean of zero and a standard deviation of 0.316.

Michaely (1991) provided additional evidence by investigating the ex-dividend day behavior of share prices before and after the passage of the 1986 Tax Reform Act. He found no evidence of excess returns around the ex-dividend day before and after tax reform. The evidence indicated that during the latter part of the 1980s the ex-dividend day price drop was equal to the dividend per share. The change occurred before tax reform, however, thus providing no evidence of tax effects. A more detailed investigation of the time series behavior of the ex-dividend day excess return reveals a similar puzzle. Eades, Hess, and Kim (1994) found substantial time series variation in the ex-dividend day behavior of share prices. These variations do not correspond to changes in the tax code.

Some studies found evidence of ex-dividend day behavior that seems consistent with an unspecified complicated version of the tax hypothesis. Barclay (1987) found different ex-dividend day share-price behavior before federal income taxes were introduced in the United States. The ex-dividend share-price drop equalled the dividend per share. Recall, however, that before 1910 the New York Stock Exchange (NYSE) lacked liquidity. In such a market, the mechanical reduction (which equals the dividend per share) in the ex-dividend day opening share price can result in such finding.

In summary, the ex-dividend day evidence is inconclusive. Some results seem consistent with the tax hypothesis, and some suggest that other economic forces must explain at least part of the ex-dividend day share-price behavior. In the absence of a theory to link this behavior to taxes, arguing that the evidence supports the tax hypothesis is extremely difficult. Is this evidence consistent with L&R's results? In the next section we integrate the theory and evidence presented in these two branches of the literature.

5.4 Ex-Dividend Day and Cross-Sectional Studies

In this section we demonstrate that L&R's results are evidence of time series risk-adjusted return variations only. As such they do not contradict the evidence presented by B&S. The L&R evidence is consistent with the results of the ex-dividend day studies. The following analysis indicates that finding a tax-based explanation for these empirical regularities is difficult.[18]

---

[18] These observations are based on Kalay and Michaely (1993).

5.4.1 The L&R Experiment Revisited: Time Series or Cross-Sectional Return Variations?

Determining whether L&R's documented dividend effect is evidence of time series or cross-sectional return variations is important. As mentioned previously, the L&R experiment defines a stock as having a positive dividend yield only during its ex-dividend period. Hence firms that pay quarterly dividends are classified as offering a zero dividend in two-thirds of the months. This experimental design makes it difficult to interpret the positive dividend yield coefficient found. Is it evidence of higher risk-adjusted returns during the ex-dividend period (time series)? Or does it also indicate that cross-sectional long-term risk-adjusted returns are positively correlated to dividend yields?

Kalay and Michaely (1993) (K&M) replicated the L&R experiment by documenting a positive and statistically significant dividend yield coefficient both for weekly and monthly data. In and of itself, this evidence indicated substantial time series return variations. The estimate of the dividend yield coefficient they find is 0.246 for the weekly and 0.226 for the monthly experiment—almost identical for both periods. The difference between the risk-adjusted returns for the ex-dividend week and the returns for other weeks was similar to the difference between the returns for the ex-dividend month and the returns for other months. In other words, almost all the excess returns occurred within the ex-dividend week. This result provides strong evidence of time series return variations.

To test further for cross-sectional return variations, K&M repeated the L&R experiment with quarterly data. They assumed that expected quarterly dividends were equal to the mean quarterly dividend yield of the previous calendar year. This procedure provided a direct test of cross-sectional return variations because the documented time series return variation within the quarter does not affect the results. In other words, the evidence indicated strongly that stocks have a larger return during the ex-dividend week (or month). The question remains: Do stocks with larger dividend yields have larger risk-adjusted returns throughout the quarter? The answer is no, they do not! The outcome of the experiment was an insignificant dividend yield coefficient.

Now we can sum up the evidence. During the ex-dividend period, risk-adjusted returns on stocks are unusually high but are unrelated to the dividend yield. Thus L&R, who examined whether stocks experience higher risk-adjusted returns during the ex-dividend period, found an effect. In contrast, B&S, who examined whether returns on stocks that yield high dividends are higher throughout the year, found no dividend effect. It is important to note that the results of the two studies are not conflicting.

5.4.2 Tax Effects and Time Series Return Variations

As previously noted, Brennan's (1970) capital asset pricing model states that a security's pre-tax return is linearly and positively related to its systematic risk and its expected dividend yield. The model predicts cross-sectional return variation; that is, stocks with higher dividend yields should offer larger risk-adjusted pre-tax returns throughout the year.[19] The empirical evidence, however, indicates that stocks experience only time series return variations. What can we learn from such evidence? Is this empirical regularity an outcome of taxes?

The answer isn't simple. It seems clear that long-term investors would require a tax premium during ex-dividend periods only if they could avoid the dividend tax penalty during other periods. Can they do so? To illustrate, let's consider an investor trying to own stock XYZ without receiving its dividends. Suppose that the stock pays quarterly dividends, with the ex-dividend days being the last business day of March, June, September, and December. A possible strategy involves buying the stock, for example, on January 1 and selling it cum-dividend after the next dividend announcement, with the investor thereby realizing only capital gains. On April 1, the investor can buy the stock ex-dividend, keep it until the end of June, and so on. The dividends are paid to the investor's trading partners. This trading strategy results in two classes of investors: those receiving only short-term capital gains and those receiving mostly cash dividends. If dividends are taxed more heavily than capital gains, the pre-tax return during the ex-dividend period will exceed the pre-tax returns during other periods. In this

---

[19] With unlimited short selling possibilities, tax arbitrage is possible in a multiperiod version of Brennan's model: Sell a well-diversified, low-yield portfolio short and buy a well-diversified high-yield portfolio, and liquidate the positions within twelve months. In this case both capital gains and dividend income are treated as ordinary income. The difference between the returns on the high-yield and low-yield portfolios constitutes profit opportunities. If the nonsystematic risk is eliminated and the portfolios are constructed so that they have the same beta, the differential returns constitute arbitrage profit.

  If such trading is allowed, no equilibrium exists. Short-term traders are at equilibrium only when no expected risk-adjusted return differential between high- and low-yield portfolios exists. But in such a case the long-term investor benefits from a shift to low-yield stock. Equilibrium requires restrictions on the economy. The restrictions can be no (or limited) short selling, wealth limitations, and less than perfect diversification possibilities. With such restrictions, an equilibrium exists in which risk-adjusted pretax return is correlated with dividend yield.

case, time series risk-adjusted return variations are evidence of a dividend tax effect.

Note, however, that investors attempting to own the stock only during non–ex-dividend periods must realize short-term capital gains. Under U.S. tax laws, short-term capital gains are taxed as ordinary income. In other words, because the attempt to avoid dividend income involves realization of short-term capital gains, investor pays the same taxes he or she would pay on dividend income and therefore requires an identical tax premium. Thus, even though long-term investors prefer capital gains to dividend income, they do not require larger pre-tax returns during the ex-dividend period only. [20,21]

The economic incentives for long-term investors should not lead to excess returns during the ex-dividend period. If many long-term investors prefer to sell stock before the last ex-dividend day, the cum-dividend share price could be depressed, creating larger returns during the ex-dividend period.[22] But, if these investors time their trades to economize on the taxes they would otherwise pay on the last dividend, they surely will require compensation for the dividends distributed during their holding periods. Therefore a tax-based price pressure that results in excess returns during the ex-dividend period should be accompanied by a *tax premium* for stocks with higher dividend yields. Thus providing a tax-based explanation of time series return variation in an economy that shows no cross-sectional return variations is difficult.

5.4.3 Tax-Induced Clienteles: Empirical Evidence

Litzenberger and Ramaswamy (1980) presented evidence that seems consistent with a tax-induced clientele effect. A clientele effect

---

[20] An argument can be made that a constant tax premium per unit of time is the preferred compensation. A different premium structure can force the long-term investor (LTI) to own the stock longer or sell it sooner than his consumption investment decisions dictate. Also, note that the LTI is almost indifferent as to the timing of the purchase around the ex-dividend day. With quarterly dividends, the investor has to own the stock for at least four ex-dividend periods to qualify as an LTI. The investor can avoid the fifth ex-dividend period just as easily by buying the stock before the current ex-dividend day. Finally, Constantinides (1983, 1984) pointed out that investors have incentives to realize short-term losses and to defer capital gains for as long as they can. Therefore the long-term buyers and the short-term traders constitute, almost by definition, a larger fraction of the market than the long-term sellers. They can be expected to offset any temporary price pressure resulting from the population of long-term sellers.

[21] Corporations are willing to pay a tax-related premium to own the stock during an ex-dividend month.

[22] The empirical evidence is inconsistent with this conjecture. A positive excess return prior to the ex-dividend day has been found. See Eades, Hess, and Kim (1984), and Lakonishok and Vermaelen (1986).

exists in the economy when investors in higher (lower) tax brackets buy stocks with low (high) dividend yield. L&R assumed that a larger dividend yield coefficient implies higher investors' marginal tax rates. They divided the stocks into five subsamples based on expected dividend yield. Group I contains the lowest yield stocks and group V the highest yield stocks. They found a smaller dividend yield coefficient for the higher yield groups and interpreted it as evidence of a tax-induced clientele effect. However, direct tests uncovered no relationships between investors' marginal tax rates and their portfolios' dividend yields.[23]

Figure 5.1 helps to resolve the issue by providing a simple explanation for this empirical regularity. Consistent with the evidence, it illustrates a situation in which all the stocks have higher ex-dividend day expected returns that are not related to dividend yield. In the cross-sectional regression the same return differential (between the ex-dividend and non–ex-dividend periods) is related to the larger dividend resulting in a smaller regression slope for the higher yield groups. This association is mechanical and is not evidence of a tax-induced clientele effect .

5.4.4 Implications of Ex-Dividend Day Studies

The results discussed have clear implications for ex-dividend period studies: We need to reexamine the common assumption that individual investors prefer capital gains. To have a lower capital gains tax, an investor must own the stock through four ex-dividend periods. As a result, the investor can be indifferent between buying cum-dividend or ex-dividend.

5.5 The Case of Citizens Utilities

The following case illustrates a different piece of evidence on the potential effects of taxes on the market valuation of dividends. In 1956, Citizens Utilities created two classes of identical common stocks that differed only in their dividend payout. Common stock Series A pays cash dividends and Series B pays stock dividends. Based on a 1969 IRS ruling, the stock dividends are tax exempt. The corporate charter

---

[23] See Peterson, Peterson, and Ang (1985) and Lewellen, Stanley, Lease, and Schlarbaum (1978). Chaplinski and Seyhun (1990) found that about half the dividends paid by corporations during 1979 were received by tax-deferred and tax-exempt recipients.

Figure 5.1 Risk-Adjusted Monthly Returns versus Dividend Yield

Plots of risk-adjusted monthly returns as a function of their respective dividend yield. The assumption is that these returns are higher during the ex-dividend months but are unrelated to dividend yields. Each *x* represents a risk-adjusted return and the corresponding dividend yield. Regression lines I–V are the outcome of a Litzenberger and Ramaswamy tax-induced clientele test performed under these conditions. The highest yield group, V, is associated with smaller yield coefficient. The vertical axis intercept □, contains two-thirds of the observations. See Kalay & Michaely (1993).

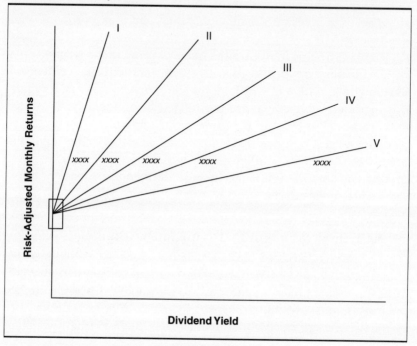

specifies that the two classes of shares should get dividends of equal market value. Long (1978) compared the market value of the two classes of shares. He found that the firm paid consistently 8 to 10 percent more stock dividends than cash dividends. The relationship between these payments was extremely stable and predictable. Therefore no reason existed to expect that investors had any difficulty in estimating the ratio of cash to stock dividends in future years. Long found that, if anything, claims for cash dividends commanded a small premium over the claims for capital gains (stock dividends). Interestingly, Poterba (1986) found that the two series have different ex-dividend day behavior. The price drop of the cash dividend series was smaller than the dividend per share, whereas for the stock dividend series it was not smaller.

More recently, Hubbard and Michaely (1996) examined the relative valuation of the cash dividend series relative to the stock dividend series of Citizen Utilities after the 1986 tax reform. The reduction in the differential taxation of cash dividends in relation to capital gains had no effect on the relative market valuation of the two series. Although the Citizen Utilities case uncovered evidence inconsistent with the tax hypothesis, it is evidence based on a sample of just one firm. Further, it is a utility stock known to attract investors with preferences for high dividends.

5.6 Conclusions

Long-term capital gains are taxed at a lower rate than dividend income for many investors. In addition, capital gains are not taxed until the gains are realized. This postponement option of the incidence of the tax lowers the effective tax rate even further. Accordingly, theory suggests that long-term investors should require a pre-tax rate of return premium to induce them to hold stocks paying dividends; theory also implies that stocks yielding higher dividends should earn larger pre-tax risk-adjusted returns throughout the year.

The documented empirical evidence, however, is inconsistent with this implication. The most recent evidence in the U.S. market indicates no difference between pre-tax risk-adjusted returns on stocks that yield high and low dividends. This evidence is inconsistent with Brennan's (1970) model. The evidence does indicate that stocks exhibit higher pre-tax risk-adjusted returns during ex-dividend periods (i.e., time series return variations). Existing theories do not link time series return variations to taxes. In our opinion, theorists will find it difficult to develop this link in an economy that exhibits no cross-sectional return variations.

The question remains: Why do stocks experience higher pre-tax risk-adjusted returns during ex-dividend periods? So far we have failed to explain the returns by risk shifts within a simple CAPM framework. Therefore, there is good reason to believe that the time series return variation is linked to taxes. We conjecture that eventually a more complete theory of taxes will explain this evidence. Table 5.2 summarizes much of the research discussed in this chapter.

Table 5.2 Summary of Research on Tax-Related Dividends

Author(s) of Study	Parameter Examined	Sample Period	Main Findings	Hypothesis Consistent with Results
Black and Scholes (1974)	Risk-adjusted rate of return of high-yield compared to low-yield stocks before and after taxes	1947–1966	Statistically insignificant dividend yield coefficient using both before and after tax returns	Investors are not averse to receiving payments of cash dividends.
Litzenberger and Ramaswamy (1979)	Risk adjusted rate of return during the ex-dividend months compared to risk-adjusted returns in non–ex-dividend months	1936–1977	Positive and statistically significant dividend yield coefficient	Investors dislike cash dividends and require compensation to receive them.
Blume (1980)	Dividend yield coefficient	1936–1976	Positive and statistically significant dividend yield coefficient	Investors dislike cash dividends and require compensation to receive them.
Gordon and Bradford (1980)	Dividend yield coefficient	1926–1978	Positive and statistically significant dividend yield coefficient	Investors dislike cash dividends and require compensation to receive them.
Litzenberger and Ramaswamy (1982)	Dividend yield coefficient for stocks with different dividend yield	1936–1977	Higher dividend yield coefficient for stocks with lower dividend yield	Findings are interpreted as evidence of tax induced clienteles.
Miller and Scholes (1982)	Dividend yield coefficient for stocks with different dividend yield	1940–1978	Insignificant positive and negative dividend yield coefficients and higher coefficients for stocks with lower dividend yield	Evidence is interpreted as inconsistent with the tax effect hypothesis.
Kalay and Michaely (1993)	Risk-adjusted rate of returns of high-yield stocks compared to risk-adjusted returns of low-yield stocks.	1936–1988	Risk-adjusted rates of return of high-yield stocks not different from risk-adjusted returns of low-yield stocks.	The data exhibits only time series return variation and as such is inconsistent with the tax effect hypothesis.
Elton and Gruber (1970)	Ex-dividend price drop compared to dividend per share	1967	Lower ex-dividend day price drop than dividend per share and higher relative drop for high-yield stocks	Evidence is interpreted as consistent with tax penalty on dividend payments.
Kalay (1982a)	Ex-dividend price drop compared to dividend per share	1967	Lower ex-dividend day price drop than dividend per share and higher relative drop for high-yield stocks	Short-term trading eliminates the relationships between the relative price drop and taxes.

Author(s) of Study	Parameter Examined	Sample Period	Main Findings	Hypothesis Consistent with Results
Eades, Hess, and Kim (1984)	Ex-dividend day rate of returns for taxable and nontaxable distributions	1962–1980	Higher returns during the ex-dividend period for both taxable and nontaxable distributions	Evidence casts doubt on the tax-based explanation of the ex-dividend day share price behavior.
Barclay (1987)	Ex-dividend day share price behavior before the introduction of taxes	1900–1910	Prior to 1910, equal ex-dividend day price drop and dividend per share	Results are consistent with the traditional explanation of the ex-dividend day behavior of share prices.
Karpoff and Walking (1988)	Correlation of ex-dividend day return and transaction costs	1964–1985	Positive correlation between ex-dividend day returns and transaction costs after the introduction of negotiated commissions (1975) for high-yield stocks	Evidence is consistent with profit elimination by short-term trading.
Michaely (1991)	Ex-dividend relative price drop around the Tax Reform Act of 1986	1986–1989	Ex-dividend price drop equal to dividend per share before and after 1986 tax reform	Evidence is consistent with profit elimination by short-term trading.
Eades, Hess, and Kim (1994)	The time series behavior of ex-dividend period returns	1962–1988	Dramatic variations in ex-dividend period returns	Variations do not correspond to changes in the tax code and thus are inconsistent with the traditional tax hypothesis.
Long (1978)	Relative prices of two classes of shares of Citizen Utilities stocks, one paying cash dividends and the other stock dividends	1956–1977	Higher market price of the series paying cash dividends than market price of the series paying stock dividends	Evidence suggests that investors like to get cash dividends and are willing to pay a premium for it.
Poterba (1986)	Ex-dividend relative price drop of Citizen Utilities	1965–1984	The ex-dividend price drop/dividend ratio is smaller than one for the series paying cash dividends and equal to one for the series paying stock dividends	Evidence is consistent with the tax hypothesis.
Peterson, Peterson, and Ang (1985)	Investors shielding dividends from taxes by creating offsetting interest payments	1979	Investors paying taxes on dividend income, with an estimated mean marginal tax rate on dividend income of 40 percent	Investors should have a tax-based aversion to cash dividend payments.

Chapter 6

Dividend Policy and Agency Problems

A key assumption in the Miller and Modigliani (1961) and other "dividend irrelevance" literature is that all nondividend decisions—the firm's operating, investment, and other financial decisions—are independent of the firm's dividend policy. While it is admittedly a simplifying assumption, we can understand the effects of the dividend policy decision on share valuation more easily without commingling the influences of other major management decisions that may affect share price. This assumption implies that when dividends are paid, the equity of the firm is maintained at its target level by the issuance of additional shares of common stock.

In practice, however, firms rarely sell equity to offset dividend payments and maintain a constant capital structure.[1] Therefore, in contrast to the dividend irrelevance assumption, dividend policy can affect asset composition, capital structure, investment plans, and therefore the value of the firm. In this chapter we consider how dividend payments affect the assets of the firm, security values, and the contractual arrangements among the different parties to the complex structure that we call *a firm*.

6.1 Agency Relationships

The various suppliers of capital to the firm (shareholders, bondholders, holders of convertible securities, etc.) and the firm's suppliers

---

[1] Research and practice suggests several reasons for the relative infrequency of seasoned equity offerings: (1) Transaction costs are higher for stock issues than for debt issues or for bank loans; (2) information asymmetries may cause managers to refrain from issuing shares if, for example, they believe the shares to be undervalued by the market; and (3) bylaws that obstruct equity issues and the like.

73

of labor (management and other employees) all share in the results of the firm's activities. We call the various classes of parties with relationships to the firm *claim holders*. Yet, since shareholders are the owners of the firm, their interests dominate (or should dominate) managers' actions. The other claim holders typically have much less influence over the firm's decisions. This disparity of influence is referred to as an *agency relationship*. In an agency relationship one party is in charge of decisions that affect several other classes of claim holders, including the decision makers. If the parties who share in decision outcomes, but not decision-making authority, cannot enforce implicit or explicit contracts that they have negotiated with the decision makers (because of legal constraints, unobservable actions, etc.), decision makers may take self-serving actions that are not in the best interests of other claim holders.

A corporation, being the focal point of many explicit and implicit contracts, gives rise to many agency relationships. All these relations potentially are affected by corporate decisions regarding investments, financing, dividends, and the like. In this chapter we emphasize a particular set of agency problems that arise from the differential effects of the decision to pay dividends to claim holders with vested interests in the firm.

6.2 Agency Relationships and Dividends

We cannot enumerate all the potential conflicts of interest that may be involved in corporate decisions, even when the decision is restricted to the payment of dividends. Accordingly, we focus on two of the most important types of agency relationships—those between

- shareholders and debt holders and
- management and shareholders.

Many of the insights gained by analyzing these two relationships, however, apply to other agency relations in a firm. For example, the effects of dividend payment on the relation between shareholders and debt holders apply equally well to the relations between shareholders and holders of other securities—holders of convertible bonds, holders of warrants, holders of preferred shares, and so on. Similarly, analysis of the effects of dividend payment on the relationship between shareholders and management also applies to the relations between shareholders and other suppliers, such as other employees and subcontractors. The agency aspect of dividends has to do with the differential effect that a cash dividend to shareholders has on other parties.[2]

6.3 Shareholders versus Debt Holders

In this section we assume that the interests of decision-making managers and shareholders are in perfect agreement or alignment. Shareholders elect members of the board of directors who hire, promote, compensate, and fire managers. In this section we assume that this linkage is sufficient to ensure alignment of interests. Accordingly, we assume that all management decisions regarding the firm are consistent with those the shareholders would make for themselves and use the terms *managers* and *shareholders* interchangeably.

Shareholders and debt holders share the value of the cash flows generated by the firm's operations.[3] Debt holders are entitled to receive interest payments periodically and to receive the face value of their claim, or principal, upon the debt's maturity. Shareholders, as residual claimants, are entitled to all remaining value once the obligations to bondholders have been satisfied.

If the value of the firm exceeds the value of the contractual obligations due to the debt holders, managers, in the interest of the shareholders, pay off the debt claim. To do so, they use either the firm's cash balance or cash received for securities issued to finance the payment so that shareholders can keep the residual value.[4] However, when the value of the firm falls below the value of the debt service obligations when they come due, the debt holders can be paid off only if the shareholders are willing to make up the gap between the firm's value and the debt service obligation. Clearly the shareholders can do better; they can forfeit ownership of the firm to the bondholders rather than service the debt. This action is the economic essence of default: Rather than pay off debt obligations that exceed the firm's total worth, the shareholders let the bondholders take over the remaining value of the firm and walk away.

---

[2] As far as the analysis presented in this chapter is concerned, dividend payments are no different from share repurchases. Both transactions represent cash distributions to shareholders and reduce the asset base of the firm. Keep in mind, however, that dividends and share repurchases are not identical. We highlight the differences between these two mechanisms for distributing cash in Chapter 10.

[3] We use the terms *debt holders* and *bondholders* synonymously, as though the only debt outstanding were in the form of bonds.

[4] *Value of the firm* refers to the sum of the present value of projects the firm has undertaken plus the net present value of the firm's future investment opportunities.

The option of shareholders to default on their debt service obligation means that shareholders and debt holders unevenly share the results of the firm's operations. In other words,

- shareholders, who exclusively receive all value remaining after debt holders have been fully paid, are the sole beneficiaries of their firm's upside potential; and

- debt holders, who will not be fully paid should the firm encounter bad times and its value drop below the value of the promised payments, bear the downside risk.

This uneven, or asymmetric, sharing of the value of the firm is the reason that an agency relationship exists between shareholders and debt holders. The asymmetric division of firm value entails differing objectives for these two classes of claim holders.

- Debt holders, who would like to increase the likelihood that they will be paid in full, try to minimize the downside risk of the firm, which increases the *safety* of their claim.

- Shareholders would like to

    maximize the upside potential of the firm, *possibly even when such an increase means an increase in the downside risk;* and

    appropriate as much value of the firm as possible prior to the debt's maturity so that they will receive some value even if the firm later defaults on its debt obligation.

The second shareholder objective, appropriation, has an immediate implication for the optimal dividend policy from the shareholders' perspective. All else being equal, shareholders would like to receive as large a dividend as possible. Large dividends mean that even if the firm eventually defaults, the shareholders will have received some return on their investment prior to the default. In other words, dividends are a means to transfer a firm's assets from the *common pool* shared by *all* the security holders of the firm to the *exclusive ownership* of the shareholders. Obviously, for the same reason, debt holders dislike dividends. Dividend payments increase the chance that the remaining value of the firm will not satisfy debt service obligations. Dividend payments make the cash flows of the debt holders more risky by increasing the chance of default and by reducing the value of the assets that can be used to repay the debt holders partially in case of delinquency.

6.3.1 The Differential Impact of Dividends

We develop the algebra that formally relates the decline in the value of the debt and equity due to the payment of dividends in Appendix 6A. However, here we provide the intuition of this development.

To understand how the divergent interests of the shareholders and the bondholders are affected by the decision to pay dividends, consider what happens to a firm's share value and debt value when the shareholders decide to pay a dividend. Upon the payment of the dividend (in the perfect world of Miller and Modigliani), the firm's value declines by exactly the value of the dividend paid.[5]

What happens to the respective values of the equity and the debt claims upon this payment? Since the value of the firm is reduced by the amount of the dividend, *both* values fall. In particular, the value of the debt falls because, upon payment of the dividend, the debt claim becomes more risky. Hence, the decline in the value of the firm as a whole is shared by the shareholders and the debt holders.

Clearly, the debt holders are worse off: They do not receive the dividend, and the value of their claim falls upon payment of the dividend. Less obvious, but equally true, is the fact that the equity holders are better off: They receive the full dividend payment, yet the value of their equity claim falls by less than the full dividend as the bondholders share some of the dividend's effect on the value of the firm.

The result is that the shareholders' gain is the bondholders' loss! By paying dividends, the shareholders transfer funds from the common pool to their pockets, making the bondholders' claim more risky and less valuable.

Note that this result holds not just for debt holders; a dividend that is paid exclusively to the shareholders reduces the value of the common pool of assets that are supposed to serve *all* claim holders: shareholders, debt holders, preferred-stock holders, warrant holders, etc. Dividends therefore lower the value of *all* claims but are received exclusively by shareholders. Because both shareholders and bondholders share the reduction in the value of the firm resulting from a dividend payment while only the shareholders receive the dividends, all else being equal, shareholders have an incentive to pay themselves as large a dividend as possible. Debt holders, in contrast, would like to retain as much of the value of the firm as possible until their debt is fully paid,

---

[5] Unless the dividend payment is accompanied by simultaneous issuance of an equal amount of equity, which rarely occurs.

which means that they prefer to minimize dividend payments. Note that this conclusion holds for *any* distribution that goes exclusively to shareholders.

A case in point is the attempt by the management of Marriott Corporation to spin off its hotel management business in 1992. During this action the firm planned to create a new subsidiary comprising only the hotel business and to distribute the stock in the new subsidiary to the shareholders as a special stock dividend. The result of this action would have been to reduce the common pool of assets available for distribution among *all* the claim holders, leaving the debt holders of the original Marriott Corporation and other claim holders of the corporation with less secure claims. Marriott's bondholders and preferred shareholders immediately appealed for court protection to block the distribution. At the time of the announcement, Moody's Investor Service, Inc., downgraded the rating of Marriott's debt from investment grade to junk-bond grade. Marriott eventually completed the spin off after compensating its security holders for the reduction in the safety of their claims.

How does the effect of dividend payment on debt's risk depend on the firm's leverage? With the payment of a dividend of any size, the risk of debt increases because the firm's leverage increases. When a firm has low levels of debt, the chance that the firm will default is small, making the debt virtually free from default risk. Accordingly, with low leverage the payment of dividends will have little impact on the value of the debt. On the other hand, when the firm is highly leveraged, every dollar counts and dividend payments can greatly increase the risk of the debt. Therefore, all else being equal, the lower the leverage of the firm, the less the debt holders subsidize the payment of dividends to the shareholders. In sum, the incentive for shareholders to pay dividends is stronger when their firm's leverage is high than when it is low.

6.3.2 Dividend Restrictions

Understanding the incentives for shareholders to expropriate value by paying excessive dividends, debt holders restrict the ability of shareholders to pay dividends. This limitation is accomplished by introducing covenants into debt contracts that restrict dividend payments.

Kalay (1982b) examined a large sample of dividend restrictions that bond covenants impose on shareholders. He showed that the typical dividend constraint defines a pool of payable dividends

- a fraction of the firm's net earnings accumulated since the bonds' issuance, plus

- the cumulative funds raised by the sale of new common stock since the bonds' issuance, plus

- a maximum sum payable out of the value that existed prior to the bonds' issuance, less

- the cumulative sum paid to the shareholders, either as dividends or as share repurchases, since the bonds' issuance.

In addition to direct restrictions on dividend payment, indirect constraints on shareholder ability to pay dividends are imposed. A case in point is a requirement for minimum net worth. At any time, *net worth* is paid-in capital plus accumulated earnings less accumulated dividend payments, so a minimum net worth requirement is analogous to a restriction on the payment of dividends.[6]

Based on the preceding analysis, we would expect shareholders—who benefit from dividend payment at the expense of bondholders—to pay the maximum dividend allowed by the bond covenants. Under the terms of the debt contract, shareholders can benefit only by raising the dividend payout, but they can raise dividends only to the limit set by the bond covenants. Kalay examined a sample of actual dividend payments relative to the pool of payable dividends. He reported that firms do *not* pay the maximum allowable dividend. Firms typically maintain a substantial dividend slack of about 12 percent of the value of the firm, on average. Such slack may imply that managers prefer to maintain some flexibility in the firm's dividend policy—for example, to maintain a fixed dividend policy even when profits decline temporarily. Paying the maximum possible dividend means increasing the chance of a forced reduction in dividend payout in subsequent periods should economic conditions worsen.

In a theoretical analysis of optimal dividend constraints, John and Kalay (1982) showed that, optimally, bondholders do not impose the most restrictive dividend indentures possible and that shareholders do not pay the maximum dividend possible. In their analysis, bondholders realized that retaining some flexibility is optimal. Similarly, shareholders did not abuse this flexibility; they also found that paying less

---

[6] Typical constraints on dividend payment, direct or indirect, do not distinguish between dividends and share repurchases. Since both cash distributions equally reduce the pool of assets available to pay the debt holders, typical covenants limit their extent equally.

than the maximum dividend permissible and investing the undistributed funds in profitable investments is optimal. Thus the observed dividend constraints are consistent with theoretical predictions.

6.3.3 Similar Conflicts

The conflicts of interest between shareholders and debt holders with respect to dividend payment are not unique to shareholder–debt holder relations. Similar conflicts of interest exist between shareholders and *any other senior-security holder*. An example is the conflict of interest between shareholders and holders of convertible bonds.

Convertible debt is effectively straight debt and an option to convert to stock packaged together. Consequently, dividend payment affects both the value of the debt and the value of the conversion option.

- The payment of dividends reduces the asset pool used to pay interest and principal; therefore, the debt portion becomes more risky and less valuable when dividends are paid.

- The payment of dividends reduces the value of the *remaining assets*, which also makes the option to convert the bonds to stock less valuable.

Both effects make dividend payment a way for shareholders to expropriate value from the holders of convertible bonds.

6.4 Shareholders versus Managers

The conflicts of interest considered in the preceding section are between different suppliers of capital to the firm. In this section we consider the interests of all suppliers of capital as a group. The conflicts of interest considered here, then, relate to the separation of ownership and control in large corporations.

6.4.1 Ownership versus Control

The shareholders own the corporation, but management controls its daily operations. Such separation is often a by-product of the requirement for economies of scale: To be able to provide a product or a service efficiently, organizations need to operate on a large scale, a size that cannot be financed by a few owner-managers. Consequently, most big corporations are financed by a large and diffuse group of investors who delegate decision making to professional managers. These managers often do not contribute capital to the firm beyond their human capital.

In theory, managers are appointed by boards of directors to serve as agents of the shareholders. Boards are supposed to monitor the performance of managers to ensure that management decisions are aligned with the interests of the shareholders. In practice, however, monitoring top management is difficult. Managers are privy to more information than are boards and investors. Inferior information inhibits an accurate assessment of the desirability of managerial decisions. Sometimes even verifying a decision is impossible.

To illustrate the difficulty of assessing managerial activities, let's consider, for example, the decision to acquire another firm. Managers may acquire firms for reasons that have little to do with shareholders' interests; managers may desire to build empires, reduce the firm-specific, or diversifiable, risk, and so on. Yet, it is often impossible to determine whether an acquisition was a good long-term investment.[7] Again, this situation is a classic agency relation where managers make decisions, but the outcome of the decisions is shared by the owners of the firm and managers (either directly through bonus plans, options, and other rewards or indirectly through subsequent employment contracts, prestige, and the like).

6.4.2 The Easterbrook Analysis

Easterbrook (1984) suggested that dividends may help reduce the agency costs associated with the separation of ownership and control. The starting point of his argument is the observation that, when the ownership of the firm is dispersed, individual investors have little incentive to monitor managers. An investor who monitors management bears all the monitoring costs, yet benefits only in proportion to his or her *partial ownership* of the firm's stock. However, taking the perspective of all the shareholders as a group, monitoring may be desirable since it can reduce the agency costs of separate ownership and control by more than the costs of monitoring. Easterbrook argues that dividend payments force managers to raise funds in the financial markets more frequently than they would without paying dividends. Thus dividends subject managers to frequent scrutiny by outside professionals, such as investment bankers, lawyers, and public accountants. Unlike

---

[7] Subsequent events in the life of the surviving firm, independent of the acquisition, can confound the "pure" contributions of the acquisition.

small investors, these outsiders who are directly or indirectly involved in a firm's new financing have strong incentives to scrutinize the firm and monitor its managers before endorsing the issue. The value of these individuals is tied to their reputations; consequently, they may lose their reputations if they manage an unsuccessful security offering or misrepresent the issue. Management is professionally scrutinized more frequently when dividends are paid, and dividend-paying managers have fewer chances to behave in their own self-interests as opposed to the shareholders' interests. Recognizing the value of this monitoring role of the capital markets, shareholders insist that dividends be paid. While shareholders cannot directly declare dividends, the actions of Kirk Kerkorian in 1994 and 1995 against the management of the Chrysler Corporation illustrate that shareholders can impose their dividend preferences. Kerkorian wanted Chrysler to distribute to shareholders some of the $6.6 billion in cash the firm had stockpiled. Failing to convince Chrysler's management to take such action, Kerkorian mounted a proxy fight and subsequently attempted a takeover of Chrysler. Although Kerkorian didn't succeed in taking over the management of Chrysler, its management was forced to increase its quarterly dividend and to buy back shares, thereby paying out a significant portion of its cash reserves.

Easterbrook suggests that dividends may also serve shareholders in forcing managers to take an action that managers would otherwise avoid, such as increasing the leverage of the firm. As the analysis in the preceding section showed, shareholders benefit from increasing the risk of existing debt securities. One way to increase this risk of debt is to increase a firm's leverage—for example, by paying dividends and lowering the value of the firm's equity. Debt holders, who understand the motives of shareholders, restrict shareholders' ability to increase leverage by requiring covenants that limit the firm's debt levels. Yet, within the constraints imposed by debt covenants, shareholders prefer to raise their firm's leverage to the maximum allowable level.

Managers, as the agents of the shareholders, are supposed to choose the maximum allowable leverage. However, the value of the human capital of managers is tied to survival of the firm. Accordingly, managers are less diversified than investors, and they disproportionately bear the unique risk of the firm, which shareholders can easily diversify away. For example, if their firm defaults on a debt contract, managers may lose their jobs and have their reputations tainted, reducing their future income potential. Consequently, risk-averse managers would like to minimize their firm's risk to minimize personal risk exposure.

Easterbrook argues that dividends can reduce the ability of managers to maintain leverage at too low a level. By continuously reducing the value of equity that is retained in the firm, dividends restrict managers' ability to reduce the firm's leverage. Thus dividends prevent managers from self-serving actions that are costly to the shareholders.

Based on agency costs, the two explanations for dividends suggested by Easterbrook imply three relationships between the dividend policies and characteristics of firms.

- Firms that have large shareholders, especially when these shareholders are involved in the management of their firms, have less need for monitoring by outside professionals; large shareholders have strong incentives to monitor managers tightly themselves. Accordingly, we expect closely held firms to have lower dividend payouts than otherwise identical firms that are more prone to owner–management conflicts of interest.

- Firms with low levels of debt will suffer little if managers reduce leverage—leverage is low to begin with, so the added safety to debt holders from further lowering leverage is minimal. Therefore shareholders of firms with low leverage have little demand for dividends as a way of maintaining leverage. Accordingly, we expect low-leverage firms, such as high-growth firms, to pay low dividends.

- Firms with high leverage also are those where value shifting is potentially costly. We expect such firms to pay large dividends. In other words, Easterbrook's analysis suggests a positive relationship between leverage and dividend payout.

6.4.3 The Jensen Analysis

Jensen (1986) suggests another argument based on agency costs for the desirability of dividends that is similar in spirit to Easterbrook's analysis. The starting point for Jensen's argument is again that managers cannot be perfectly monitored, which means that managers can choose actions that best serve their interests rather than the shareholders' interests. Jensen further argues that cash is the asset that managers can misuse most easily. Managers with large balances of excess cash, or money not needed for positive NPV investment, which he calls *free cash flow*, may use this cash in ways not in shareholders' best interests—for example for unwise acquisitions. Under these conditions, shareholders' best interests may be served if cash balances not needed for investment are minimized. Jensen's analysis implies that dividends, which extract surplus cash from management control, benefit shareholders. Increasing leverage, which entails an increase in routine interest payments, is another way to reduce the amount of cash under management control.

6.4.4 Managerial Compensation

The last conflict of interest that we consider in this section has to do with the way firms reward managers. Managerial compensation often depends on the value of the firm's capital.

- Managers often are compensated through bonus plans that are proportional to profits; profits, in turn, are larger when more capital is employed.

- The return on managers' human capital also is tied to the success of the firm they manage; managers prefer a large equity cushion to avoid the unpleasant personal consequences of defaults.

- Top management often receives options to buy stock. The value of these options depends on the equity value of the firm.

- Managers' social status typically is correlated with the amount of assets they control.

Accordingly, managers have strong incentives to retain profits. Dividends reduce firm size, the value of executive bonus plans and stock options, and social status, but they increase default risk. Thus, despite the preferences of shareholders of leveraged firms to receive dividends, managers prefer to pay as few dividends as possible. As managers are hired indirectly by shareholders, we expect managers to pay more dividends than they want to pay, but dispense as little as they can by justifying additional investments as prudent business decisions. Obviously, since managers are typically privy to more information than investors, such claims are often hard to dispute.

The conflict between Chrysler's management and Kerkorian in 1994 illustrates this point. Kerkorian claimed that the cash reserves maintained by Chrysler's management were excessive, but Chrysler's management argued that they were necessary to bridge periods of cash shortfalls anticipated during new-model development. Inside documents subsequently obtained by reporters at the *Wall Street Journal* revealed, however, that internal projections at Chrysler did not predict cash needs and, in fact, anticipated an almost doubling of cash reserves. Obviously, without such documents, assessing the reasonable magnitude of Chrysler's cash needs would have been pure speculation.

6.5 Empirical Evidence on Agency Problems and Dividends

6.5.1 Shareholders and Debt Holders

The differential effects of dividend payments and share repurchases on the security holders of the firm have been the subject of extensive empirical investigations. Here, we discuss only the main conclusions of the evidence.

Many of the empirical studies examined the consequences of *changes* in dividend policy. The underlying premise is that firms' financial policies in general, and dividend policies in particular, depend on numerous factors, some of which are unknown. The solution to this problem is to examine *changes* in policies. When we examine policy changes, each firm effectively serves as its own control under two different policies—before and after the dividend change.

Taken in isolation, using dividends and share repurchases to transfer assets from the common corporate pool to shareholders implies that these payments should *lower* the value of debt. This prediction, however, is difficult to test empirically because dividend changes may not only transfer value to the exclusive ownership of the shareholders, but also convey information about the value of the firm (which we discuss in Chapter 7). To understand this difficulty, consider a firm that increases its dividends as a signal that its prospects have improved. On the one hand, the increased dividends make the bondholders worse off by reducing the asset base from which their claims are paid. On the other hand, the debt holders now learn that the prospects of the firm are better than they thought prior to the announcement of the dividend increase. In some cases the former effect may dominate, and in other cases the latter effect may prevail.

Handjinicolaou and Kalay (1984) were the first to examine the reaction of bond investors to announcements of dividend changes. They found little reaction to dividend increases and a negative reaction to dividend decreases. They interpreted their findings as being more consistent with dividend changes conveying information about firm prospects than with dividends serving as a means for shareholders to expropriate value from bondholders. Dhillon and Johnson (1994) reexamined the issue, looking only at *significant* changes in dividends. Specifically, they examined large dividend changes and dividend initiations and omissions. Using these more pronounced dividend changes, they found that market reactions to announcements of significant dividend changes are consistent with predictions based on agency theory.

- Following the announcement of a dividend initiation, share prices rise by an average 0.72 percent, while bond prices decline by an average 0.70 percent.

- Following the announcement of dividend increases of at least 30 percent, share prices rise by an average 1.82 percent, while bond prices decline by an average 0.50 percent.

Brickley (1983) provides an alternative study that is consistent with a dividend explanation based on agency theory. His study examined the valuation impact of specially designated dividends (SDDs), or extra and special dividends. The logic for Brickley's analysis is that changes in regular dividends, which reflect management's dividend *policy*, potentially convey more information than SDDs, since the latter are earmarked by management as temporary dividends. Examination of SDDs, which minimize potential signaling effects, therefore represent a purer test of the agency aspects of dividends—separated from the information aspects of dividends. Consistent with this hypothesis, Brickley's results illustrate that investor reaction to SDDs is weaker than the reaction to comparable changes in regular dividends. Further, he found that earnings changes following regular dividend changes are more pronounced than earnings changes following SDDs. In a related study, Jayaraman and Shastri (1988) reported that, although SDD announcements are met with share-price increases and bond-price declines, the changes are not statistically significant.

The overall picture emerging from the study of investor reaction to dividend announcements is that shareholders and debt holders perceive dividends as a means of transferring assets from the common corporate pool to the exclusive ownership of the shareholders. Such transfers enrich shareholders at the expense of debt holders, holders of preferred stock, warrant holders, and others.

6.5.2 Shareholders and Managers

Several empirical studies have examined the agency relationship between managers and shareholders (or other suppliers of capital) as they relate to dividends. Lang and Litzenberger (1989) compared investor reaction to dividend changes by managers suspected of overinvesting (investing in negative NPV projects) versus managers who are less suspect. They show that managers who optimally invest generate a market-to-book ratio (called *Tobin's Q ratio*) that exceeds 1 because the market value reflects the investment (the book value) *plus* the net present value of the investment. Using the same logic, a Q ratio of less than 1 indicates overinvestment. An increase in the dividend payout by a firm with a Q ratio of less than 1 is good news because it means fewer dollars spent on suboptimal investment. For a firm with a Q ratio exceeding 1, however, such a dividend increase merely reflects optimal investment decisions. A mirror argument applies to dividend decreases. Lang and Litzenberger found that the reaction to dividend changes by firms having a low Q ratio is almost four times as large as the reaction to dividend changes by firms having a high Q ratio. This evidence, they conclude, supports the argument that dividends may constrain management's ability to invest beyond the levels that shareholders desire.

Agrawal and Jayaraman (1994) took another approach to examining the hypothesis that dividends reduce the opportunity for managers to use free cash flows in a self-serving manner. Since both interest payments and dividends reduce the pool of excess cash that managers can misuse, Agrawal and Jayaraman examined the free–cash–flow motive for dividend payments. They compared the dividend policies of debt-free firms to those of comparable firms that were leveraged. If dividend policy is influenced by concerns that managers may overinvest excess cash, unleveraged firms should distribute more of their profits as dividends than leveraged firms, which distribute some of their operating profits as interest.[8] In line with this expectation, Agrawal and Jayaraman reported that the dividend payout ratios of all-equity firms were significantly higher than the dividend payout ratios of leveraged firms. They also compared firms within the group of all-equity firms where managers have significant share holdings to firms in which managers have little equity stake. They reported that firms with high managerial

---

[8] Note, however, that this prediction is somewhat weakened by the incentive that shareholders have in leveraged firms to issue dividends, which are partially subsidized by the debt holders.

share holdings—presumably firms where the interests of managers and shareholders are more aligned—have lower payout ratios than firms with low share holdings. Overall, these results suggest that dividends do serve as a means to reduce the conflict of interest between managers and shareholders regarding the use of free cash flows.

Jensen, Solberg, and Zorn (1992) examined the joint determination of dividends, insider ownership of stock, and leverage. They provided empirical evidence that dividends serve as a means of reducing the conflict of interest between managers and shareholders. After controlling for differential profitability, growth prospects, and investment opportunities, they found that dividend payouts are negatively related to leverage and to insider holdings. These results are consistent with Jensen's free cash flow explanation of dividend policy. In other words, dividends are less important in reducing the free cash flow problems when debt service obligations provide managerial discipline and/or when insiders have large equity holdings, aligning their interests better with nonmanagerial shareholders.

Finally, Lambert, Lanen, and Larcker (1989) examined changes in the dividend policies of firms that adopted executive stock option plans. They found that for these firms dividends are reduced relative to the dividend levels of a control sample of firms that hadn't introduced such plans.[9] Again, these results are consistent with self-serving management behavior since option-owning managers avoid diluting the value of their options by paying large dividends. Their findings indicated that dividend policies are set, at least partially, according to management preferences, rather than purely to maximize shareholder wealth. Further, their results implied that managers may choose other self-serving actions when their actions are difficult to monitor or govern by contracts. This conclusion is the basic tenant of theories of dividends based on agency relationships.

6.6 Conclusions

Dividend payments present an example of the classic agency situation. The level of dividend payments is in part determined by shareholder preferences as implemented by their management representatives. However, the impact of dividend payments is borne by a variety

---

[9] Smith and Watts (1992) examined a similar question and found that the dividend yields of firms where managers receive option-based compensation are lower than the dividend yields of similar firms where managers do not own options.

of claim holders, including debt holders, managers, and suppliers. In this chapter we examined the implications of these agency relationships on the choice of dividend policies, capital structure, and management behavior.

We emphasized two sets of agency relationships in the chapter:

- the shareholder versus debt holder conflict, and
- the shareholder versus management conflict.

In the context of shareholder and debt holder relationships, we illustrated why shareholders, as the sole recipients of dividends, prefer to have large dividend payments, all else being equal. Conversely, creditors prefer to restrict dividend payments to maximize the firm's resources that are available to repay their claims. The empirical evidence discussed is consistent with the view that dividends transfer assets from the corporate pool to the exclusive ownership of the shareholders, which negatively affects the safety of the claims of debt holders.

In terms of shareholder–manager relationships, all else being equal, managers, whose compensation (pecuniary and otherwise) is tied to firm profitability and size, are interested in low dividend payout levels. A low dividend payout maximizes the size of the assets under management control, maximizes management's flexibility in choosing investments, and reduces the need to turn to capital markets to finance investments. Shareholders, desiring managerial efficiency in investment decisions, prefer to leave little discretionary cash in management's hands and to force managers to turn to capital markets to fund investments. These markets provide monitoring services that discipline managers. Accordingly, shareholders can use dividend policy to encourage managers to look after their owners' best interests; higher payouts provide more monitoring by the capital markets and more managerial discipline. The empirical evidence discussed in this chapter, summarized in Table 6.1, is consistent with the monitoring role of dividends.

Table 6.1 Summary of Research on Agency-Related Dividends

Author(s) of Study	Parameter Examined	Sample Period	Sample Size	Main Findings	Hypotheses Consistent with Results
Kalay (1982b)	Dividend constraints implied by bond covenants	1956–1975	150	Indentures restrict dividend payment Average reservoir of payable dividends of 11.7 percent of total dividends allowed	Bond covenants are structured to control shareholder–bondholder conflicting interests.
Brickley (1983)	Price reactions to announcements of specially designated dividends (SDDs)	1969–1979	165	Positive price reaction to SDD announcements; weaker reaction to SDD than to regular dividend increases	Since SDDs are transitory, which means that they do not signal future prospects, the market reaction to their announcement means that dividends also play a nonsignaling role.
Handjinicolaou and Kalay (1984)	Bond price reaction to dividend changes	1975–1976	255	Negative reaction of bond prices to dividend cuts and hardly any reaction to dividend increases	Bondholders react more to the information conveyed by the dividend change than to the wealth transfer they entail.
Jayaraman and Shastri (1988)	Share- and bond-price reactions to specially designated dividends	1962–1982	2,023	Positive stock price reaction to SDD announcements; effectively no bond price reaction	Dividends are signals of future prospects with little evidence for wealth transfer.
Lang and Litzenberger (1989)	Relative share-price reaction to dividend changes of over- and under-investing firms	1979–1984	429	Larger reaction to dividend changes by underinvesting firms than the reaction to dividend changes by overinvesting firms	Dividends serve as a constraint on management's ability to invest beyond the levels that shareholders desire.

Author(s) of Study	Parameter Examined	Sample Period	Sample Size	Main Findings	Hypothesis Consistent with Results
Lambert, Lanen, and Larcker (1989)	Dividend policies of firms that adopt executive stock option plans	1927–1980	221	Decline in dividend payments following adoption of executive stock option plans	Besides shareholder interests, dividend policies reflect the self-serving interests of managers.
Smith and Watts (1992)	Financing, dividend, and compensation policies of firms	1965–1985	94	Low dividend yields in firms where managers receive option-based compensation	Dividend policies reflect the self-serving interests of managers
Jensen, Solberg, and Zorn (1992)	Simultaneous determination of dividends, insider ownership of stock, and leverage	1982 and 1987	565 and 632	Negative correlation of insider ownership with dividend and leverage	Dividends, debt, and insider ownership are substitute means to control agency relations in the firm.
Dhillon and Johnson (1994)	Stock and bond price reactions to large dividend changes	1978–1987	131	Bond-price reactions opposite in sign to share-price reactions to large dividend changes	Dividend changes entail wealth transfers between shareholders and bondholders.
Agrawal and Jayaraman (1994)	Dividend policies of all-equity firms in relation to those of leveraged firms	1979–1983	71	Higher dividends paid by all-equity firms and firms with low managerial holdings than by comparable leveraged firms.	Dividends and debt are substitute mechanisms for minimizing managerial agency costs.

Appendix 6A

The Differential Impact of Dividends on Shareholders and Bondholders

In this appendix, we consider the changes in values of stock and debt of a firm when a dividend of D dollars is paid. Upon payment of the dividend, the value of the *firm as a whole* changes. We denote this change ΔF. In a perfect world, such as the one described by Miller and Modigliani, the value of the firm will fall by exactly the dividend payment, or[10]

$$\Delta F = -D.$$

What happens to the respective values of the equity and the debt claims on this payment? Since the value of the firm is reduced, *both* values fall. In particular, the value of the debt falls because, upon payment of the dividend, the debt claim becomes more risky. Obviously, the debt's value does not fall by the full amount of the dividend paid. Let's label the drop in value of the debt (say, bonds) by ΔB, where ΔB is negative. Similarly, we denote the drop in value of the shares ΔS. As the decline in the value of the firm as a whole upon payment of the dividend is shared by the shareholders and the debt holders,

$$\Delta B + \Delta S = \Delta F = -D.$$

Clearly, the debt holders are worse off. They receive no dividends, yet the value of their claim declines upon payment of the dividend. At the same time, the equity holders are better off. They receive the full dividend payment, but the value of their equity claim declines by less than the full amount of the dividend; the bondholders share some of the dividend's effect, the decrease in the firm's value. Therefore we can say that

$$\Delta S = \Delta F - \Delta B = -D - \Delta B > D.$$

---

[10] Unless the dividend payment is accompanied by simultaneous issuance of an equal amount of equity, which rarely occurs.

The overall change in the wealth of the shareholders, the dividend receipt together with the decline in the value of their claim, is

$$D + \Delta S = D + (-D - \Delta B) = -\Delta B.$$

Thus the shareholders' gain is the bondholders' loss! By paying dividends, the shareholders transfer funds from the common pool to their pockets and make the bondholders' claim more risky and less valuable.

Since the shareholders *and* the bond holders share the reduction in the value of the firm resulting from a dividend payment, while only the shareholders receive the dividend, all else being equal, shareholders have an incentive to pay themselves as large a dividend as possible. Debt holders, however, prefer to minimize dividend payments. This conclusion is true for *any* distribution that goes exclusively to shareholders.

Chapter **7**

Dividend Policy and Asymmetric Information

In a symmetrically informed market, all interested participants have the same information about a firm, including managers, bankers, shareholders, and others. However, if one group has superior information about the firm's current situation and future prospects, an informational asymmetry exists. Most academics and financial practitioners believe that managers possess superior information about their firms relative to other interested parties.

In this chapter we explore the use of dividend policy by corporate "insiders," or managers, to communicate their superior private information to the market. We examine both the theory and the empirical evidence on the potential use of dividend policy as a communication mechanism.

7.1 Perfect Capital Markets and Information

Recall from Chapter 3 that, under perfect capital markets (PCM), we assumed that

> information is costless and available to everyone equally. This assumption implies that *all* individuals are symmetrically informed.

In their famous *dividend irrelevance* proposition, which we discussed in Chapter 3, Miller and Modigliani (1961) argued that under PCM the level of a company's dividend payout should have no effect on the value of its shares of stock. The value of the firm's shares is the present value of the stream of future cash flows from the firm's assets in place (past investments) and future growth opportunities (future investments), adjusted for any additional investment required to maintain or generate cash flows. As long as the securities sold to finance any incremental current dividends are fairly priced, a dividend payment is merely an exchange of current cash for future cash of equal market value. As Miller (1988) later stated, an incremental current dividend is "not much different in principle from withdrawing money from a passbook savings account."

However, the irrelevance of dividend policy to a firm's value seems to be inconsistent with the empirical evidence on dividends. Of particular interest in this chapter is the empirical research documenting the significant impact that dividend announcements have on stock prices. This research shows that announcements of large dividend increases are met with upward share-price movements; announcements of dividend cuts are associated with share-price declines.

Miller and Modigliani suggested that managers may announce such dividend changes in an effort to move market expectations closer to those of management's about future earnings prospects. During the past twenty-five years, this *dividend information* proposition has been the backdrop for a number of empirical studies that attempted to identify what information, if any, is conveyed by dividend announcements.

Dividend changes (increases and decreases), dividend initiations (first-time dividends or resumption of dividends after a lengthy hiatus), and elimination of dividend payments are announced regularly in the financial media. In response to such announcements, share prices usually increase following dividend increases and dividend initiations, and share prices usually decline following dividend cuts and dividend eliminations.

Before examining empirical studies based on large samples of data, let's consider a few specific examples of dividend changes and resulting market reactions.

- Figgie International announced a cut in its quarterly dividend from 12.5 cents to 6 cents a share on November 17, 1993. On the announcement Figgie's stock price declined by 9 percent, from $14.25 to $13.00.

- Bethlehem Steel Corporation announced that it was omitting its quarterly dividend on January 29, 1992. Its share price fell 14 percent on the announcement, from $16.00 to $13.75.

- Wal-Mart Stores announced an increase in its quarterly dividend from 5.25 cents to 6.75 cents on March 6, 1997. Wal-Mart's share price increased from $26.50 to $27.25 on the announcement.

- Procter & Gamble Company announced an annual dividend increase from $1.80 to $2.02 on July 8, 1997. On the announcement, P&G's share price increased from $72.06 to $74.69.

As is usually the case, these examples reflect share-price decreases for dividend cuts and share-price increases for dividend increases. The abnormal returns associated with these dividend announcements were significant.

A resolution of the observed market reaction to dividend announcements is possible if corporate insiders can communicate their private information to the market through dividend decisions. A formal way of studying this possibility is to explore the idea that dividends could be a signal of a firm's prospects. Formal arguments in the form of *dividend signaling models* have been used to analyze whether dividends can be used credibly to convey new information to the market. These signaling models generate testable empirical implications regarding the announcement effect of dividend changes on stock prices.

The idea that dividend payouts can signal a firm's prospects seems to be well accepted among the chief financial officers (CFOs) of large U.S. corporations. In a survey of these executives conducted by Abrutyn and Turner (1990), 63 percent of the respondents ranked a signaling explanation as the first or second reason for dividend payouts.

7.2 Signaling Models

The following brief look at some of the recent theoretical work in the area of dividends provides a framework for understanding how dividend announcements can convey relevant new inside information to the market. Although the idea of dividends signaling information to the market historically was present as a heuristic proposition, only recently has a rigorous logical structure been provided by the dividend signaling models. Examples of these models include those developed by Bhattacharya (1979), John and Williams (1985), and Miller and Rock (1985).

The basic thrust of all these models is that managers have private information about future prospects and choose dividend levels to signal that private information. The signal is credible (or believable) if other firms, whose future prospects are not as good, cannot deceptively mimic the dividend actions of the firms with good future prospects. These theories provide a rationale for dividends—especially dividend changes—and generate hypotheses about the announcement effects of dividends that have been observed in the empirical literature.

Although the technical details of the different signaling models differ, the central intuition of these models can be presented by discussing one of the models. We can use the John and Williams (1985) model to describe the basic structure underlying the signaling argument.

7.2.1 Signaling with Dividends

We illustrate crucial assumptions of the John and Williams model—and the intuition underlying the "signaling equilibrium" in it—with a numeric example.[1] First, however, we need to describe the setting. It is one in which the corporate insiders know more than the investors about the future prospects of the firm (i.e., the quality of its investment opportunities and future cash flows). While some of the information can be conveyed to the market fairly easily through audited earnings reports and financial statements, other crucial information may be more difficult to communicate.

Let's say that management is confident of the economic viability of a new high-tech product being developed by its research and development (R&D) department. It may be difficult to communicate to investors the projected level of profitability of this product. On the one hand, if management simply makes a public statement that it expects the product to be highly successful, a likelihood exists that other firms whose R&D is not going well will make similar assertions. On the other hand, the releases of too much detail by management of the firm with the new product to support its claims may compromise the firm's competitive advantage.

The effect of this informational asymmetry is most important when a firm has incentives to establish its true market value. For example, the desire to establish maximum value may occur when (1) the firm is selling shares of stock or other (risky) securities in the market, (2) current shareholders are selling their shares to raise cash for personal reasons, or (3) the firm is facing a takeover threat. When the private or inside information about a firm's prospects is favorable, the market may undervalue the firm's shares. Under these conditions, security sales to raise a specific level of necessary funds will result in a greater reduction (or

---

[1] To be a credible signal, the action taken (e.g., a dividend increase), must be prohibitively expensive for firms that do not possess favorable information to mimic (e.g., by making the *same* dividend announcement). Therefore the firms without favorable information do not increase dividends. If the signal is credible, investors will attach a higher value to the signaling firm than the nonsignaling firm. The result is referred to as a *signaling equilibrium* because investors are able to assign different values to firms based on the content of the signal, or lack thereof.

dilution) in existing shareholders' fractional ownership of the firm than when the favorable information is reflected in a higher share price. More shares in the undervalued firm will have to be sold to raise the necessary funds, or a takeover may be successful at a price that is too low.

Reducing this underpricing is more valuable to the shareholders of firms with more favorable inside information. If the payment of a dividend can "proxy" for the favorable inside information, managers, acting in the interests of their current shareholders, may distribute a cash dividend if it signals that "better" firms distribute larger cash dividends. The favorable aspects of the dividend payment may more than offset the higher taxes on dividends relative to capital gains. In this scenario, outsiders bid up the share prices of firms paying larger dividends, reducing underpricing to such a degree that the payment of taxable dividends is justified.[2]

To complete the argument, we assert that the market will believe that firms with more favorable private information will choose to pay larger dividends and adjust share prices accordingly. The marginal benefits of distributing dividends will differ from firm to firm. For firms with favorable inside information, higher share prices must, at a minimum, compensate shareholders for incremental personal taxes on dividends. In contrast, for firms with no or less favorable inside information, the tax costs of the same dividend must exceed the gains from reducing the level of underpricing. Consequently, a pricing mechanism must exist for shares that separates firms with more from those with less favorable inside information, based on the dividend signal.

7.2.2 Numeric Examples

Some simple numeric examples illustrate the underlying intuition of signaling models. Consider the case of the cosmetic industry where firm values are crucially dependent on the success of their R&D efforts. For simplicity, let's make the following assumptions:

> Two firms differ *only* in the level of success of their R&D efforts. However, market participants cannot distinguish between the two firms.

---

[2] Different signaling models have focused on differential potential costs of paying cash dividends. John and Williams (1985) and Ambarish, John, and Williams (1987) focused on the personal tax disadvantage of cash dividends. Miller and Rock (1985), Woolridge and Ghosh (1985), and John and Lang (1991) studied models in which dividend payouts were tied to suboptimal investments by the firm. In John and Mishra (1990) unsystematic risk of insider holdings and suboptimal investment drove the signaling costs.

Their relative levels of R&D successes are known only by the firms' respective managements, the insiders. If, after the fact, the value of the products resulting from the R&D is high, the present value of each firm will be $1,000 million dollars; if the R&D proves to be unsuccessful, each firm's value will be $900 million. The cash flow from current operations, based on the successes of prior investments, is $10 million for each firm. Further, each firm requires $30 million for optimal investment. The current consumption needs of the shareholders are $20 million. Shareholders can achieve their consumption needs of $20 million in one of three ways: (1) by receiving cash dividends, (2) by selling shares, or (3) by some combination of dividends and security sales. We assume that the incremental personal tax on cash dividends over that on capital gains is 25 percent. The personal tax liability, equal to 25 percent of cash dividends, is paid at the end of the period from future wealth. Currently, each firm has 1 million shares outstanding.

7.2.2.1 *"Better" Firm—No Dividend Case*

Consider the case where the firm with the higher quality R&D pays no dividends. (We refer to this firm as the "better" firm and the firm with the lower quality R&D as the "poorer" firm.) To invest $30 million, the better firm needs to raise $20 million from external sources to supplement the $10 million cash flow from operations. Since current shareholders receive no dividends, they must sell stock on personal account to raise $20 million. Recall that we have assumed no personal taxes on security sales. Therefore, in total, $40 million worth of the firm is sold in the market—$20 million by the firm and $20 million by the shareholders.

At the time of the stock sales the market is unable to decipher the quality of the two firms, so it assigns a value based on an *average* (expected) value of the two firms. Let's say that the market assesses the probability of a firm having high-quality R&D as 1/20, or 5 percent. Under these conditions, the average value of the two firms will be

$$\left(\frac{1}{20}\right)(\$1,000 \text{ million}) + \left(\frac{19}{20}\right)(\$900 \text{ million}) = \$905 \text{ million}.$$

To raise the necessary $40 million, the market requires 40/905 of the total outstanding shares of the firm (40/905 × $905 million = $40 million). After receiving their $20 million from selling shares, the current shareholders of the better firm will have a total wealth of

$$\$20 \text{ million} + \left(1 - \frac{40}{905}\right)(\$1,000 \text{ million}) = \$975.84 \text{ million.}$$

Recall that the "better" firm will be worth $1,000 million once its R&D program reaches fruition.

7.2.2.2 "Better" Firm—Dividend Case

Now, consider the case where the managers of the better firm decide to pay an aggregate dividend of $16.04 million. Accordingly, the shareholders must raise the additional $3.96 million *net of taxes* on personal account by selling shares to satisfy their consumption demand of $20 million; they incur an additional tax liability of $4.01 million (25 percent of each dollar of cash dividend received). This tax liability will be paid at the end of the period from the wealth (the future cash flows) of the shareholders. Now, the better firm must raise an additional amount ($20 million + $16.04 million) = $36.04 million at the firm level and $3.96 million at the investor level for a total of $40 million in stock sales. If this firm's dividend policy cannot be mimicked by the poorer firm, then the market assigns the value of $1,000 million to the firm paying the high dividends at the dividend announcement. In other words, the firm paying the high dividend can be identified as the better firm. Similarly, the market would assign the value of $900 million to the firm paying the low dividends. Again, only the poorer firm will pursue a low-dividend payout policy. In other words, if the market established a value of $1,000 million for a firm paying $16.04 million in dividends and $900 million to a firm paying less, would the optimal dividend policy chosen by the better firm be $16.04 million and that of the poorer firm be zero?

The wealth of shareholders of the better firm paying dividends of $16.04 million is $20 million − ($16.04 million × 0.25) + (1 − 40/1,000)($1,000 million) = $975.99 million. Contrast this amount to the $975.84 million in wealth the shareholders had without the dividend payment. Under these conditions, shareholders are better off if the better firm signals its quality with the high dividend in spite of the tax disadvantage of dividends.

Does it also pay a poorer firm to signal deceptively using the dividend policy of the better firm? Compare the shareholders' wealth with no dividend and the $16.04 million dividend for the poorer firm.[3]

---

[3] Since the market will attach a value of $900 million to all firms paying dividends of less than $16.04 million, it does not pay to use an intermediate dividend policy.

7.2.2.3 *"Poorer" Firm—No Dividend Case*

On the one hand, in the no-dividend case, the wealth of the current shareholders of the poorer firm would be $20 million + (1 − 40/900)($900 million) = $880 million.

7.2.2.4 *"Poorer" Firm—Dividend Case*

On the other hand, if the poorer firm chooses to pay the $16.04 million dividend, the shareholders' wealth would be

$$\$20 \text{ million} - (\$16.04 \text{ million} \times 0.25) + \left(1 - \frac{40}{1,000}\right)(\$900 \text{ million})$$

$$= \$879.99 \text{ million}.$$

Since the wealth of the poorer firm's shareholders is higher in the no-dividend case, this firm is better off not mimicking the dividend policy of the firm with the higher quality R&D.

7.2.2.5 *Summary*

In the preceding examples, we showed that, if the market prices firms based upon their dividend payouts (i.e., $1,000 million for the firm paying no less than $16.04 million in dividends and $900 million for the other firm), the optimal dividend policy chosen by the better firm will be to pay out $16.04 million. For the poorer firm, zero payout is optimal. The examples have illustrated the conditions necessary to establish a signaling equilibrium with taxable dividends.

7.2.3 John and Williams Model

In their general model, John and Williams (1985) relaxed the simplifying assumptions that we just made. The following were three of their important results.

- In the signaling equilibrium, firms expecting higher future operating cash flows optimally pay larger dividends.

- The optimal dividend policy involves dividend smoothing relative to future operating cash flows so that dividend variability is lower than operating cash flow variability.

- The optimal dividend is higher for smaller tax disadvantage of dividends relative to capital gains.

The John and Williams (J&W) model provides a compelling explanation for the generous payout policies pursued by firms, even when cash dividends have adverse tax consequences. It explains why firms pay cash dividends even when alternative methods of distributing cash exist, such as share repurchase, which do not have adverse tax consequences. The J&W model also explains why a firm may find it optimal to pay cash dividends and raise new equity financing or repurchase stock in the same planning period. The argument for simultaneously paying dividends and obtaining new financing is that dividends are paid to reduce the underpricing of the securities issued to raise new outside financing. When cash from operations is sufficient to meet the investment needs of the firm—and partially satisfy the liquidity needs faced by current shareholders—the firm may repurchase shares and pay cash dividends in the same planning period.

7.2.4 Bhattacharya Model

Bhattacharya (1979) developed a model in which managers signal the quality of an investment project by "committing" to a dividend policy. The project quality, measured as the expected profitability of the project, is private information known only to managers. A crucial assumption of the model is that, if the payoffs from the project are not sufficient to cover the committed dividends, the firm will resort to outside financing to cover the shortfall. However, outside financing involves transaction costs. A firm with a genuinely high-quality project would have lower expected transaction costs to meet the same level of precommitted dividends than would a firm with a low-quality project. Accordingly, it would be unprofitable for the latter firm to mimic the dividend policy of the firm having a high-quality project.

This first model of dividend signaling represented a significant step toward explaining why firms pay dividends. However, the model was also subject to several criticisms. For example, Bhattacharya did not clarify what he meant by firms committing to a certain level of dividends. Because an announced dividend is not a contractual obligation, but only a payment to the residual claimants (shareholders), the firm is not obliged to maintain the dividend by issuing costly external financing if a cash flow shortfall occurs. Realizing this lack of obligation, the market would not attach any importance to precommitted dividends.

7.2.5 Miller and Rock Model

In the Miller and Rock (1985) model managers are assumed to have private information about realized earnings. From these earnings the firm finances its dividend payments and its new investment. Neither the earnings nor the new level of investment are directly observed by investors. Since at any time a fraction of the shareholders are selling their shares, managers want to communicate their private information to the market so that shareholders do not have to sell underpriced shares. In the Miller and Rock (M&R) model, the "better" firms under-invest and pay large enough dividends to obtain higher prices for their shares. The equilibrium levels of dividends are sufficiently high to make it unattractive for "poorer" firms to reduce their investments enough to pay out the same levels of dividends.

The M&R model also generates predictions regarding the an-nouncement effect of dividend changes on share prices. However, this model has nothing to say about the level of cash dividends paid by a firm. In fact, the dividend term in the model denotes the sum of cash dividends and stock repurchases net of any external financing. In other words, if any adverse tax consequences exist for cash dividends, the M&R model implies that firms would pay zero cash dividends and un-dertake all cash distributions through share repurchases. Therefore the M&R model is not able to resolve the dividend puzzle.

7.3 Other Theoretical Models

In this section we will discuss several alternative theoretical mod-els of signaling with dividends.

7.3.1 Dividend Smoothing

Another documented empirical finding about dividend policy is that corporations smooth dividends. As we documented in Chapter 1 for the aggregate economy—and address again in Chapter 8 for indi-vidual firms—the patterns of cash dividends display a substantial de-gree of stability. A firm's dividend payout may not change over a pe-riod of time, even though earnings may change substantially.[4]

Why firms smooth dividends in well-functioning capital markets has puzzled financial economists. John and Nachman (1986) and Kumar (1988) have addressed this problem in theoretical models. John and Nachman (J&N) use a dynamic version of the John and Williams (1985) model. In the latter model, the dividends optimally paid by firms are a product of two terms: (1) the total extent of financing done

---

[4] For example, among more than 13,000 widely held corporations, only 14 percent of the firms changed their dividends in 1992; 11 percent increased their dividends, and 3 per-cent cut their dividends.

at firm level and at shareholder level, and (2) the level of optimism in the private information of the firm. Therefore, when the firm has highly optimistic private information, its optimal strategy would be to raise only enough external financing to undertake its investments. In this case the first term is small and the second term is large. In contrast, when the private information of the firm is not significantly different from that of the market, the firm may optimally raise a large amount of external financing and hold a fraction of these funds in reserve for future investments. In this case, although the second term is small, the first term is large. Even though management's private information about the firm's prospects is dramatically different in the two cases, the optimal dividends would be approximately the same. In other words, dividends would be highly stable even though the realized earnings may be volatile. In summary, the J&N model provides a rationale for firms paying a smooth series of cash dividends even though such dividends have some tax disadvantage over alternative methods of distributing cash.[5]

7.3.2 Dividends versus Share Repurchases

As mentioned before, one of the main questions involving dividend puzzles is why firms use cash dividends instead of alternatives such as share repurchases, which impose a lower tax burden on shareholders.[6] As we showed earlier, the J&W model provides a rationale for using cash dividends rather than share repurchases: Firms do not repurchase shares to avoid taxes because it is precisely the tax costs that drive the signaling role of cash dividends. Ambarish, John, and Williams (1987) developed a model whereby firms may use dividends or stock repurchases as signals. It indicates when firms would use cash dividends and when firms would use share repurchases for signaling.

Other work, such as that reported by Ofer and Thakor (1987), Barclay and Smith (1988), and Brennan and Thakor (1990), also addressed a firm's choice between cash dividend and share repurchases. In these cases, share repurchases also have a disadvantage in that informed investors can refrain from selling underpriced stocks back to the firm and sell when stocks are overpriced. Therefore, share repurchases suffer from the costs of adverse selection.[7] Since dividends are paid pro rata

---

[5] Kumar (1988) also addressed the relative stability of dividends for long periods of time by using an alternative argument.

[6] We discuss stock repurchase in detail in Chapter 10.

[7] By *adverse selection*, we mean that market participants with more information will take actions that adversely affect those without superior information.

on each stock, leaving shareholders without an option to receive or not receive cash, dividend distributions do not provide an advantage to informed participants. Building on this argument, Brennan and Thakor provided an explanation for why firms choose dividends over share repurchases in spite of the adverse tax treatment. They argued that, given the adverse selection problem associated with share repurchases, uninformed shareholders prefer cash dividends to repurchases, provided that the tax disadvantage is not too large. However, informed shareholders would prefer share repurchases to cash dividends. If the method of distribution were based on shareholder voting, Brennan and Thakor held that, for larger distributions, repurchases would be chosen and that, for smaller distributions, cash dividend would be preferred. Their logic is that, for a fixed cost of obtaining information, the number of investors who choose to be informed will depend on the dispersion of share holdings and the cost of becoming informed. For a large distribution it pays to become informed. Accordingly, more shareholders would become informed and would vote for repurchases. Alternatively, for small distributions most shareholders would remain uninformed; only the investors with large holdings would become informed. Thus more shareholders would vote for cash dividends.

7.3.3 Choice of Signals

We have discussed the role of dividends as a signal of a firm's prospects when corporate insiders have more information than the market does. Even though dividends have adverse tax costs, they can play an important role in communicating private information to the market. When we argue that costly dividends can be a signal, the question naturally arises of whether less costly alternative signals exist that can convey the private information to the market. In other words, are dividends the most efficient way of communicating inside information? Corporate leverage, share repurchases, insider buying, and the level of corporate capital expenditures are some of the alternative signals that have been proposed. Would cash dividends survive as a signal in competition with any or all of these alternative signals?

Recent studies, such as those by Ambarish, John, and Williams (1987) and John and Lang (1991), did not designate dividends as the only mechanism for conveying private information to the market. They found that firms choose from a variety of signals to convey their private information in a cost-effective manner.[8] The nature of the firm's

---

[8] Dividends, investments, share repurchases, or new issues of equity are signals covered in Ambarish, John, and Williams (1987).

investment opportunities determines the optimal blend of signals used in equilibrium. Mature firms use large payouts as their primary signal; growth firms deemphasize dividends and use investments as their main signal. The announcement effects of dividend changes and seasoned equity offerings[9] also reflect this difference. These models predict that announcement of dividend increases will cause larger price increases for the shares of mature firms relative to those for growth firms. For seasoned equity offerings, the model predicts larger decreases of share prices for mature firms than for growth firms. Shortly, we provide evidence consistent with these predictions for dividend changes.

These theories suggest that dividend changes by firms will be interpreted by the market in the context of the investment opportunities of the firms. Dividend announcements by mature firms will be interpreted differently by the market from those by growth firms. Before we examine the empirical studies on this phenomena, let's examine a recent announcement on August 28, 1997, in a PR Newswire story:

> The Board of Directors of Windmere-Durable Holdings, Inc., (NYSE: WND) announced today that it eliminated the company's regular quarterly cash dividend of $0.05 per share in order to reinvest all earnings into its business. The Board of Directors reevaluated Windmere-Durable's divided policy in light of the Company's strategic repositioning for growth and the resulting cash requirement. "The financial results, as recently announced, of Windmere-Durable are gaining momentum, and the company is positioned to grow at an accelerated rate," commented David M. Friedson, Windmere-Durable's Chairman, President, and Chief Executive Officer. "Because of this improvement in our business outlook, we believe it is in the best interest of the company and its shareholders to eliminate the dividend and invest in our future growth."

Even though this statement announced elimination of the dividend, the firm's share price increased from $18.25 to $19.00 upon release of the information. The abnormal returns on the shares for three days, adjusting for concurrent market movements, were 4.09 percent.

In contrast, Compaq Computer Corporation paid a dividend of 3 cents per share for the first time on October 16, 1997, accompanied by

---

[9] Seasoned equity offerings are equity issues made by a firm after the firm has gone public, i.e., made its first equity issue (called the initial public offering (IPO)).

a two-for-one stock split. Upon the announcement, however, Compaq's share price declined from $38.62 to $34.75, for an abnormal return of –5.37 percent. Both of the events cited are consistent with the theory of Ambarish, John, and Williams (1987) and the empirical study of dividend initiations by John and Lang (1991), which argue that dividend changes have to be examined in the context of the investment opportunities and strategies of the firm in question.

John and Mishra (1990) suggested that insider trading could be an important signal by a firm. They argued that the trading activity of corporate insiders would be influenced by the private information they have. Because of the Security and Exchange Commission's (SEC's) reporting requirements, the details of insider trading (purchase or sale and the extent of trading) are available to the market with a delay.[10] John and Lang (1991), examined insider trading around announcements of dividend changes. Their model implies that the announcement effect of dividends will be influenced by the nature of a firm's investment opportunities and the productivity of its current capital expenditures. One of the model's predictions is that the market should *not* interpret all dividend increases as good news. In some cases, dividend increases may signal the end of outstanding investment opportunities. In general, the interpretation of the informational content of a dividend increase has to be based on insider trading activity immediately prior to the dividend announcement. In cases of heavy insider selling, a dividend increase will elicit a negative share-price response. In cases of negligible insider selling or heavy buying, the announcement's effect will be positive. The evidence presented by John and Lang on insider trading around announcements of initiation of dividends largely supports the model's predictions.

7.4   Empirical Evidence

Extensive empirical evidence is available on several aspects of the use of dividends to convey the private information of insiders to

---

[10] Under SEC Rule 144(e)-1, "insiders" are prohibited from liquidating more than the minimum of (1) 1 percent of the outstanding shares of the class of securities, or (2) the average weekly trading volume in the class of securities, within any three-month period, unless a (secondary distribution) registration of the offering is filed with the SEC. In addition, Sections 16(a) and 16(b) of the Exchange Act require that changes in "insider" ownership positions be reported to the SEC within ten business days of the close of the month in which the change takes place. These rules make it illegal for "insiders" to secretly change their holdings in the firm.

investors in the market. Earlier empirical studies were called *tests of the information content of dividends.*

The ability of dividends to convey information to the market has been empirically tested to answer three questions:

1. Do unanticipated changes in dividends, when announced, cause share prices to change in the same direction?

2. Are unanticipated announcements of changes in dividends accompanied by revisions in the market's expectations of future earnings in the same direction as the dividend change?

3. Do dividend changes predict future earnings beyond those predicted by past earnings?

7.4.1 Announcement Effects

Several empirical studies exist on the announcement effects of dividend changes on share prices. These studies almost uniformly show that the announcements of dividend changes cause a similar change in share prices.

Pettit (1972) documented that announcements of dividend increases are followed by significant price increases and that announcements of dividend decreases are followed by significant price drops. Aharony and Swary (1980) showed that these relationships hold even after controlling for contemporaneous earnings announcements. Most studies found an average excess return of about 0.4 percent for a dividend increase and –1.3 percent for a dividend decrease. Three studies of large changes in dividend policy—Asquith and Mullins (1983) (dividend initiations), Healy and Palepu (1988), and Michaely, Thaler, and Womack (1995) (dividend omissions)—showed that the market reacts dramatically to such announcements. The average excess return is about 3 percent for initiation and –7 percent for dividend omissions. Kalay and Loewenstein (1986), documented that the timing of dividend announcements contains information. They found that early dividend announcements, on average, connote good news and that late dividend announcements connote bad news. In summary, and addressing the first question, regarding whether unanticipated changes in dividends cause stock price change in similar direction at announcement, most studies document that dividend increases and dividend initiations result in significant positive share-price reactions and that dividend decreases and dividend omissions invoke significant negative share-price responses.

7.4.2 Changes in Market Expectations

Ofer and Siegel (1987) demonstrated that the market revises its expectations based on announced changes in dividends. They documented that financial analysts revise their earnings forecasts by an amount that is positively related to the size of the announced dividend change. They also provided evidence that analysts' revisions are positively correlated with the market reaction to the announced dividend change. The results of the study are consistent with a positive answer to the second question posed, regarding unanticipated dividend changes accompanied by revisions in market expectations.

Dyl and Weigand (1998) hypothesized that initiation of cash dividends coincides with a reduction in the risk of a firm's earnings and cash flows. Based on a sample of 240 firms listed on the NYSE or the American Stock Exchange (AMEX) that initiated dividend payments during the period January 1972 through December 1993, they showed that the variance of daily returns drops from an average value of 0.001329 to 0.001138 and that the average beta falls from 1.397 to 1.2118.

7.4.3 Predictions of Future Earnings

If dividends are meant to convey private information to the market, predictions about the future earnings of a firm based on dividend information should be superior to forecasts made without dividend information. Further, a dividend change should be followed by a subsequent earnings change in the same direction.

A number of studies test these implications of the information content of dividends. Watts (1973) examined the proposition that knowledge of current dividends improves the predictions of future earnings over and above those based on information contained in current and past earnings. Based on a sample of 310 firms with complete dividend and earnings information for the years 1946–1967, and annual definitions of dividends and earnings, Watts tested whether earnings in the coming year $(t + 1)$ can be explained by current (year t) and past (year $t - 1$) levels of dividends and earnings. For each firm in the sample, Watts estimated the current and past dividend coefficients (while controlling for earnings). Although the average dividend coefficients for the firms were positive, the average significance level was low. In fact, only the top 10 percent of the coefficients were marginally significant. Using changes in earnings and dividend levels yielded similar results. Gonedes (1978) also obtained only weak evidence that current dividends improve the predictability of future earnings. Benartzi, Michaely, and Thaler (1997) also concluded that dividend changes seem to respond to earnings changes in the immediate past and not to signal future unexpected earnings changes.

Other studies, however, suggest that extreme dividend changes contain some information about future changes in earnings. Healy and Palepu (1988) showed that earnings changes following dividend initiations and omissions are at least partially anticipated at the time of dividend announcement.

Lipson, Maquieira, and Megginson (1998) examined the performance of newly public firms and compared those firms that initiated dividends with those that did not. Earnings increases following the dividend initiation and earnings surprises for initiating firms are more favorable than those for noninitiating firms. Their results suggest that dividends signal differences in performance between otherwise comparable firms.

Brook, Charlton, and Hendershott (1998) found that firms poised to experience large, permanent cash flow increases after four years of stable cash flows tended to increase their dividends before their cash flows increase. They also found that these firms also had a high frequency of relatively large dividend increases prior to the influx of cash and concluded that investors appear to interpret the dividend changes as signals of future profitability.

The evidence on the relationship of future earnings to dividend changes—the third question posed—appears weaker with respect to the information content of dividends than the results concerning announcement effects and changes in market expectations. The evidence presented suggests that the signaling role of dividends is weak. However, the theoretical models argue that dividends may be an efficient (low-cost) signal only in conjunction with other signals (e.g., investment expenditures or the level of insider trading). These models also emphasize that the market may interpret the dividend signal differently for different firms based on knowledge of the investment opportunities for the firm in question. In other words, the same dividend signal from a growth firm might be interpreted less favorably than from a mature firm. This explanation provides one possible reason why the predictability of future earnings based on dividends is weak. If the market bases its interpretation of dividends on other information about the firm, studies that do not properly control for other factors will provide unreliable results.

7.5 Dividend Signaling Considering Investment Opportunities and Insider Trading

We now examine two recent studies that found evidence suggesting that the information content of dividends may depend on the observable features of its investment opportunities and insider trading activity. In short, the information content of dividends must be conditioned upon other important variables.

7.5.1 Lang and Litzenberger Study

Lang and Litzenberger (1989) provided interesting evidence suggesting that the announcement effect of large dividend changes (increases as well as decreases) is significantly affected by investment opportunities of the firm. Specifically, the announcement effect of a dividend increase is significantly more positive for firms that appear to overinvest.

The nature of investment opportunities used in the study is captured by Tobin's Q.[11] Data on Q ratios are not readily available, so Lang and Litzenberger used empirical estimates of the average Q ratio of a firm to characterize it as an overinvesting firm. If a firm's investments exhibit decreasing marginal productivity of capital or declining rates of return as a function of accumulative investment, an average Q ratio of less than 1.0 implies a high likelihood of overinvestment. If a firm has undertaken the value-maximizing level of investment, its average Q will exceed 1.0.[12]

Lang and Litzenberger found that the average abnormal returns at the announcement of dividend is more than three times larger for firms with average Qs less than 1.0 than for firms with average Qs greater than 1.0. The difference was significant at the 1 percent level. Similar results were found for dividend decreases and dividend increases, when examined separately.

These results are consistent with the predictions of the Ambarish, John, and Williams (1987) model wherein the nature of investment opportunities affects the dividend and investment strategies of firms

---

[11] Tobin's Q is a measure of the marginal efficiency of capital, computed for any asset or investment project as the ratio of the market value of the asset to its replacement cost. Value-maximizing firms, which invest optimally, will choose all projects with Q ratios of at least 1.0. Firms that choose projects with Q ratios of less than 1.0 are overinvesting (i.e., they are investing in projects with a negative net present value), decreasing the wealth of the shareholders.

[12] For details of Lang and Litzenberger's calculation of Tobin's Q, see their 1989 article.

when corporate insiders have private information. Ambarish, John, and Williams make differential predictions for announcement effects of dividend changes for firms with different classes of investment opportunities. For mature firms (with a firm average Q ratio of less than 1.0), the predicted announcement effect is larger than that for growth firms (with an average Q ratio exceeding 1.0). Consistent with these predictions, the evidence shows an inverse relationship between the Q ratio and the dividend change announcement effect. The evidence indicates that the dividend change is differentially interpreted by the market based on firms' investment opportunities.

7.5.2 John and Lang Study

In this section we examine the John and Lang (1991) study of insider trading around corporate announcements of dividend initiations and changes. John and Lang constructed a theoretical model of insider trading around dividend announcements and tested the model's prediction empirically.

Given the reporting requirements and regulation of insider trading, the direction and extent of insider trading could be an important item in the menu of signals a firm uses to communicate with a less-informed market. If insider trading and dividends are the main signals, the cost-effective blend of signals used will depend on the investment opportunities facing the firm. The announcement effects of dividend changes are derived explicitly. One of the novel features of the John and Lang (J&L) model is the implication that all increases in dividends (or initiations of dividends) do not connote "good news." Interpretation of the dividend increase is conditional on the current state of the firm's investment opportunities, which are revealed through the other signal used (i.e., trading of corporate insiders). Therefore, in some firms, higher than expected dividend announcements would generate a positive share price response when accompanied by significant insider buying. Alternatively, for other firms, higher than expected dividend announcements would result in a negative stock price response when accompanied by unusually intense insider selling.

Dividend initiations are commonly viewed as unambiguous signals of good news. Contrary to this position, the J&L model predicts that the initiation announcement will generate a positive share-price response only when insider selling has not occurred prior to the announcement. The model predicts a significant difference in the share-price response to dividend initiation between firms with and without prior insider selling. Using data on dividend initiations and concurrent insider trading, John and Lang tested this prediction.[13,14]

The average announcement day excess return for the firms with insiders purchasing shares is significantly higher than that for the group with insiders selling shares (by about 2.5 percent). John and Lang also present evidence indicating that the most recent insider sales seem to be the most informative of insider trading activity for understanding share-price response around dividend initiations.

Dividend initiations are an example of unexpected dividend increases from zero dividends to some positive level. Therefore the evidence can be interpreted in the context of the J&L model and its predictions for dividend increases. It indicates that the announcement effect of dividend initiations is significantly affected by the extent and direction of insider trading activity during the quarter prior to the announcement. As we have said, contrary to the existing notion from earlier studies, all dividend initiations do not convey "good news." With regard to insider buying, the excess return of 2.51 percent is significantly higher than for insider selling. Overall, the evidence is consistent with the main predictions of the J&L model:

- the informational content of dividend increases has to be read in conjunction with the second signal (i.e., insider trading), and

- the announcement effect of dividend increases should be significantly different for firms with net insider buying from those with net insider selling.

---

[13] The dividend initiation data came from 1988 Compustat database. The procedure for selecting the sample is to search for firms paying a cash dividend following at least five years of no cash dividend payments. The dividend initiation announcement dates are taken from the 1987 Daily Master Tape and the *Wall Street Journal Index*. Officers, directors, and principal shareholders who hold more than 10 percent of total common shares outstanding are defined as insiders whose trading records for this study come from *Value Line Investment Survey*. The *Value Line* entry contains the monthly aggregate number of insiders' open market purchase and sale records of fifteen months prior to the *Value Line* quarterly reporting date. The final sample contained seventy-two firms (for which data of all the above categories were available).

[14] John and Lang computed a single standardized measure of the intensity of insider trading in a given time period prior to the announcement of dividend initiation, called ISPI. This index is for the case of insider sales only and +1 for the case of insider purchases only. The index lies between −1 and +1 for the mixed cases. To investigate the impact of ISPI on the dividend initiation announcement effect, daily returns are adjusted by the market model, that is, by subtracting (beta) × (market return) from the unadjusted returns, to compute the abnormal returns for the announcement day (day 0) and the next day (day +1).

7.6 Conclusions

In this chapter we examined the theoretical and empirical studies of the role of dividends in signaling the superior information that corporate insiders have about the prospects of a firm to a less informed market. We examined several theoretical studies of the communicating function of dividends. The empirical evidence is consistent with many hypotheses generated by dividend signaling models of the announcement effects of dividend initiations, dividend increases, dividend omissions, and dividend decreases. Overall, announcements of dividend increases generate abnormal positive security returns, and announcements of decreases generate abnormal negative security returns.

The dividend policy of a firm can be entirely independent of its investment policy in the idealized setting of perfect capital markets. However, theoretical studies show that the information content of dividends can be influenced by a firm's investment opportunities. If corporate insiders have superior information about the firm's prospects and its investment opportunities relative to investors, then independence may not hold.

The least-cost blend of signals chosen by a firm, including the dividend component, may be determined by a firm's investment opportunities. Ambarish, John, and Williams characterized the different dividend policies implemented by growth firms and mature firms. They predicted that announcement effects of dividends for no or low growth firms—Tobin Q values less than 1.0—will be larger than those for growth firms—Tobin Q values greater than 1.0. John and Lang also predicted that the announcement effects of dividend increases may depend on the investment opportunities available to the firm. In addition, the J&L model provides some testable implications relating the announcement effects for dividend changes to the extent and direction of insider trading immediately prior to the announcement.

The evidence presented in Lang and Litzenberger shows that the announcement effect of dividend changes is significantly larger for firms with a low Tobin Q ($Q < 1.0$) than for firms with a high Tobin Q ($Q > 1.0$). John and Lang present evidence of differential announcement effects of dividend initiations as a function of insider trading in the previous quarter. Their evidence suggests that the market is using its information about the direction and extent of insider trading in interpreting whether a dividend initiation is "good news" or "bad news." Treating concurrent insider trading as an additional signal seems to provide a useful perspective for understanding the informational content of corporate dividends.

Information about the prospects of a firm may include the firm's current projects and its future investment opportunities. The firm's dividend policy, either exclusively or in combination with other signals, such as capital expenditure announcements or trading by insiders, may communicate this information to a less informed market. Tables 7.1 and 7.2 summarize the research discussed in this chapter.

Table 7.1 Summary of Selected Dividend Signalling Models

Author(s) of Study	Signal(s)	Main Empirical Implications
John and Williams (1985)	Cash dividends	Dividend increases elicit share-price increases. Share-price response should be higher with higher external financing and larger adverse tax consequence of dividends over capital gains.
Bhattacharya (1979)	Cash dividends	The announcement effects of dividend increases are positive. Dividend payouts are lower, with larger adverse tax consequences and higher flotation costs of external financing.
Miller and Rock (1985)	Cash dividends (net of external financing).	The announcement effects of dividend increases are positive. The announcement effects of increases in external financing are negative.
Ambarish, John, and Williams (1987)	Cash dividends and investments	The announcement effects of dividend increases (different for growth firms and mature firms) and share repurchases are positive. The announcement effects on equity issues are positive (negative) for growth (mature) firms.
John and Mishra (1990)	Investments and insider trading	The announcement effects for capital expenditure announcements are positive (negative) for growth (mature) firms. The announcement effects are positive (negative) for insider buying (selling).
John and Lang (1991)	Dividend initiations and insider trading	The announcement effects for dividend initiations accompanied by concurrent insider buying (selling) are positive (negative).

Table 7.2 Summary of Studies of Announcement Effects of Dividends

Author(s) of Study	Type of Announcement	Data Study Period	Sample Size	Announcement Effect Two-Day Excess Return (percentage)	Hypothesis Supported by the Result (Author's Interpretation)
Pettit (1972)	Dividend changes	1967–1969	135	Increases: +0.935 Decreases: –3.69	Substantial information is conveyed by the announcement of dividend changes. The market is efficient in incorporating information into share prices.
Aharony and Swary (1980)	Dividend changes	1963–1976	149	When earnings announcements precede or follow dividend announcements: For dividend increases +0.72 and +1.03, respectively. For dividend decreases –3.76 and –2.82 respectively.	Changes in quarterly cash dividends provide information beyond that provided by quarterly earnings numbers. Stock market adjusts efficiently to quarterly dividend information.
Asquith and Mullins (1983)	Dividend initiations	1964–1980	168	+3.7	Initiating a dividend policy conveys positive information to the market.
Kalay and Lowenstein (1986)	Whether dividend announced early or late	1981	Early: 72 Late: 76	Early = +0.331 Late = –0.124	The market interprets deferral of dividend announcements as conveying negative information.
Healy and Palepu (1988)	Dividend initiations Dividend omissions	1969–1980	Initiations: 131 Omissions: 172	Initiations = +3.9 Omissions = –9.5	Share price increases upon dividend initiations. Share price decreases upon dividend omissions. Further, a firm's earnings performance changes significantly around either a dividend initiation or omission.

(continued)

Table 7.2 (cont.)

Author(s) of Study	Type of Announcement	Data Study Period	Sample Size	Announcement Effect Two-Day Excess Return (percentage)	Hypothesis Supported by the Result (Author's Interpretation)
Lang and Litzenberger (1989)	Dividend initiations	1979–1984	429	For *Q*>1.0, average daily abnormal return = +0.3 For *Q*<1.0, average daily abnormal return = +1.1	The average return for firms with *Q*s less than 1.0 is significantly larger (three times) than for firms with *Q*s greater than 1.0. Dividend changes for overinvesting firms signal information about investment policies.
John and Lang (1991)	Dividend initiations	1975–1985	265	All firms, +3.23 For insider selling group, 2.2 less than that for the remaining group.	The announcement effect of dividend initiations is lower when accompanied by insider selling by 2.2 percent than otherwise. The evidence is consistent with insider trading being a signal jointly with dividend increases.
Dyl and Weigand (1998)	Dividend initiations	1972–1993	240	Variance drops: 0.001329 to 0.001138 Beta drops: 1.397 to 1.218	Dividend initiations convey information to the market regarding the lower risk (variance and beta) of the firm. The risk is lower in the year following dividend initiation.
Lipson, Macquieira, and Megginson (1998)	Dividend initiations	1980–1990	1628 IPOs 114 initiations	+1.53	Dividend initiations are associated with favorable subsequent earnings surprises. Dividend surprises are more favorable for dividend initiating firms than for firms that went public at the same time and did not choose to initiate dividends.
Benartzi, Michaely, and Thaler (1997)	Dividend increases Dividend decreases	1979–1991	1025	Increases = +0.81 Decreases = –2.53	Share price increases with dividend increases and decreases with dividend decreases. There is no evidence that dividend changes have information content about future earnings changes.

Chapter **8**

Corporate Dividend Policy Decisions

*I*n Chapter 3 we concluded that, under conditions of perfect capital markets, dividend policy is irrelevant. Following a managed dividend policy—whereby managers attempt to achieve a desired dividend payment pattern—does not add value relative to a residual policy, which simply pays out cash flows from operations in excess of investment needs. However, once we've introduced market imperfections, or frictions, the conclusion that a managed dividend policy is irrelevant is not so clear.

In this chapter we consider whether managers behave as though they believe that the dividend policy decision is important. For those who do, we examine how they go about making dividend policy decisions and whether they follow a consistent strategy in making these decisions.

8.1 Dividend Patterns of Individual Firms

When we looked at the economywide pattern of corporate dividend payments versus earnings in Chapter 1, we noted that dividend payments have been much less volatile than earnings over time. On the surface, this evidence suggests that, in aggregate, corporate decision makers who manage the dividend flow do not simply pay out a residual dividend, nor do they pay out a constant percentage of earnings. If they did, dividend volatility would be much higher than the data indicate. But let's consider the pattern for some individual companies and examine whether individual company dividend patterns reflect a managerial tendency to manage dividends. Figure 8.1 shows the dividend

119

Figure 8.1 Dividends versus Earnings Patterns

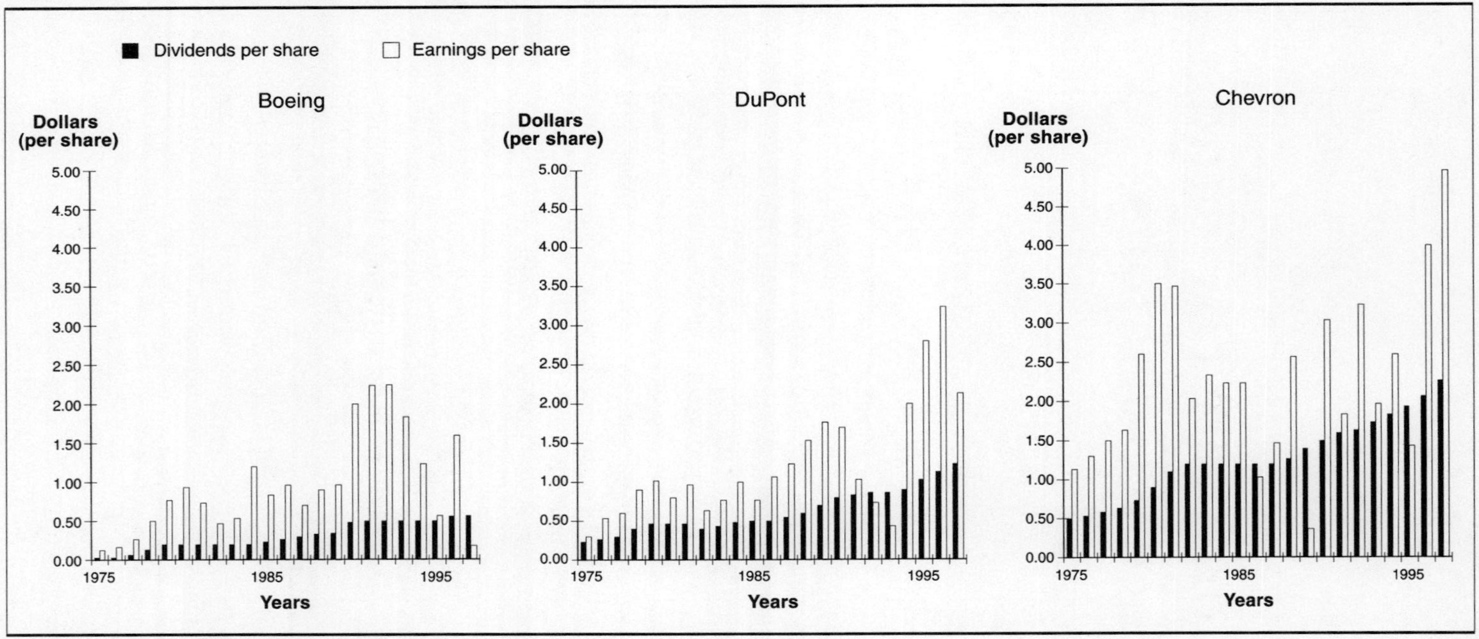

■ Dividends per share   □ Earnings per share

Source: Annual Industrial Compustat Tapes.

Figure 8.1 (cont.)

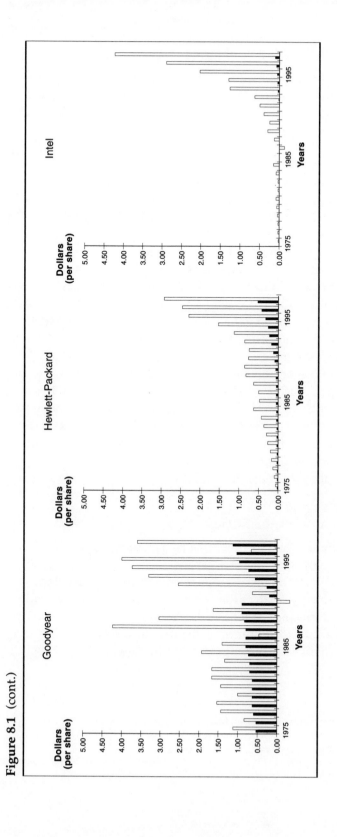

versus earnings patterns for six firms for the period 1975 through 1997.[1] Both dividends and earnings have been adjusted for stock splits. The dollar values are "nominal"; therefore they have not been adjusted for inflation.

Five of these six firms are blue chip members of the Dow Jones Industrial Average (Boeing Company, Chevron Corporation, E.I. duPont de Nemours & Company (DuPont), Goodyear Tire & Rubber Company, and Hewlett-Packard Company). Two are considered to be high-growth firms (Hewlett-Packard and Intel Corporation). Obviously these firms aren't a random sample, but the individual patterns suggest that, even though the payout levels differ, the payout patterns are consistent with the aggregate patterns discussed earlier.

Note that dividends per share appear to be much less volatile than earnings per share. Table 8.1 illustrates the levels of volatility for these firms as measured by their standard deviations, the coefficients of variation of EPS and DPS, and the average payout ratios, DPS/EPS, over this twenty-three year period.[2]

If managers followed a residual dividend policy, we would not expect to see such a consistent relationship between the low volatility of dividends relative to earnings as measured by either the standard deviation or the coefficient of variation. In short, both the visual evidence and the absolute and relative calculations of volatility suggest that at least these firms manage their dividend payout policies. We have more to say about the payout level later in the chapter.

8.2 The Lintner Survey

Lintner (1956) conducted a classic study on how U.S. managers go about making dividend decisions. He carefully reviewed the academic and popular finance literature that dealt with dividend policy and listed fifteen variables that were identified as having a bearing on dividend decisions. Among these variables were firm size, plant and equipment expenditures, willingness to use external financing, use of stock dividends, earnings stability, and ownership by control groups.

---

[1] These data have been taken from the *Annual Industrial Compustat Tapes.*

[2] Recall from Chapter 1 that the coefficient of variation is the standard deviation of a series of numbers divided by the average value. Standard deviation represents the absolute measure of volatility, whereas the coefficient of variation represents the relative measure of volatility.

Table 8.1 Volatility and Payout of a Sample of Individual Firms

Firm	Standard Deviation of EPS	Standard Deviation of DPS	Coefficient of Variation of EPS	Coefficient of Variation of DPS	Average Payout Ratio: DPS/EPS
Boeing	1.28	0.30	0.65	0.55	0.30
Chevron	0.84	0.39	0.40	0.33	0.72
DuPont	0.88	0.40	0.45	0.36	0.65
Goodyear	1.16	0.18	0.67	0.28	0.31
Hewlett-Packard	0.75	0.15	1.02	0.67	0.11
Intel	1.63	0.07	2.83	1.55	0.01

Source: Annual Industrial Compustat Tapes.

Next, he chose a sample of more than 600 listed, well-established industrial companies. From this sample, he chose 28 firms for intensive follow-up interviews. Although these firms were not statistically representative, they provided the diversity in terms of the fifteen variables that Lintner sought.

Lintner then conducted interviews with several of the managers responsible for the dividend decisions in each of these 28 firms, usually presidents, financial vice-presidents, treasurers, or directors. These interviews focused on the concrete, tangible elements that affected dividend decisions, especially when dividends were changed.

For the majority of firms the first question asked during consideration of a dividend decision was: Should the existing dividend be changed? Managers did not consider how much the dividend should be without referring to the existing dividend level.

Once convinced that a dividend change was desirable, managers asked a second question: What should be the magnitude of the dividend change? Again, the existing dividend level served as the benchmark. The real decision variable therefore was the *change* in the dividend, not the new dividend level itself. Lintner observed that an inherent resistance to changing the dividend (inertia) and a concern for increasing the dividend too much (conservatism) were prominent in dividend change decisions.

Managers had a consensus view that shareholders prefer a stable rate and that the market puts a premium on stability and gradual growth. Accordingly, managers considered having to reverse dividend changes as undesirable. A dividend increase was made only when management believed that it could be sustained in the future. Accordingly, a forecast of future earnings played an important role in a given period's dividend decision. A dividend decrease was made only if adverse circumstances were not expected to be overcome quickly; managers had a strong aversion to dividend cuts.

Lintner found that managers believed that they needed a tangible financial indicator to justify a dividend change. He found that earnings dominated all other factors, including investment requirements, as a basis for dividend decisions.

As another by-product of the interview process, Lintner discovered that managers believed that, as part of their fiduciary responsibility to shareholders, they should design a dividend policy that distributed a portion of any substantial change in earnings, either an increase or decrease, as a dividend change. They had a notion of "fair share" with respect to their shareholders' claims to dividends relative to earnings. The majority of firms had an ideal or "target" payout rate, or dividends per share divided by earnings per share. However, this target level was just that, a target toward which to move and not a restrictive year-by-year constraint. In his sample, Lintner found payout targets that varied from 20 to 80 percent of earnings; a 50 percent target was most common.

In addition, most of the firms had a standard with respect to the speed at which they would move toward their payout targets; these adjustments ranged from one-sixth to one-half. For example, let's assume that a target payout was 50 percent and that the speed of adjustment factor was 25 percent. Using these parameters, if EPS increased from $2.00 to $3.00, the first-year dividend increase would be ($1.00)(0.50)(0.25), or $0.1250. This calculation represents the earnings increase times the target payout ratio times the adjustment factor. The full $0.50 dividend increase (EPS change times target payout ratio) might take several years to achieve, assuming that the new EPS level remains constant.

Managers developed their target payout levels and adjustment factors over time. Among other factors, these parameters were determined by growth prospects for the firm, cyclical movement of investment opportunities, working capital needs, and internal cash flows. Once these parameters had been established, managers maintained the target payouts and adjustment factors over extended periods of time. Current capital expenditure or working capital needs did not tend to affect the current dividend decision. If current internal cash flows were insufficient to cover both dividend and investment requirements,

Lintner concluded that managers would scrutinize the necessity of the proposed investments. Managers would raise outside capital to fund the investments or cancel or postpone them. Lintner concluded that dividends represented the primary and active decision variable relative to investments and were not the by-product of investments.

Therefore, in deciding on a dividend change, managers looked at current earnings and applied their internal target level of payout to those earnings. Current earnings times the target payout level less last period's dividend determined the potential dividend change. This potential change was then multiplied by the speed of adjustment factor to determine the actual dividend change. In addition, firms preferred to keep dividend changes in multiples of $0.05. An example will clarify this decision-making process.

8.2.1 A Dividend Change Example

Using the information that Lintner obtained from managers in his survey, let's follow a step-by-step example of the decision process. We assume that Targhee Corporation paid a $2.50 dividend in the prior year on earnings of $6.25 per share. Targhee has a target payout rate of 40 percent and a speed of adjustment factor of 30 percent. Then Targhee's earnings increase from $6.25 to $8.00. Eight dollars times the target payout rate of 40 percent suggests a target dividend of $3.20 versus last year's dividend of $2.50. Will Targhee increase its dividend by $0.70, or $3.20 – $2.50? No! Targhee nominally would increase the dividend by the target change of $0.70 times the adjustment factor of 30 percent, or by $0.21. Given a preference for changes in $0.05 increments, Targhee would announce a *change* in dividend of $0.20 per share, resulting in a total dividend of $2.70 per share.

8.3 The Lintner Model

Convinced that managers conscientiously manage dividends systematically, Lintner developed a mathematical model to represent the verbal descriptions of the dividend decision process he had heard. But did managers' actual behavior follow this reported process? His regression model was

$$\Delta D_{it} = A_i + C_i(r_i E_{it} - D_{i(t-1)}) + U_{it},$$

where

ΔD_{it} = the change in dividends per share observed from period $t - 1$ to t for firm i;

A_i = the intercept term for firm i;

C_i = the speed of adjustment coefficient for firm i;

r_i = the target payout ratio for firm i;

E_{it} = the earnings after taxes per share in period t for firm i;

$D_{i(t-1)}$ = the dividends per share paid out last period for firm i; and

U_{it} = the error term for firm i in period t.

Lintner tested his regression model with actual corporate dividend data and found an r^2, or explained variance, of 85 percent. In other words, 85 percent of the variation in dividend changes year to year were explained by this compact mathematical model. Importantly, the intercept term, A_i, was significant and positive. This evidence indicated that managers consciously do avoid dividend cuts even when earnings decline, consistent with Lintner's impression from his interviews.

Thus Lintner's results show us that managers do try to do what they described verbally; or, that is, they

- stabilize dividends with gradual, sustainable increases whenever possible,
- establish an appropriate target payout ratio, and
- avoid dividend cuts, if at all possible.

To further examine its usefulness, Lintner tested his model for time periods outside of the period he used to develop the model. The regression coefficients were practically the same. In other words, the model worked over longer periods of time, not just for a specific time period.

8.4 The Impact of Dividend Policy on Investment

One potentially troubling aspect of Lintner's discussions with managers responsible for dividend decisions was the implication that "dividends may be the tail that wags the dog." In other words, did the desire to maintain a predictable dividend payout influence the firm's investment decisions?

Perhaps the most basic law of corporate finance decision making is that firms should take all positive NPV projects. If dividend policy dominates investment policy in management's hierarchy of priorities, could it be that value-enhancing projects are being canceled or postponed?

Fama (1974) examined the extent to which dividend decisions and investment decisions are related. We won't go into the details of his methodology here because the relationship of investments to dividends is only tangentially related to the purpose of this book. In brief, Fama found independence between the dividend and investment decisions of managers. In other words, Fama concluded that investments are not a function of the level of dividends paid. Rather, firms appeared to take on desirable investments while maintaining their dividend payout policies. Flexibility in external financing could account for this independence; that is, if good investments projects required outlays that exceeded free cash flow less the desired dividend, firms would secure external financing.

What does the financial press have to say about the interaction of dividends and investment? According to an article in the June 4, 1994, issue of *The Economist:*

> Contrary to popular assumption, the current high level of profits that British firms are devoting to dividend payments does not explain the firms' low level of investment. Dividends and investment are not direct competitors because firms can get cash not only from profits, but also by borrowing from banks or the capital markets and by raising money from their shareholders through rights issues. It is more likely that British firms are restraining investment because they perceive high levels of risk and, accordingly, seek high returns. (p. 15)

8.5 Dividend Patterns of Individual Firms Revisited

Having the background of the Lintner study, let's reexamine Figure 8.1. For Boeing, Chevron, and DuPont, we see a consistent and steady pattern of dividend growth. Note that dividends were not cut even during periods when earnings declined—a two-year period for Boeing (1981–1982) and three-year periods for DuPont (1991–1993). In short, these three firms seem to fit the Lintner model well.

We observe the same pattern of resisting dividend cuts when earnings declined for Goodyear until 1991. In 1988, Goodyear experienced a 28 percent decline in earnings, followed by a 46 percent decline in 1989, and a 126 percent decline in 1990. Over these three years, Goodyear basically held the line on dividends. Finally, in 1991, Goodyear drastically reduced dividends, from $0.90 per share to $0.20 per share. This reluctance to cut dividends is consistent with what managers told Lintner more than four decades ago.

Recently, an article in the *Wall Street Journal* discussed a dividend decision by General Motors' board of directors.[3] At its next meeting, the GM board was expected to raise the automaker's dividend. However, the article goes on to state:

> Company officials have emphasized, however, that they would recommend increasing the dividend only to levels that will be sustainable in a downturn. One of the reasons GM ran into trouble in the early '90s was that top management increased the dividend to a high of 75 cents quarterly, only to have to slash it to 40 cents and then further to 20 cents.

Hewlett-Packard and Intel, examples of high-growth companies, also conform to the pattern predicted by Lintner's model. However, Table 8.1 shows relatively low dividend payout levels for these firms compared to the four more mature firms. This anecdotal evidence suggests that the target payout ratio is set with an eye toward growth and investment needs. Once the target payout level has been set, however, managers still try to achieve a stable, steady growth pattern.

8.6 Subsequent Dividend Model Research

Although Figure 8.1 suggests that managers are still making dividend decisions consistent with Lintner' survey results and model, other researchers have conducted subsequent surveys of management views on dividend policy and have formally retested Lintner's model and have developed more sophisticated models to describe dividend behavior.

Baker, Farrelly, and Edelman (1985) conducted a survey of corporate financial managers to identify the factors they considered most important in determining their firms' dividend policies. One of the survey objectives was to compare contemporary determinants of dividend

---

[3] Blumenstein (1997).

policy using a much larger sample of firms (318 usable responses and a 57 percent response rate) with Lintner's survey results. Baker, Farrelly, and Edelman conclude:

First, the results show that the major determinants of dividend payments today appear strikingly similar to Lintner's behavioral model developed during the mid-1950's. In particular, respondents were highly concerned with dividend continuity. Second, the respondents seem to believe that dividend policy affects share value, as evidenced by the importance attached to dividend policy in maintaining or increasing share price. Although the survey does not uncover the exact reasons for their belief in dividend relevance, it does provide evidence that the respondents are generally aware of signaling and clientele effects. (p. 83)

Brittain (1964, 1966) and Fama and Babiak (1968) reevaluated Lintner's model. These authors concluded that Lintner's basic model continues to perform well relative to alternative specifications using both economywide earnings and dividend data and data for individual firms. Specifically, Fama and Babiak concluded:

The regressions on the firm data, the simulations, and the prediction tests provide consistent evidence on dividend models for individual firms. The two-variable Lintner model (4), including a constant term, D_{t-1}, and E_t, performs well relative to other models; in general, however, deleting the constant and adding the lagged profits variable E_{t-1} leads to *slight* [emphasis added] improvement in the predictive power of the model. (p. 1160)

In a recent comprehensive study, Benartzi, Michaely, and Thaler (1997) provided additional evidence that relates to Lintner's model. They stated:

The conclusion we draw from this analysis is that Lintner's model of dividends remains the best description of the dividend setting process available. Changes in dividends mostly tell us something about what has happened. Earnings have gone up quickly in year −1 and 0, and dividends are adjusted to reflect that. If there is any information content in this announcement, it is that the concurrent change in earnings is permanent rather than transitory. (p. 1032)

8.7 Conclusions

After four decades, Lintner's research remains the definitive study of management dividend behavior—a finance "classic." As a result of his work, along with confirmation by other researchers, we can safely conclude that in the United States financial managers typically view dividend decisions as an important part of their job. The typical firm does not follow a residual policy nor leave its dividend payout to chance. Rather, firms manage their dividends as Lintner's model proposed.[4]

However, in spite of the fact that managers view dividend decisions as important, we *cannot* conclude that the market rewards a carefully managed dividend policy with a higher share price. As Miller (1977) suggested with respect to the capital structure decisions, dividend policy decisions might be a "neutral mutation,"—policies that cause no harm but create no value. As the empirical evidence discussed suggests, the benefit of a managed dividend policy, if any, seems to escape systematic detection.

---

[4] We discuss dividend policies in other countries in Chapter 9.

Chapter **9**

Dividend Policy:
The Global Perspective

*I*n Chapter 1 we provided evidence of the importance of cash dividends as a payout mechanism to shareholders of firms based in the United States. Similarly, dividends also are important in other countries where public companies are a common form of corporate organization. However, economic environments around the world differ in terms of laws, regulations, and customs. Consequently, dividend policies systematically vary from country to country. For example, cash dividend payments are smaller and less relevant for firms in Japan, Switzerland, and Israel but are relatively more important in Canada and the United Kingdom. The frequency of dividend payments also varies from country to country. Dividends typically are paid quarterly in the United States and Canada, but most firms in Finland, Italy, and many other countries pay dividends annually.

In this chapter we present an overview of dividend policies in other countries. We provide descriptive statistics on their dividend payouts and describe the characteristics of their different laws and regulations, especially tax laws. We also examine the academic research that analyzes the potential effects of differing economic environments on the dividend decisions. We focus on countries in Europe, the Pacific Rim, and North America. These countries have developed sophisticated economic and capital market systems and their financial markets are studied frequently by researchers.

Before we begin a discussion of the global perspective of dividends, we emphasize that, even in countries where dividends traditionally are smaller and less relevant to investors, financial policy makers are well aware of the consequences of dividend policy. Consider the following dividend-related news from Japan whose economy has been sluggish in the 1990s.

- During a decline in trading volume, the exchanges looked for new ways to attract investors. The Foundation of the Japanese Security Association (Nihon Shoukengyo Kyokai) published an article on April 17, 1991, raising the question, "How do we attract the Japanese individual investor?" The first item stressed in the article was the importance of dividend policy.

- On March 2, 1992, *Barron's* reported that the powerful Japanese Ministry of Finance (MOF) was planning to allow Japanese life insurance companies to pay dividends out of capital gains rather than be restricted solely to life insurers' interest and dividend earnings. The implication of this change is global because "Japanese life insurance companies no longer will feel impelled to span the globe for high yields to pay out to policyholders." *Barron's* concluded that the MOF's clear aim is to encourage a repatriation of Japanese capital.

- As Japan's economy showed no signs of recovery, the *Wall Street Journal* reported on September 14, 1993, that "more than a dozen companies, including Nippon Steel and other big steelmakers, have suspended or cut their dividends to conserve cash."

These examples suggest that, even in Japan, lawmakers, financial institutions, corporations, and investors realize the importance of dividend policy.

9.1 Descriptive Statistics on Dividend Policies around the World

Let's consider some descriptive statistics on cash dividend practices in various countries that we have compiled from numerous studies. Table 9.1 presents the average dividend yield for firms, along with payment frequency, sample period, and special institutional features associated with dividend payments in those countries.

9.1.1 Dividend Size and Frequency

The average annual dividend yield in the European industrial countries, such as Germany, France, Switzerland, and Italy, is between 2.5 percent and 3.5 percent. This yield is less than the 4 percent average annual dividend yield in Canada and the United States.

Table 9.1 Descriptive Statistics of Typical Dividend Policies in Various Countries

Author(s) of Study	Country	Average Dividend Yield (percentage)[a]	Sample Size	Sample Period	Dividend-Paying Firms (percentage)	Payment Frequency	Important Institutional Features
Eckbo and Verma (1994)	Canada	3.1–10.5 Avg. 5	592–860 firms	1976–1988	47–67		Cash dividend decreases as voting power of manager-owner increases.
Booth (1987)	Canada	3.4	300 firms	1963–1982			Dividend tax credit is given.
Booth and Johnston (1984)	Canada	4	242–461 ex-dividend days	1970–1980			The tax reform of 1971 and subsequent reforms affected policies.
Lakonishok and Vermaelen (1983)	Canada	4.4 annually	555–671 ex-dividend days	1971–1972		Quarterly	The tax reform of 1971 taxed capital gains and changed dividend tax credit.
Bailey (1988)	Canada		9 firms with dual shares	1976–1983		Quarterly	There are two classes of equity: one pays cash and the other is capital gains.
Leithner and Zimmermann (1993)	United Kingdom	6.12	500 firms	1962–1986			Unique to the United Kingdom, share prices and dividends follow a cointegrated real process.
Ang, Blackwell, and Megginson (1991)	United Kingdom		12 dual-class funds	1969–1982			Tax reforms are frequent and an imputation dividend system existed during part of the sample period.

[a] The definition of dividend yield varies slightly among the studies.

(continued)

Table 9.1 (cont.)

Author(s) of Study	Country	Average Dividend Yield (percentage)	Sample Size	Sample Period	Dividend-Paying Firms (percentage)	Payment Frequency	Important Institutional Features
Kaplanis (1986)	United Kingdom	3.3	Options on 14 shares	1979–1984		Semi-annually	Shares go ex-dividend on the first Monday of the two-week account period.
Poterba and Summers (1985)	United Kingdom		633 ex-dividend days	1955–1981		Semi-annually	Frequent tax reforms have occurred with government changes.
Leithner and Zimmermann (1993)	Germany	3.43	467–638 firms	1959–1986		Annually	Only a specified portion of earnings can be distributed.
Behm and Zimmermann (1993)	Germany		32 major firms	1962–1988			Average payout ratio is about 38 percent. Tax credit on dividends was provided after 1977.
Capitelli (1989)	Switzerland		230 firms	1974–1986		Annually	The dividend is known with certainty at the beginning of the ex-dividend month.
Leithner and Zimmermann (1993)	Switzerland	2.46	49–65 major firms	1959–1986		Annually	The belief that Swiss firms maintain constant dividend per share is supported by the data.
Loderer (1989)	Switzerland		108 traded firms	1986	95		Firms raise considerable equity and simultaneously pay dividends.

Author(s) of Study	Country	Average Dividend Yield (percentage)	Sample Size	Sample Period	Dividend-Paying Firms (percentage)	Payment Frequency	Important Institutional Features
Leithner and Zimmermann (1993)	France	3.6	481–968 firms	1963–1987		Annually	In Europe, shareholders must typically approve a proposed dividend.
Michaely and Murgia (1995)	Italy	3.13	132–220 firms	1981–1990	85	Annually	Dividends on common (registered) and savings (bearer) stocks are taxed at different rates.
Hietala (1990)	Finland	5	50–60 firms	1974–1985		Annually	Dividends are actually paid on the ex-dividend day.
Hayashi and Jagannathan (1990)	Japan		7,106 ex-dividend days	1983–1987		Semi-annually	Dividends are not declared until several weeks after the ex-dividend day.
Kato and Loewenstein (1995)	Japan	0.7–2.5 Avg. 1.5	18,869 ex-dividend days	1981–1991	77–96.6	Semi-annually	The proximity of ex-dividend days to fiscal year-end, not the dividend per se, dominates returns.
Gn (1994)	Singapore		90 firms	1978–1992	66	Annually	Firms frequently tend to keep their existing dividend levels unchanged.

(continued)

Table 9.1 (cont.)

Author(s) of Study	Country	Average Dividend Yield (percentage)[a]	Sample Size	Sample Period	Dividend-Paying Firms (percentage)	Payment Frequency	Important Institutional Features
Bartholdy and Brown (1994)	New Zealand	About 4, taxable and nontaxable	335 ex-dividend days	1982–1987			Prior to 1985, dividends were either taxed or not, depending on the funds' source. Firms paid both types.
Procianoy and Snider (1994)	Brazil		40 firms	1987–1992	Profitable firms required by law to pay a fraction of their earnings as dividends		Taxes were levied on dividends but not on capital gains before 1989 and vice versa after 1990.
La Porta, Lopes-de-Silanes, Shleifer, and Vishny (1997)	33 different countries		4,103 firms	1994			Dividend policies were compared for common law versus civil law countries.

Most firms in these European countries pay dividends only once a year. Again, this practice is in contrast to the United States and Canada, where dividends are typically declared quarterly and sometimes even monthly. The European country that seems unique in its firms' dividend policies is the United Kingdom. There, average dividend yields are higher (6.12 percent, according to one study) and dividends are paid semiannually. In recent years, most Japanese firms have increased their annual dividends and now declare dividends more frequently (twice a year rather than once). Moreover, firms have to pay dividends in order to be listed on the Tokyo Stock Exchange. Nevertheless, dividend yields remain relatively low (less than 2 percent) because the increases in dividends still have not caught up with the rise in stock prices during the 1980s.

As a final demonstration of the variety of dividend policies in different countries, we present the time series of payout ratios for four major economies in Figure 9.1. The payout ratio is defined as the amount of dividend paid as a percentage of after-tax profits.

Figure 9.1 Payout Ratios in Four Major Countries

Dividend payouts as percentage of post-tax profits

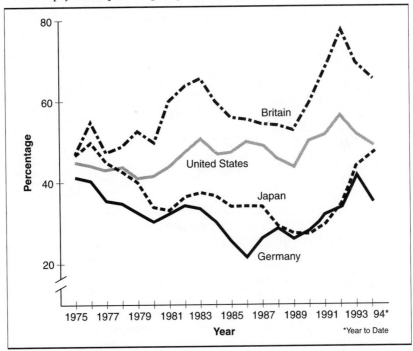

Source: The Economist, June 4, 1994, p. 109.

9.1.2 Institutional Features

The differences in dividend practices throughout the world can be attributed to unique institutional features in various countries. In most European countries and Japan, shareholders must typically approve the proposed dividend. In Germany, Switzerland, Brazil, and several other countries, the law specifies the minimum percentage of earnings that must be distributed as dividends. However, corporations in these countries usually are able to exploit loopholes in the tax code to circumvent these requirements. In Switzerland, firms raise considerable equity and simultaneously pay dividends. The information provided to the market concerning forthcoming dividend payments ranges from being available at the beginning of the ex-dividend month in Switzerland to the absence of any dividend announcement prior to the ex-dividend day in Japan.[1]

9.1.3 Tax Differences

A variety of tax codes, which change frequently as tax reforms are passed in various countries, also can have an important effect on dividend policies. Dividends and capital gains are the alternative sources of return for shareholders, but, in many countries, there are no capital gains taxes or they were introduced for the first time only recently. For instance, in Canada capital gains taxes were introduced in the tax reform of 1971 and in Japan in the tax reform of 1988. In Israel, the government attempted to introduce capital gains taxes in 1994 but backed down under public pressure in 1995. In contrast, capital gains have been taxed in the United States since early in the twentieth century. Under the U.S. tax code, capital gains received a preferential tax treatment relative to dividends between 1921 and the Tax Reform Act of 1986, when the rates were equalized. However, since the Omnibus Reconciliation Act of 1993, capital gains again have been taxed at a lower rate than dividends in the United States.[2] In 1997, the capital gains tax rate was lowered again relative to dividends.

Dividend tax laws vary greatly among countries.[3] The Canadian tax code calls for a dividend tax credit, although the details change

---

[1] Some Japanese executives, however, make occasional voluntary announcements on the sizes of their dividends prior to ex-dividend day. See Kato, Loewenstein, and Tsay (1997).

[2] For more details, see the tax discussion in Chapter 5.

[3] The purpose of this discussion is to provide a "flavor" for the tax differences among countries without going into specifics. The details are both overwhelming and outside the scope of this book.

from time to time (e.g., the tax reform of 1971). A dividend tax credit is part of the tax code in Japan and also was adopted in Germany in 1977.[4] In the United Kingdom, a dividend imputation system is used off and on, depending on whether the Conservative Party or the Labour Party is in power.[5] A complicated dividend imputation system also was in place in Australia until recently. In New Zealand, until 1985, dividends were taxed or not taxed, depending on the source of the funds that financed the dividend. In Italy, dividends on registered stocks and savings stocks are taxed at different rates. The tax code for individuals in the United States is costly for shareholders. Dividends are subject to taxation both at the corporate and the individual level. Further, the United States has no tax credit or imputation system, although from time to time small amounts of dividend income are exempted from taxation. Tax laws for corporate income from dividends also are different in various countries, although the general rule in most of them is that corporate investors enjoy a preferential tax treatment of dividend income.

American investors are well aware of the various tax laws in different countries. On November 16, 1994, the *Wall Street Journal* reported that:

> In a scene reminiscent of the dividend capture game of a few years ago, some giant American investors such as pension funds are playing a different game that might be called the dividend dump. They are bobbing and weaving, darting in and out of emerging-market stocks to avoid collecting dividends because the withholding tax is so high.
> (p. C1)

Those less interested in the details of specific studies may wish to skip to the summary of this chapter. In addition, Table 9.1 summarizes

---

[4] An amusing anecdote associated with the German dividend tax credit was reported by *The Economist* on December 18, 1993: "Ekkehard Wenger is at it again. On December 20th the University of Wuerzburg Professor, scourge of German managers and champion of small shareholders, plans to demand that Daimler-Benz pay out more than half its equity in one big dividend . . . of profit that was earned between 1977 and 1989, and taxed at 56%. Under Germany's tax laws, if profits are paid out in dividends, the tax already paid on them is restored, and shareholders pay tax on their portion instead. Individuals would gain, because they need pay an average of only 30–40% on dividend income. . . . If past form is any guide, his performance at the extraordinary shareholders' meeting will be showy and abrasive; his proposal will be summarily dismissed. Yet that may not be the end of the story, for Mr. Wenger's wishes often come true" (p. 70).

[5] In an *imputation system* the personal tax liability on dividends is reduced by the amount of taxes the corporation paid on the income that was used to pay out the dividend. The rationale for this system is the desire to avoid double taxation of corporate income.

the important institutional features for most of the research described in Sections 9.2–9.4.

9.2 Dividend Payout Patterns around the World

Despite the statistical differences in the characteristics (size, yield, frequency, etc.) of the dividend streams of corporations in various countries—and the range of tax laws, regulations, and institutional features—we can point to some similarities in corporate dividend policies in various countries. Specifically, dividend smoothing seems to be a management tendency everywhere.

In Chapter 8 we discussed Lintner's (1956) classic study on corporate dividend decisions in the United States.[6] Numerous researchers have replicated Lintner's methodology and have observed similar corporate payout decisions in different countries. These researchers, using variations of Lintner's model, have documented patterns of dividend streams similar to those he found for U.S. companies. The evidence suggests that managers tend to maintain smooth dividend payout patterns; they pay out stable amounts of dividends and avoid sudden changes, especially cuts in dividends. This practice transcends national boundaries.

For example, Leithner and Zimmermann (1993) analyzed dividend streams for four major European markets: West Germany, the United Kingdom, France, and Switzerland. In Switzerland, individual firms often explicitly formulated a policy of stable dividends per share. Variance ratio tests supported the hypothesis that management attempts to smooth the time path of dividends in all four countries. To test for long-term target payout ratios in these countries, Leithner and Zimmermann used a market portfolio value as a proxy for permanent earnings. They found that dividends and market portfolio values showed a long-term relationship in the United Kingdom but not in any of the other countries under investigation.

Two other studies tested the Lintner hypothesis directly in two European countries. McDonald, Jacquillat, and Nussenbaum (1975) examined the French market and documented results consistent with

---

[6] Recall that Lintner polled managers, discovered that they generally had a target dividend payout ratio on earnings, and that they made considerable efforts to smooth changes to achieve the target. Therefore changes in dividends only partially adjusted to changes in earnings. In his statistical analysis, Lintner found that managers typically stabilized dividends with gradual, sustainable increases. Managers were extremely reluctant to cut dividends and did so only when adverse circumstances were likely to persist.

Lintner. The variation in current dividends was explained by current earnings and past dividends, not by investment or external financing levels. Behm and Zimmermann (1993) examined the empirical relationship between dividends and earnings in Germany. They followed Lintner and the subsequent literature and tested models relating dividends to different earnings measures of firms. Behm and Zimmermann reported results that generally were consistent with Lintner. Firms smooth dividends relative to earnings, but dividend changes are related positively to current earnings and negatively to lagged dividends. However, Behm and Zimmermann also reported that dividend decisions may not be based on a long-term target payout ratio, as suggested by the Lintner model. Apparently, long-term payout ratio averages deviate substantially from implied target ratios.

Dividend smoothing policies also are common in Pacific Rim countries. For example, Kato and Loewenstein (1995) reported a relatively stable payout ratio during the 1980s for the median firm in Japan. Gn (1994) studied corporate dividend policy dynamics in Singapore. He claimed that zero dividend changes were more common in Singapore than they were in the United States, and that the majority of Singapore firms tended to keep dividend payouts unchanged for at least three years. Gn developed a variation of the Lintner model that incorporated frequent zero changes. The empirical results were consistent with the model.

Nevertheless, in a recent study Dewenter and Warther (1998) directly compared dividend policies in Japan and the United States. They observed that Japanese firms (especially firms belonging to business groups, or *keiretsus*) adjust their dividends to earnings changes more quickly than do U.S. firms (i.e., the Japanese firms make larger dividend changes, in response to earnings changes, resulting in a more volatile dividend pattern). Moreover, Japanese firms are less reluctant to omit or cut dividends than their U.S. counterparts. Interestingly, the share-price reaction to dividend omissions and initiations is smaller in Japan than in the United States, which is consistent with the conjecture that Japanese firms face less information asymmetry and/or agency conflicts than do U.S. firms.

Other studies that did not test the Lintner hypothesis directly still examined the time series of dividend payments. Loderer (1989) documented that in Switzerland firms issue equity frequently through rights offerings at low prices (for example, 43 percent of the traded firms did so in 1986). He was puzzled that, at the same time, almost all (98 percent) of the equity-issuing firms also paid dividends. This evidence suggested that Swiss firms follow their payout target ratios closely.

Procianoy and Snider (1994) examined the time series of payout ratios for Brazilian firms. Before Brazil's unique tax reform in 1989, investors were taxed on dividend income but not on capital gains. Since 1990, capital gains have been taxed but dividend income has been tax free. The Procianoy and Snider study benefited from a complete reversal in the Brazilian tax code regarding dividends, making it an exceptionally clean experiment. Furthermore, since 1990, all investors, including pension funds, mutual funds, and corporations, have been subjected to identical taxes. Thus the complications associated with tax-induced clienteles that we discussed in Chapter 5 have been avoided. Because dividend income has been exempt from taxes since the 1990 reform and, accordingly, became more desirable to taxpaying investors, we would expect larger payout ratios after 1990. Procianoy and Snider reported, however, that payout ratios did not increase. Their evidence provides another example of the strong tendency for managers everywhere to maintain smooth dividend payouts, even in changing economic environments.

9.3 Taxes and Dividend Payout Policies in Various Countries

In addition to studies on the dividend payout practices in various countries, many researchers have examined the different institutional features in these countries to analyze how market imperfections may affect dividend policies. Much of the research in the global arena is comparable to the studies conducted in the United States. It sheds light on some puzzles associated with dividend policy by examining how a variety of economic and market settings affect dividend decisions.

A popular avenue of research is examining the impact of different tax regulations on dividend policies. In particular, many studies analyze share-price behavior around ex-dividend days. The idea is that if taxes are relevant—and if investors are subjected to different tax treatment for dividend and capital gains income—then share-price drops on the ex-dividend day will not equal the dividend per share.[7]

---

[7] To understand our discussion of taxes in this chapter, please refer to the complete treatment of taxes in Chapter 5.

9.3.1 Share-Price Behavior around Ex-Dividend Days

Many of the ex-dividend share-price behavior studies in different countries consider tax reforms during a sample period. This design enables the researchers to evaluate the effects of the relevant changes in the tax code on security prices.

Lakonishok and Vermaelen (1983) examined the ex-dividend day behavior of Canadian companies on the Toronto Stock Exchange before and after the tax reform of 1971. This reform introduced taxes on capital gains and made dividend income more attractive for investors. Lakonishok and Vermaelen calculated the ratio of the share-price drop on the ex-dividend day to the dividend per share. They were puzzled by the low ratio observed, which was much lower than the comparable ratios documented in the United States. They also noticed, however, that the ratios generally were lower in 1972 than in 1971. They interpreted this result as being inconsistent with the tax-induced clientele hypothesis and consistent with the short-term trading hypothesis.[8]

Booth and Johnston (1984) also used data from the Toronto Stock Exchange. Their sample period (1970–1980) included both the tax reform of 1971 and other tax changes. Like Lakonishok and Vermaelen, they tested the tax-induced clientele hypothesis against the professional short-term trading hypothesis. Booth and Johnston used a slightly different methodology, and they reached different conclusions. They found that the data from around the 1971 tax reform did not support the professional short-term trading hypothesis. Also, the ratio of price drop to dividend on the ex-dividend day provided no evidence for the tax-induced clientele hypothesis. Finally, they also observed that the ratio was positive but significantly different from 1. They attributed this finding to a strong preference for capital gains income by Canadian investors trading around ex-dividend days.

Share-price behavior in the United Kingdom around ex-dividend days also has been studied extensively. Poterba and Summers (1985) exploited the fact that the United Kingdom has undergone several major dividend tax reforms in the post–World War II period, providing, in their words, ". . . an ideal natural experiment for analyzing the

---

[8] Recall that the tax-induced clientele hypothesis suggests that groups of investors characterized by their tax status are attracted to stocks of firms with desired dividend policies. The short-term trading hypothesis suggests that trading around the ex-dividend day is dominated by short-term traders who are indifferent (in the sense of taxes) to the form of returns (i.e., dividends or capital gains). Also see Chapter 5.

dividend tax effect (page 227)." They tested three hypotheses: (1) the tax irrelevance hypothesis, which states that taxes do not affect any aspect of a dividend decision; (2) the capitalization hypothesis, which views a dividend decision as a residual decision (i.e., dividends are paid only when all the positive net present value projects have been accepted by the firm); and (3) the standard tax-effect hypothesis, which suggests that taxes influence market behavior generally and security prices specifically. They examined ex-dividend price behavior and concluded that the tax irrelevance view was not supported by the data; returns on ex-dividend days changed with important changes in the tax code. Poterba and Summers did not stop there, however. They also examined the reaction of share prices and corporate payout ratios to the announcements of major tax reform in the United Kingdom. They interpreted their findings as being consistent with the traditional tax effect, rather than the other two competing hypotheses.

In a second article, Poterba and Summers (1984) used daily data for sixteen large U.K. firms. They observed changes in excess returns on the shares of these firms on ex-dividend days that were associated with various tax reforms and therefore also were consistent with the traditional tax effect.

Kaplanis (1986) employed a different methodology to study share-price behavior around ex-dividend days in the United Kingdom. He used a measure designed to reflect the market expectations for the forthcoming price drop on the ex-dividend day. Using option prices, he calculated the implied drop in share prices on the ex-dividend day and found that the actual price drop was very similar to the implied decline from option prices. Kaplanis also found that the implied price drop to dividend ratio was much less than 1, and was higher for securities that yielded high dividends. These results are consistent with the tax-induced clientele hypothesis and inconsistent with the short-term trading hypothesis.

In a later study, Lasfer (1995), using a different methodology and a larger sample, confirmed Kaplanis's results. Lasfer examined share-price behavior on ex-dividend days before and after the tax reform of 1988, which substantially reduced the tax differential between dividends and capital gains in the United Kingdom. He documented positive and significant excess returns on ex-dividend days before the reform and negative and insignificant excess returns on ex-dividend days after the reform. Moreover, ex-dividend day returns were significantly related to dividend yields but were not affected by measures of transaction costs, such as the bid–ask spread. Lasfer concluded from these findings that ex-dividend day share prices were affected by taxes but not by short-term trading.

In another ex-dividend study, Michaely and Murgia (1995) explained an interesting institutional feature of the Italian stock market, in which dividends on two classes of shares are taxed differently. Dividends on savings stocks are taxed at a fixed rate of 15 percent for all market participants, whereas the tax rate on dividend income from shares of common stock varies by investor. Michaely and Murgia found that for the savings stock sample the relative price drop on the ex-dividend day was almost identical to that predicted by the theory (they documented a price-drop-to-dividend ratio of 0.86). They also found no abnormal trading volume around the ex-dividend days of this sample. They explained this volume behavior by the fact that no gains from trade exist in this case, since all investors face the same tax rate. In contrast, the price-drop-to-dividend ratio for the common stock sample was very low (0.25), or lower than the theoretical ratio for any investor in this market. They attributed this result to a "registration effect." It turned out that the ex-dividend day coincided with the date on which common stocks were registered. Individuals who preferred to maintain their fiscal anonymity would sell their shares and create a downward price pressure before the ex-dividend day. The volume of trade for common stocks of Italian firms was high around ex-dividend days, which was consistent with gains from trading in these securities. Michaely and Murgia also reported positive correlations between the volume of trade and dividend yields and between the price drop on the ex-dividend day and dividend yield. These correlations are consistent with the traditional tax effect.

The most bizarre share-price behavior around ex-dividend days was observed in Japan. Hayashi and Jagannathan (1990) documented a negative price-drop-to-dividend ratio. In other words, the average stock price *rose* on ex-dividend days. The negative sign of the ratio was not consistent with an explanation that relies solely on dividend-related tax considerations. Hayashi and Jagannathan struggled to explain this finding but were unable to resolve this puzzle satisfactorily.

More recently, Kato and Loewenstein (1995) conducted a comprehensive empirical analysis of share-price behavior around ex-dividend days in Japan. Initially, they confirmed Hayashi and Jagannathan's results, but noted, however, that most ex-dividend days coincided with the end of the fiscal year for Japanese corporations. They provided evidence that excess returns around ex-dividend days were attributable to intercorporate trading activities around the end of the fiscal year to manipulate their tax liabilities, or to provide "window dressing" for their annual reports. The unique industrial structure in Japan presented a natural opportunity for such trading activities. Although tax considerations associated with dividends appeared to be of secondary importance in Japan, Kato and Loewenstein presented evidence consistent with cross-sectional variation associated with the tax effect. For example, they documented a significant positive correlation between the price-drop-to-dividend ratio and dividend yields. Moreover, they found substantial changes both in share-price behavior and volume of trade on ex-dividend days taking place before and after the major Japanese tax reform of 1988. These changes clearly are consistent with the traditional tax effect.

Ex-dividend studies also were conducted in smaller markets. Hietala (1990) studied the ex-dividend share-price behavior in Finland. The tax code in Finland is "strikingly similar" to the U.S. tax code after the 1986 tax reform. Both dividends and capital gains are regarded as ordinary income. Hietala found a price-drop-to-dividend ratio of 0.9, which is consistent with a marginal investor (seller) being an individual in the 50 percent tax bracket. However, he did not find any indication of a tax-induced clientele effect, as securities with different dividend yields exhibited similar ratios of price drops to dividends on the ex-dividend days.

Brown and Walter (1986) studied the ex-dividend day behavior in Australia. They documented a price-drop-to-dividend ratio of 0.75, which is consistent with a tax effect.

Bartholdy and Brown (1994) explored a particular tax regime in New Zealand under which companies can pay either, or both, taxable and nontaxable dividends. During the sample period (1982–1987), investors who declared a long-term "intent" were not subject to taxes on capital gains, even if they realized the gains in the short-run. Bartholdy and Brown found the price-drop-to-dividend ratio on the ex-dividend day to be less than 1 for taxable dividends. However, they could not reject the hypothesis that the ratio was 1 for nontaxable dividends. They also used alternative methodologies with similar results. They interpreted their results as being consistent with a tax effect in New Zealand but not with the short-term trading hypothesis.

In summary, overwhelming evidence exists that, for those countries in which the tax code grants preferential treatment to capital gains, either excess returns are observed on the ex-dividend day, or the price-drop-to-dividend ratio on that day is significantly lower than 1. Moreover, tax reforms in various countries seem to affect prices, investor behavior, and firms' policies in meaningful ways. The authors responsible for these studies interpreted this evidence as suggesting that taxes play an important role in dividend decisions everywhere in the world. Less support was found for the clientele hypothesis and the short-term trading hypothesis. The existence of a tax effect around ex-dividend days, however, is not an open and shut case. Recent research in the United States offers another explanation for share-price behavior around ex-dividend days (see Chapter 5).

9.3.2 Other Tests for the Tax Effect

Ex-dividend studies are the most common method used to examine the existence of the tax effect in the global arena. However, some researchers use other approaches to observe the role of taxes in dividend decisions.

Booth (1987) examined the macroeconomic effects of a change in dividend tax credits in Canada. He hypothesized that an increased dividend tax credit gives an incentive for Canadian citizens to invest in Canadian markets rather than other markets, especially the U.S. markets, in which investors do not enjoy a dividend tax credit. He found a higher concentration of Canadian ownership following the change in the dividend tax credit, especially in dividend intensive industries. This evidence is consistent with the tax hypothesis.

Bailey (1988) explored the consequences of the Canadian tax reform of 1971, which allowed firms in Canada to issue dual-class common shares, identical in every respect except that Class A shares paid cash dividends and Class B shares paid capital gains income.[9] Although conversion options were available, Bailey claimed that, if positive transaction costs were associated with a conversion, one class of shares might sell at a premium. For his sample of nine firms, he found that Class A shares had a higher volume of trade than Class B shares and that Class A shares sold at a statistically significant premium relative to Class B shares. However, as free conversion from class to class was possible, this premium was puzzling. Bailey explained that differences in the value of the cash dividends relative to the actual value of

---

[9] Specifically, in the early part of the sample period, Class B shares paid "tax deferred" dividends. For each $1 of dividends received by Class A shareholders, Class B investors received $0.85 in cash, which was not taxable at that time. At the time a Class B share was sold, the sum of all tax-deferred dividends previously received was subtracted from the purchase price for the purpose of determining the taxable capital gains. In the latter part of the sample period, Class B shares paid stock dividends instead.

the capital gains—as well as implicit and explicit transaction costs (e.g., odd-lot transaction costs associated with stock dividends)—could account for the premium. He concluded that, after controlling for some of the differences in institutional features associated with both distributions, he could not find evidence for a preference for cash dividends over an equal amount of capital gains.

Ang, Blackwell, and Megginson (1991) studied dual-class shares issued by British investment trusts. They examined the effect of taxes on the relative valuation of dividends and capital gains. Specifically, they examined twelve dual-class British investment trusts having one class of shares entitled only to stock dividends and another class entitled only to cash dividends. The values of the cash dividends were set to be equal to the values of the stock dividends. The stock-dividend shares were convertible without cost to cash-dividend shares on specified annual terms. In periods when stock dividends received favorable capital gains tax treatment, Ang, Blackwell, and Megginson found that stock-dividend shares sold at a significant premium above shares paying cash dividends of equal personal pre-tax value. The conversion rate from stock-dividend shares to cash-dividend shares during such periods was low. In other periods, when no tax advantages to capital gains income existed, cash-dividend shares sold at a premium. Further, during these periods the conversion of stock-dividend shares to cash-dividend shares increased substantially until stock-dividend shares virtually were eliminated. All the results are consistent with a tax effect.

The U.K. capital markets were tested for the tax effect in yet another way by Poterba and Summers (1984b). They followed the studies by Litzenberger and Ramaswamy (1979, 1980, 1982) for the U.S. capital markets and tested empirically the after-tax version of the capital asset pricing model (CAPM). Poterba and Summers analyzed monthly data for a sample of 3,500 British firms, correcting for information effects that might bias the results. The results were consistent with a tax effect. The different tax regimes in Britain produced different tax penalty coefficients on dividends. The changes in these coefficients were in the right direction, although some appeared to be too high relative to their expected size.

Capitelli (1989) also used the after-tax version of the CAPM with Swiss data. Using monthly security price data from the Zurich Stock Exchange, he argued that in Switzerland, since dividend payments were known before the beginning of the ex-dividend month, information effects were not a concern. The coefficient of the dividend yield variable was positive and significant, which was consistent with a tax effect. Capitelli also interpreted other findings as being consistent with a clientele hypothesis.

In summary, similar to the ex-dividend studies, other tests for tax effects have indicated the important role of taxes in affecting security prices, investor behavior, and firm's decisions on dividend policies.

9.4 Conflict of Interest, Information, and Payout Policy

International dividend researchers have focused on the role of taxes in explaining dividend decisions, but a few studies are available for foreign countries on other facets of dividend policy.

Eckbo and Verma (1994) studied the relation between share ownership concentration and dividend policy in Canada. Their hypothesis was that, in light of heterogeneous interests, dividend policy is determined according to who has the voting power. They noted that in Canada, where firms are generally more closely held, manager-owners derive benefits from free cash flows, and pay high taxes on dividends. At the same time, corporate investors or institutions are largely exempt from paying taxes on cash dividends. Eckbo and Verma found higher dividend yields for firms with a concentration of corporate/institutional shareholders and lower dividend yields for firms with higher manager-owner voting power. Therefore, consistent with Eckbo and Verma's hypothesis, manager-owners and corporate/institutional shareholders had opposing preferences for cash dividends. The resulting dividend policy reflected the relative power of each group to impose its preferences on the other.

A recent contribution to the agency literature from an international perspective was provided by La Porta, Lopez-de-Silanes, Shleifer, and Vishny (1997). They argued that by paying dividends, insiders return corporate earnings to minority shareholders rather than exploiting them by using the funds for private benefit. They hypothesized a relationship between dividend policies and the protection that the legal system provides to outsiders or minority shareholders in one of the following ways: (1) dividends are the outcome of an effective system of legal protection where minority shareholders use their legal powers to force companies to pay out cash, or (2) dividends are a substitute for legal protection that relies on firms' needs to raise external financing. These latter firms are not able to sell securities without providing routine dividend payments. In other words, dividends protect investors in an environment where they have poor legal protection.

In their empirical analysis, La Porta et al. examined 4,103 firms in thirty-three countries. They divided the countries into two categories: countries with strong legal protection for minority shareholders (generally countries governed by common law), and countries where investors' legal protection is weak (generally countries governed by civil law). They then compared dividend policies for firms in the two categories of countries.

The researchers found support for the first hypothesis. Firms operating in countries with better legal protection pay, on average, higher dividends. Furthermore, faster growing firms in these countries pay relatively lower dividends than do slower growing firms. Presumably, they do so because their shareholders are well protected by the legal system and are willing to wait for future dividends when the firm has good current investment opportunities. In contrast, in countries with less legal protection, investors demand dividends whenever they can get them.

Amihud and Murgia (1997), who are interested in dividends as a signaling device, studied the German market. This study is another example of research that uses the different institutional features in a foreign country to shed light on a theory that was proposed for the U.S. economy. Specifically, they reexamined the John and Williams (1985) dividend signaling model in which higher taxes on dividends served as the necessary signaling cost. Amihud and Murgia noted that, unlike in the United States, in Germany the majority of investors actually have a tax preference for dividends. Therefore tax considerations do not work against dividends in Germany. Consequently, they claimed that share prices should react differently in Germany than in the United States to announced dividend changes. However, they found that share-price reaction to dividend announcements was very similar in both countries. They interpreted this result as being inconsistent with the hypothesis that taxes are the costs that allow dividends to serve as a signaling device.

9.5 Conclusions

Cash dividends as a payout mechanism are an important method of rewarding shareholders everywhere in the world where public companies are a common form of corporate organization. However, economic environments differ from country to country in terms of laws, regulations, and customs. Consequently, dividend policies vary among countries in terms of relevance, payment frequency, dividend size, and the decision-making process. Table 9.1 provides descriptive statistics of typical dividend policies in various countries.

Corporate dividend policies are similar in certain respects all over the world. Specifically, the smoothing of dividends appears to be a common management practice everywhere.

Much of the research in the global arena has examined the different institutional features in various countries to analyze the impact of market imperfections on dividend policy. The idea is to shed light on some puzzles associated with dividend policies by examining how a variety of economic and market settings affect dividend decisions.

A popular avenue of research is examining the impact of different tax regulations on dividend policies. The majority of the researchers interpret their evidence as suggesting that taxes play an important role in dividend decisions everywhere in the world. However, we must be a bit cautious about this interpretation because of some recent research in the United States (see the discussion in Chapter 5 of the research by Kalay and Michaely 1993).

Chapter *10*

Common Stock Repurchases: An Alternative to Dividends

The United States is one of the few countries that provides its corporations with an option for distributing cash to their shareholders other than in dividend payments. This alternative mechanism is a common stock repurchase.[1] In a common stock repurchase, the corporation pays out cash in return for all or part of the shares owned by individual shareholders. Consequently, the outstanding equity of the company is reduced in a share repurchase.

This significant alternative method of cash distribution has not escaped corporate America. Under the headline "U.S. firms buy back stock at a record-setting pace," the *Los Angeles Times* reported on March 23, 1996:

> U.S. companies are conducting the most intensive share-repurchasing effort in the market's history. This year, more than 300 companies have announced plans to buy back a total of $40 billion worth of stock. In the first two weeks of March alone, a list of companies that includes Monsanto Co., Sears, Roebuck & Co., Bristol-Meyers, Squibb Co., and BankAmerica Corp. announced plans to repurchase a total of more

---

[1] Share repurchases are also fairly common in Canada and the United Kingdom and have recently started to gain popularity in other European countries, especially open market share repurchases. Moreover, a few countries in Europe and the Far East have been studying the possibility of introducing share repurchases.

153

than $9 billion of publicly held stock. If this trend continues, compa-
nies will retrieve more than $160 billion of publicly held stock in 1996,
shattering the record of $98.8 billion set last year. (p. D-3)

In this chapter we discuss common stock repurchases, examine
possible reasons for stock repurchases, and compare and contrast common stock repurchases to dividend payments. We review both the theoretical and empirical literature concerning share repurchases.

10.1 Motives for Common Stock Repurchases versus Dividend Payments

Common stock repurchases and dividend payments can be
spurred by motives that have both similarities and differences.

10.1.1 Similar Motives

The academic research identifies numerous motives for share repurchases that are similar, but not identical, to those for declaring cash
dividends. As with a dividend payment, a corporation may choose to
declare a stock repurchase for lack of profitable investment opportunities. Also comparable to dividends, common stock repurchases can be
used by a company to convey superior inside information possessed
by the management to the market. The announcement of a repurchase
plan may reflect management's expectations about the firm's future
prospects. Moreover, like cash dividends, common stock repurchases
may create conflicts of interest between the corporation's shareholders
and other claimants. A repurchase plan can be viewed, at least in some
instances, as an action taken to benefit shareholders at the expense of
bondholders and other claimants. Finally, stock repurchases can cause
substantial changes in the capital structure of the firm, especially if the
repurchase is debt financed. The changes in capital structure are similar, in principle, to those of a debt-financed dividend payment, although the magnitude of the changes is typically much larger with a
common stock repurchase.

10.1.2 Dissimilar Motives

In spite of the similarities noted, significant differences exist between motives for cash dividends and common stock repurchases.
First, the tax treatment of common stock repurchases is different from

that of cash dividends. For individuals, cash dividends are taxed as ordinary income, whereas income from share repurchases is treated as capital gains. Therefore, in periods when the tax code provides preferential treatment of capital gains, private investors may prefer to receive the firm's distribution in the form of a common stock repurchase.

Second, a cash distribution to shareholders in the form of a share repurchase is generally disproportional. That is, only the shareholders who choose to tender or sell back all or a fraction of their shares to the firm are entitled to receive the cash distribution. Consequently, a common stock repurchase may revise the proportions of the shareholders' holdings and thereby affect the ownership structure of the firm.[2] Corporate control issues may be a possible explanation for some of the upswing in share repurchases, serving as a strong defensive mechanism against a hostile takeover (see Section 10.3).

Managers or other insiders may choose not to sell their shares in a repurchase offer, thereby increasing their concentration of voting power. Furthermore, a shareholder who is willing to tender shares must have a reservation price that is lower than the repurchase offer price.[3] In contrast, the remaining shareholders, who choose not to participate in the tender, must have reservation prices that are higher than the offer price.[4] Therefore, a potential raider will have to make a higher offer in order to attract enough shares to complete a successful takeover.[5]

In summary, a corporation may adopt a share repurchase program for several reasons: (1) to convey positive inside information to the market, (2) to transfer wealth from some claim holders to other groups of claim holders, (3) to change the capital structure of the firm, (4) to minimize taxes, or (5) to change the ownership structure of the firm,

---

[2] With a cash dividend, all shareholders receive their pro rata share of the distribution. Other differences between a repurchase plan and cash dividends may include using repurchased stocks for stock option programs, retirement programs, and acquisition plans. In such cases, a repurchase plan may be less expensive than newly issued stock. Also, some trust funds allow the consumption of income (dividends) but require reinvestment of capital gains (stock repurchases).

[3] By *reservation price* we mean the lowest acceptable price to the seller.

[4] To make this argument, we must assume that all shareholders are rational and well informed. Otherwise, a disproportionate distribution, such as a share repurchase, may provide an incentive for informed investors to take advantage of uninformed investors with a subsequent transfer of wealth between these investor groups.

[5] Of course, a successful defense against a takeover is not always in the best interest of the firm's shareholders, who might be better off with an alternative management team.

perhaps for corporate control reasons. However, the disproportionate nature of stock repurchases versus cash dividends is a major differentiating feature of these two types of distributions.

To see how the disproportionate nature of stock repurchases works in practice, consider the case of Reebok International Ltd., which used this method for corporate control reasons, as reported in the *Wall Street Journal* on August 30, 1996:

> Reebok International Ltd. said it has agreed to repurchase approximately 17 million common shares for $612.7 million or $36 a share under its recently launched self-tender offer. . . .The buyback will reduce the number of common shares outstanding to about 55.5 million from 72.5 million. It will also boost the stake held by Chairman and Chief Executive Paul Fireman and his family—who didn't tender theirs—to 22% from 16.9%. The move, in effect, makes the company less vulnerable to a hostile bidder, since under the company's bylaws and Massachusetts law, investors representing two-thirds of the shares outstanding must approve a merger. At the time Reebok announced the share-repurchase plan last month, it said the move was part of a "long-term commitment to shareholder value." But in a companion document filed with the Securities and Exchange Commission, Reebok disclosed that from time to time over the past year, "senior management of the company has been approached by third parties expressing an interest in discussing the possible acquisition of, investment in, or merger or combination" with Reebok. . . . The repurchase program also allows disgruntled shareholders to pull out of the stock. (p. A5)

10.1.3 Survey Results on Common Stock Repurchases

A straightforward method to reveal the reasons for share repurchases is through a survey of share repurchasing firms. Wansley, Lane, and Sarkar (1989) conducted such a survey. They sent questionnaires to chief financial officers of repurchasing and nonrepurchasing firms in an attempt to identify the motives for a share repurchase program. Repurchasing companies' financial officers stated that the reason for a repurchase was management's belief that the stock was undervalued and that it was confident about the firms' positive prospects. Nonrepurchasing companies' officers suggested that an important reason for a repurchase was a lack of investment opportunities and excess cash.

In a recent survey by Howard Willens, 110 senior financial officers of S&P 500 companies commented on the role of share repurchases in their companies' financial planning. The responses suggested that the majority of the companies with a buyback program in place simultaneously increased their dividends. The survey also revealed that almost all the responding financial officers believed that share repurchase programs are "more effective than raising dividends in providing downside stock-price protection in a falling market." In contrast, many of these financial officers claimed that in hard times for their firms, dividend streams receive a higher priority than share repurchases.

However, survey responses can suffer from nonresponse and incorrect response bias. Therefore we supplement these survey results with other methods of inferring management motives for share repurchases, such as stock market reactions and the interpretation of knowledgeable observers, to identify the intentions of firms that repurchase their shares.

10.2 Methods of Common Stock Repurchases

Common stock repurchases take five principal forms:

- fixed-price tender offers,
- open-market share repurchases,
- Dutch-auction repurchases,
- transferable put-rights distributions, and
- targeted stock repurchases.

10.2.1 Fixed-Price Tender Offers

In a fixed-price tender offer, the company offers to purchase its stock at a specified price. The offer also includes the number of shares sought and the expiration date. The typical fixed-price repurchase offers a 20 to 25 percent premium over the prevailing market price. The percentage of outstanding shares sought by the corporation commonly ranges from 15 to 19 percent, with an expiration date of three to four weeks. If the offer is oversubscribed, the firm usually reserves the right to purchase more than the specified amount or to purchase shares on a pro rata basis. If the offer is undersubscribed, the company may buy all the tendered shares, extend the offer, or withdraw it. The fraction of the outstanding shares actually purchased is typically in the range of 15 to 17 percent.[6]

10.2.2 Open-Market Repurchases

In an open-market repurchase, the firm buys back a fraction of its outstanding shares at market prices over a long period of time—months or even years. This form of share repurchasing became very popular during the 1980s, outnumbering fixed-price tender offers ten to one.[7] Because of its less dramatic nature, an open-market repurchase may be less effective as a signal than a fixed-price tender offer.[8] However, the corporation saves in terms of the price that it pays for its shares, since it does not offer a premium above the market price. In either case, the shareholders enjoy potential tax advantages vis-à-via cash dividends.[9] Firms tend to announce repurchase programs after they have experienced a period of falling share prices, a practice that was especially prevalent after the market crash of October 1987, as well as the market correction of October 1997.[10] For example, the following information was reported in the *Wall Street Journal* on October 29, 1997:

> Led by International Business Machines Corp.'s $3.5 billion share buyback announcement early yesterday—which appeared to help halt three days of stock market losses—several companies went bargain hunting, announcing stock repurchases or simply buying up large blocks of their shares. "It was a vote of confidence that helped

---

[6] These summary statistics come from four sources: Jensen and Smith (1985), Asquith and Mullins (1986), Lakonishok and Vermaelen (1990), and Comment and Jarrell (1991).

[7] See Comment and Jarrell (1991), and Barclay and Smith (1988).

[8] The average abnormal return during the announcement period of an open-market repurchase program is about 3 percent. Ikenberry, Lakonishok, and Vermaelen (1995) found, however, that, on average, firms that announce open-market repurchases are 15 percent undervalued when long-term (four-year) performance is considered.

[9] Barclay and Smith (1988) argue that the tax benefits of open-market repurchases are mitigated by the costs associated with the use of inside information by managers who advance their own interests at shareholders' expense. They present evidence that bid–ask spreads widen when firms engage in repurchases and interpret this evidence as being consistent with their hypothesis. More recent evidence reported by Miller and McConnell (1995) and Singh, Zaman, and Krishnamurti (1994), however, contradicts the earlier results of Barclay and Smith. Miller and McConnell attribute the earlier results to an artifact of Barclay and Smith's sample period. They showed in various tests that neither relative nor absolute bid–ask spreads widen following announcements of open-market share repurchase programs by NYSE firms. Singh, Zaman, and Krishnamurti documented similar results to those of Miller and McConnell for NASDAQ firms.

[10] See Vermaelen (1981) and Comment and Jarrell (1991).

bring people back in," said Barry Berman, head trader for Robert W. Baird & Co. in Milwaukee. "It woke people up and got them focused on the positives of the marketplace." (p. A3)

10.2.3 Dutch-Auction Repurchases

An emerging alternative to the fixed-price tender offer is the Dutch-auction repurchase method. The first company to use this method was Todd Shipyards in 1981. By the late 1980s, more than twenty firms a year utilized Dutch-auction repurchases.[11] In a Dutch-auction repurchase, the firm specifies a range of purchase prices for the shares and the total number of shares sought. Each interested shareholder submits an offer to sell back to the firm a number of shares at a minimum acceptable selling price within the specified range. The corporation compiles these sell offers, rank orders them from low to high by the shareholders' minimum acceptance prices, and pays the lowest price that will purchase the number of shares desired. In accordance with the fairness provision in the Security Exchange Commission Act of 1934, this price is then paid to all the shareholders that offered to tender their shares at an equal or lower price. In a typical Dutch auction, the minimum price in the specified range is slightly above market price (about 2 percent) and the maximum price is comparable to fixed-price tender offer prices (on average 17 percent). Consequently, the average premium in Dutch-auction repurchases is lower than the premium in fixed-price tender offer share repurchases.[12]

10.2.4 Transferable Put-Rights Distributions

Another recent innovation in repurchase methods is the transferable put-rights distribution.[13] It gives shareholders the right to sell shares back to the firm at a specified exercise price before the expiration day. Shareholders who choose not to exercise the right can trade this put option in a secondary market established for this purpose.[14]

---

[11] See Bagwell (1992), and Gay, Kale, and Noe (1991).

[12] See Bagwell (1992).

[13] See Gay, Kale, and Noe (1991).

[14] Kale, Noe, and Gay (1989) argue that secondary markets for transferable put-rights allow for gains from trade because shareholders with high reservation prices can sell the rights to shareholders with lower reservation prices. Moreover, since only shareholders with low reservation prices end up tendering their shares, aggregate tax payments by the shareholders are reduced and takeover costs by potential raiders are increased.

Gay, Kale, and Noe (1991) used simulation techniques to compare the efficiency of fixed-price tender offers, Dutch-auction repurchases, and transferable put-rights in terms of probability of success, expected proration, expected payment in excess of the minimum required to ensure success of the offer, and expected shortfall. They found that the Dutch auction was the most efficient repurchase method, followed by the transferable put-right. The fixed-price tender offer appeared least efficient in these respects. Gay, Kale, and Noe also reported that, from an economically desirable perspective as measured by the combined wealth changes of the tendering and nontendering shareholders, a Dutch auction and a transferable put-right dominated the traditional fixed-price tender method. If the reason for the repurchase was to prevent a takeover of the firm, once again the Dutch auction required the highest offer price by a potential bidder; the two other methods were inferior and equally effective to each other. In summary, this study suggests that the Dutch-auction method should be considered by management contemplating a share repurchase.[15]

10.2.5 Targeted Stock Repurchases

Finally, a share repurchase directed only at a specific segment of shareholders is called a *targeted stock repurchase*. One form of a targeted repurchase is directed only at small share holdings. The purpose is to save the costs of servicing small accounts. The average premium above market price for such offers is about 10 percent.[16] However, the more common targeted share repurchase aims at a single, large-block shareholder. The terms of this form of repurchase are negotiated; they provide preferential treatment of large-block shareholders and pay an average premium of about 13 percent.[17] Large-block repurchases are frequently used during a corporate control contest. The large-block seller is usually an actual or potential takeover bidder. Therefore it is not surprising that on many occasions such a repurchase is accompanied by a standstill agreement, which limits the tendering large-block shareholder from increasing his or her interest in the firm for a specified time period.

---

[15] Management should be aware, however, that an auction mechanism, by its nature, allows for strategic behavior by the participants who might influence the outcome. Indeed, Loewenstein and Wang (1997) modeled the effects of large-block shareholders on the outcome of Dutch-auction repurchases. They also documented empirical results consistent with such strategic behavior.

[16] See Bradley and Wakeman (1983).

[17] See Dann and DeAngelo (1983), and Bradley and Wakeman (1983).

10.3 Trends in Common Stock Repurchases

Aggregate statistics on common stock repurchases from official government sources are not readily available. However, until fairly recently the general impression has been that only on rare occasions do corporations use share repurchases instead of dividends to distribute cash to their shareholders. This perception has intrigued researchers since the early studies of share repurchases in the 1960s.[18] Why weren't more share repurchases (and fewer dividends) used, in light of the obvious tax advantage of share repurchases? The puzzle is best described in an article by Brennan and Thakor (1990):

> The prediction that corporations will distribute cash to shareholders by way of repurchase only, in order to avoid the adverse tax consequences of dividends, is clearly counter-factual, and the challenge remains to explain the survival of dividends in the age of income tax. (p. 993)

Consider the evidence. Table 10.1 presents the annual time series of the amount of cash distributed through share repurchases and cash dividends as compiled by numerous researchers.[19] The most striking observation is the tremendous growth of the annual dollar amounts of distribution in the form of share repurchases during the past four decades. In the early 1960s, for the first time share repurchases amounted to more than $1 billion. Significantly higher repurchase activity was observed during the period of "voluntary" dividend controls between late 1971 and mid 1974. The explosive share repurchase growth is especially evident in the mid 1980s when share repurchases grew, in constant dollars, by a multiple of roughly six in four years, or from 12 to 40 percent of total cash distribution. The growth of share repurchases slowed somewhat in the early 1990s, but picked up again in the mid 1990s. The *Wall Street Journal* reported about $75 billion in stock repurchases in 1994, close to $100 billion in 1995, and more than $100 billion in the first nine months of 1996.[20] Note that the 1986 tax reform did not reverse the repurchase growth trend, especially in constant dollars. Although the 1986 tax reform did not eliminate the tax advantage of share repurchases relative to dividends, it certainly

---

[18] For example, see Woods and Brigham (1966).

[19] See Guthart (1965), Shoven (1986), Bagwell and Shoven (1989), and Dunsby (1994).

[20] *Wall Street Journal*, September 26, 1996, p. C1.

Table 10.1 Annual Cash Distributions to Shareholders ($ millions)

Year	Share Repurchases	Dividends
1954[a]	274	9,800
1955	388	11,200
1956	414	12,000
1957	382	12,400
1958	466	12,300
1959	647	13,700
1960	598	14,500
1961	794	15,300
1962	1,057	16,600
1963	1,303	17,800
1964–1969	Not reported by referenced sources	—
1970[b]	1,213	22,500
1971	736	22,900
1972	2,121	24,400
1973	1,585	27,000
1974	2,059	29,700
1975	2,139	29,600
1976	1,904	34,600

[a] Source for years 1954–1963: Guthart (1965). The sample includes all NYSE corporations. The dollar values for repurchases are calculated by multiplying the number of shares repurchased during each year by the average price of all shares traded on the NYSE during that year.

[b] Source for years 1970–1976: Shoven (1986). The CRSP monthly stock returns file database is used to determine the number of shares outstanding for each NYSE corporation. Each decrease in the number of shares outstanding is regarded as a repurchase. The value of the repurchase is estimated by multiplying the decrease in the number of shares by the average price of the security at the end of the preceding month and the price at the end of the month in which the reduction occurred.

reduced this advantage. This observation suggests that share repurchases have gained popularity for reasons beyond tax considerations; other consequences of the disproportionate nature of common stock repurchases may have contributed to their popularity.

10.4 Tax Issues in Share Repurchases versus Dividend Payments

Since the modern U.S. income tax went into effect in 1913—and as recently as the Tax Reform Act of 1986—individual investors have been

Table 10.1 (cont.)

Year	Current Dollars		Constant 1986 (or 1992) Dollars[d]	
	Repurchases	Dividends	Repurchases	Dividends
1977[c]	3,361	29,450	5,688	49,842
1978	3,520	32,830	5,553	51,791
1979	4,507	38,324	6,532	55,535
1980	4,961	42,619	6,594	56,643
1981	3,973	46,832	4,814	56,747
1982	8,080	50,916	9,203	57,993
1983	7,709	54,896	8,451	60,179
1984	27,444	60,266	29,024	63,735
1985	41,303	67,564	42,421	69,392
1986	41,521	77,122	41,521	71,122
1987	54,336	83,051	52,585	80,370
1988[e]	47,232	69,876	55,051	81,443
1989	43,196	64,772	48,212	72,294
1990	37,030	66,392	39,579	70,963
1991	22,251	66,645	22,894	68,750
1992	22,469	69,932	27,469	69,932

[c] Source for years 1977–1987: Bagwell and Shoven (1989). The data source is 2,445 firms on the Compustat Primary, Supplementary, and Tertiary industrial files.

[d] 1986 constant dollar figures are used for the years 1977–1986 and adjust current dollar numbers using the GNP deflator from the *1988 Economic Report of the President*. See Bagwell and Shoven (1989). 1992 constant dollar figures are used for the years 1987–1992.

[e] Source for years 1988–1992: Dunsby (1994). These data are for the 1,000 largest firms from the combined industrial and research files on Compustat for each year.

subjected to higher tax rates on income from dividends than income from capital gains. The act equalized the two tax rates. Current tax law, governed by the Omnibus Budget Reconciliation Act of 1993, again gave preferential tax treatment to capital gains. In 1997, Congress passed a new tax law that provides even more preferential tax treatment for capital gains relative to dividends. In previous periods of preferential tax treatment for capital gains, the tax rates for individual investors on capital gains typically have been between 40 and 70 percent of the tax rate on ordinary income. Clearly, this preferential tax treatment of capital gains makes common stock repurchase distributions more attractive than dividend payout for many investors. However, common stock repurchases are regarded as capital gains by the

IRS only if the distribution is "essentially not equivalent" to paying a dividend (Section 302 of the U.S. Tax Code); that is, if it is interpreted to be less routine than a dividend. Another provision in Section 302 states that the repurchase must be "substantially disproportionate" to the extent that after the repurchase shareholders must hold less than 80 percent of their preoffer holding to apply for capital gains tax treatment. Nevertheless, according to Barclay and Smith (1988), "[T]he IRS has never imposed such ruling on a large public corporation. Thus, on balance, the U.S. Tax Code appears to favor repurchases over cash dividends" (p. 63).

As previously noted, from 1986 through 1993 the tax code did not provide preferential treatment of realized capital gains relative to dividends. The 1986 tax reform raised the tax rate on capital gains for individuals by making this rate the same as the ordinary income tax rate. Consequently, the tax advantage of common stock repurchases relative to dividend payments was lessened, but not completely eliminated, during that interval. The reason for this conclusion is the disproportionate nature of share repurchase distribution; that is, not all the shareholders participate equally in a common stock repurchase.

Let's consider two tax dimensions. First, capital gains are calculated as the difference between the historical buying price (or "basis") and the realized selling price. When a corporation offers to repurchase shares from its shareholders, it seems logical that those who are most eager to tender their shares have the lowest potential tax liability. The shareholders that fit this description best are those who bought the shares at high historical prices, thus establishing a high "basis" for capital gains calculations. For similar reasons, shareholders whose marginal tax rates are lower are also more likely to tender their shares. In a common stock repurchase, shareholders have a choice as to the fraction of their holdings to be tendered. Thus the aggregate tax liability for the shareholders of a repurchasing firm will be lower relative to the aggregate tax liability for the shareholders of a company that is distributing an equal amount of cash dividends. All the shareholders who receive an involuntary dividend are paying taxes on this dividend, regardless of their marginal tax rate or basis.

Second, capital gains are taxed only when realized. The deferral of tax payments translates to a lower current effective tax rate because of the time value of money. Therefore, since the price of the remaining outstanding shares is higher after a repurchase than after a distribution of an identical amount of cash dividends, the shareholders who choose not to tender their shares will accrue unrealized capital gains, thereby reducing their effective tax liability.[21]

To summarize, a common stock repurchase can be viewed as a tax-efficient way to distribute funds to shareholders even in periods when ordinary income and capital gains are taxed at the same rates. Shareholders who pay the lowest taxes have greater incentives to participate in a share repurchase; the aggregate tax bill for these shareholders is minimized for the benefit of all shareholders.

Corporate managers around the world are clearly attuned to the tax consequences of repurchases compared to those of dividends. Consider the case of Reuters Holdings, the London-based media giant, which suspended its move to buy back 5 percent of its shares in October 1996, after the British government announced that it would toughen tax laws on such deals. One analyst estimated the net present value of the repurchase to be 859 pence per share with the original tax breaks, but only 687 pence without the tax credit. "That is a big difference," the analyst said. Instead of using the special dividend structure, "Reuters might consider doubling up its regular dividend."[22]

10.5 Theoretical Implications of Share Repurchases

One avenue of theoretical research recently explored is the use of share repurchases as a signaling device when the attribute being signaled is the firm's prospects (see Chapter 7 for a detailed discussion of the signaling mechanism). Those involved in this line of research include Vermaelen (1984), Ofer and Thakor (1987), Williams (1988), Constantinides and Grundy (1989), and Hausch and Seward (1993). Brennan and Thakor (1990) and Chowdhry and Nanda (1994) presented models based on asymmetric information but which are not signaling models. A second avenue of theoretical research explored is share repurchases as a defense against takeover. Those examining this device included Bagnoli, Gordon, and Lipman (1989), and Sinha (1991).

---

[21] Consider a simple case. Assume that an all-equity firm has 100 shares of stock outstanding at a market value of $100, so the market price per share is $1. The firm is considering a $20 distribution to its shareholders. Ignoring any other effects, the market price of a share will be $0.80 if a cash dividend is declared, but will remain at $1 if shares are repurchased—only 80 shares will remain after repurchase. Even when a premium over the market price is offered for the repurchased stock, the price of the remaining shares will be higher than $0.80.

[22] *Wall Street Journal*, October 9, 1996, p. A18.

10.5.1 Signaling Models

Vermaelen (1984) presented an early signaling model of share repurchases. The offer premium, the target percentage of shares sought, and the percentage of insider holdings were perceived as signal devices—the higher each of these parameters, the more positive is the signal. The market was presumed to set share prices, assuming that managers obtained significant net benefit from truthful signaling. These benefits were related to the role of repurchases in preventing takeover bids and to the increased value of executive stock options.

In subsequent work researchers attempted to differentiate share repurchases and dividends as the signaling device. Ofer and Thakor (1987) presented an integrated theoretical model that allows signaling by both dividends and repurchases and specifies the conditions under which a corporation will prefer one distribution mechanism over the other. Specifically, a firm will choose the payout method that achieves the signaling objective most cheaply. The researchers proposed that, with only a small disparity between the intrinsic worth of an undervalued corporation and its market price, dividends will be used. In contrast, if the price disparity is large, a large dividend is needed to convey the information; thus the same information can be signaled with a much smaller cash outlay by using repurchases.

Williams (1988), and Constantinides and Grundy (1989) derived models in which dividends and repurchases are efficient signals of a company's optimal investment. In the Williams model, companies invest at the optimal level, sell stock in the capital markets to finance this investment, and are willing to distribute costly dividends to signal the quality of their investment.[23] Accordingly, the dividend payment supports the sale of shares at high prices. In the Constantinides and Grundy model, excess money raised from senior security sales to support optimum investment is used to repurchase shares. The role of the share repurchase is to align management's incentives with the market. If managers understate the firm's value, they lose more from the sale of the senior claim than they gain from the low prices of the share repurchase. If managers overstate the firm's value, they lose more from the high-priced share repurchase than they gain from the sale of the claim at high prices. The difference between share repurchases and cash dividends is that dividends are paid to all investors, including manage-

---

[23] The Williams model is a special case of the Ambarish, John, and Williams model (1987).

ment. In practice, management only occasionally participates in repurchases. In the model, management is banned from participation.

In Hausch and Seward's (1993) signaling model, they assumed dividend payments to be known with certainty, while the value of repurchases is uncertain. Shareholders do not know exactly how much they will get for the shares, especially if the repurchase is in the form of an auction. The nature of the corporation's investment opportunities determines the optimal form of the distribution to its shareholders. If the managers of a high-quality company are less risk averse, given their investment opportunities, then a stock repurchase (risky distribution) is a more efficient signal of the firm's "type," or quality. If, however, the managers of a high-quality company are more risk averse, given available investments, then dividends (certain distribution) will be used to signal the firm's quality. Hausch and Seward specify the determinants of this relative risk aversion, or "tolerance," for the type of distribution chosen.

Two additional studies also considered asymmetric information but not in the context of signaling models. Brennan and Thakor's (1990) model is different in that they did not assume asymmetry of information between managers and outsiders. Information collected by investors about the prospects of the corporation is costly, however. Since share repurchases, unlike dividends, are generally nonproportional, they require shareholders to incur information collection costs or suffer wealth transfers to better informed traders. Therefore only investors with large holdings will invest in acquiring the information. Consequently, Brennan and Thakor's model predicted that the smallest distributions would be paid with dividends despite the tax disadvantage; larger distributions would take the form of open market repurchases, and tender offers would be used for the largest distributions.

Chowdhry and Nanda (1994) present a model in which managers have no incentive to signal the value of the firm to market participants. Instead, managers attempt to distribute cash to shareholders in the least expensive way. Chowdhry and Nanda suggest that precisely because tender offer share repurchases are associated with a large price reaction, they become a costly means of distribution. Therefore the model predicts that the optimal payout policy is to distribute some cash in the form of dividends and inventory the remaining cash to future periods. At some point when the shares are sufficiently undervalued, the firm uses share repurchases to distribute the accumulated cash.

To conclude this theoretical section on the use of share repurchases for signaling purposes, we mention some recent cases where management used the signaling motive of the firm's quality as a justification for a repurchase announcement. John B. Menzer, Wal-Mart's chief financial officer suggested that the buyback "sent out an excellent message that we're dedicated to increasing shareholder value." Roger King, chairman of King World Productions, Inc., suggested that its announced repurchase (and a dividend initiation) is aimed at signaling that King World was focused on growing as opposed to selling out when he declared: "We don't have a for sale sign out there now."[24]

10.5.2 Takeover Defenses

Bagnoli, Gordon, and Lipman (1989) presented a signaling model of share repurchase in which the purpose of the signal is to defend against takeover attempts by potential raiders. In their model, managers repurchase shares to prevent takeovers, but only if the cost of doing so is not too high. This cost is defined as the difference between the repurchase price and the corporation's true value under current management, a factor that is unobservable by outsiders. A share repurchase's high premium will cause a large reduction in the firm's value. Therefore only if its value is truly high will the relative cost of the repurchase be low. A repurchase offer, then, is a positive signal to shareholders about the company's value under current management. Accordingly, the repurchase will deter a takeover, which becomes more costly at higher share prices.

Sinha's (1991) model also uses share repurchases as a defense against takeovers. Managers have resources that they allocate between investment and perquisites, and this allocation is unobservable by outsiders. Management uses a debt-financed share repurchase to bond itself to a given level of investment because of the higher probability of bankruptcy. This action, in turn, reduces the threat of takeover, since the profits to the raider of a corporation that follows an optimal investment policy are smaller. Moreover, in a share repurchase the first shareholders to tender their shares are those with the lowest reservation price. Any subsequent bidder faces shareholders with relatively higher reservation prices. Thus a debt-financed repurchase dominates a debt-financed dividend that is proportional (i.e., all the shareholders participate equally in the distribution).

---

[24] *Wall Street Journal*, March 7, 1997, p. B4, and April 15, 1997, p. B19, respectively.

10.6 The Empirical Evidence on Share Repurchases

Since the early 1980s, a vast body of empirical evidence has been accumulated on the market reaction to share repurchase decisions. The studies differ by the type of repurchase, by the characteristics of the companies and securities studied, by the sample period, and by the manner in which samples are partitioned into subsamples. Nevertheless, the purpose of these studies is to identify the motivation for a share repurchase, based on the various circumstances of the company. Many of these studies use an event study methodology that compares the daily rates of return on firm's securities around the event (e.g., share repurchase announcement) with the average realized returns on these securities in periods outside the period of interest.

10.6.1 Announcement Period Returns

Three early studies of stock returns around share repurchases are those by Masulis (1980), Dann (1981), and Vermaelen (1981). Masulis reports an average 17 percent return during the two-day fixed-price share repurchase announcement period compared to an average 0 percent return in the non-announcement comparison period. He found larger (smaller) average returns for offers seeking to purchase above (below) the sample average percentage of outstanding shares and for offers that were primarily financed with debt. He interpreted these results as being consistent with the hypotheses that share repurchases are undertaken because of personal tax savings in contrast to cash dividends and because corporate tax shields increase from debt financing of share repurchases. Masulis also reported results consistent with wealth transfers for different types of security holders and wealth transfers between tendering and nontendering shareholders.

Like Masulis, Dann and Vermaelen attempted to identify the economic forces underlying the observed price changes of securities upon the announcement of a share repurchase. Similar to Masulis's results, both studies reported excess returns of about 15 percent around the announcement of a fixed-price tender offer repurchase and a decline of about 3 percent around the expiration of the offer. Vermaelen also documents excess returns of 3 percent around the announcement of an open-market repurchase program that follows a period of negative market performance.

Dann and Vermaelen interpreted their results differently from Masulis. Dann and Vermaelen were skeptical about the tax factor and wealth transfer affects. Although they could not exclude the existence of small tax or expropriation effects completely, they presented reasons why these effects are subordinate to a positive information effect conveyed via a repurchase announcement. Through a tender offer, management seems to be disclosing inside information that the stock was undervalued. This disclosure results in the upward price revision.

10.6.2 Share Repurchases as a Signaling Mechanism

Dann, Masulis, and Mayers (1991), Hertzel and Jain (1991), and Bartov (1991) explored the hypothesis that share repurchases convey information regarding future earnings and risk changes. All three studies found that, following share repurchases, analysts revise the firms' earnings forecasts upward, earnings are higher especially in the short-run, and the systematic risk of these companies declines significantly.

Comment and Jarrell (1991) compared the relative signaling power of Dutch-auction repurchases, tender offers, and open-market repurchases. They argued that Dutch auctions are less credible signals because the tender prices are determined by outsiders, not by insiders. Also, the generally lower premiums of Dutch auctions reduce the potential of a wealth transfer from nontendering managers; therefore the signal is once again less credible. Open-market repurchases offer only small, if any, premiums. Hence, for the same reason presented in the previous studies, they concluded that the signaling power of open-market repurchases is low. They presented evidence consistent with their hypotheses and concluded that repurchases, especially in the form of tender offers, increase share prices because they are credible managerial signals.

The motive for more recent repurchases might, however, be for reasons other than signaling. The majority of companies use open-market and Dutch-auction repurchases, which have lower signaling effectiveness.[25] Moreover, Ikenberry, Lakonishok, and Vermaelen (1995) questioned whether short-term announcement premiums are a correct measure of signaling power. They reported that firms making open-market repurchase announcements were, on average, undervalued by

---

[25] Dutch auctions are a useful form of repurchases to explore shareholder heterogeneity. Bagwell (1992) presented empirical evidence that shareholders are indeed heterogeneous and that firms are facing an upward sloping supply curve for their shares. She suggested that the reasons for shareholder heterogeneity could be their tax bases, differential transaction costs, asymmetric information, or differences of opinion. Also, see Brown and Ryngaert (1992). In a recent working paper, Loewenstein and Wang (1997) demonstrated that in a Dutch-auction large-block shareholders with market power can influence the outcome of the auction, specifically the premium paid for the repurchased shares.

15 percent over a subsequent four-year period relative to firms that were not involved in open-market repurchases. They attributed this undervaluation especially to firms with low market values relative to their book values. These firms had a four-year abnormal performance of 45 percent relative to a control sample. Therefore Ikenberry, Lakonishok, and Vermaelen concluded that, even though many firms might have other reasons for open-market share repurchases, at least the high book-to-market ratio firms were sending a strong message to the market when they engaged in an open-market share repurchase program. However, it takes market participants four years to fully appreciate the extent of the message—thus the magnitude of the undervaluation of these firms.

Kamma, Kanatas, and Raymar (1992) compared the overall market responses to Dutch auctions with market responses to fixed-price self-tenders. They focused on the total returns to all shareholders over the full tender period (from before the initial announcement until after the final outcome) and on the gains achieved by nontendering shareholders relative to those who sell. They found that the sample of Dutch auctions had total returns significantly larger than those of the sample of fixed-price offers after controlling for firm-specific and tender-offer characteristics. However, unconditional total returns did not differ significantly between repurchase forms. Combined with the tendencies of fixed-priced offers (larger fraction of shares sought and higher premiums), they interpreted these results to mean that more wealth is transferred from owners who retained their holdings in the firm to shareholders who tendered their shares in fixed-price offers than in Dutch auctions. Finally, the researchers reported that firms using Dutch auctions generally are larger than firms that repurchase their shares with a fixed-price tender offer.

In another study, Lakonishok and Vermaelen (1990) presented evidence that, until the 1980s, tender offers were made mainly by smaller firms whose management felt that the shares were undervalued; they used repurchases to signal their assessment to the market. However, in recent years tender offers have been made by larger corporations, often in the context of a hostile takeover bid. They reported an average premium of 22 percent to tendering shareholders compared to excess returns of 13 percent to nontendering shareholders. Thus an investor can purchase a share after the announcement of the tender offer but before its expiration, tender the share, and earn returns of 9 percent in less than a week. Lakonishok and Vermaelen claimed that the nontendering shareholders are insiders who are willing to "give away" part of the firm and that such moves potentially are related to their benefits from consolidating voting power and preventing a successful takeover.

10.6.3 Corporate Control Issues

Denis (1990) examined the effects of a share repurchase plan as a mechanism to thwart a hostile corporate takeover, since nontendering managers increase their concentration of voting power. This defensive strategy appeared to be successful. More than 70 percent of the companies that repurchased shares for this reason retained their independence. The announcement of a defensive repurchase was accompanied by about a 1.5 percent negative excess return. During the entire corporate control contest, the cumulative abnormal returns for companies that retained their independence were 16 percent, whereas firms that experienced a control change had cumulative abnormal returns of 29 percent. Therefore successful resistance to a takeover through a repurchase was associated with large losses for the target shareholders. Denis interpreted this result as suggesting that the main reason for such a defensive activity is management entrenchment.

A share repurchase program as a defensive mechanism in a corporate control contest also has been studied by Dann and DeAngelo (1983), Bradley and Wakeman (1983), Klein and Rosenfeld (1988), and Mikkelson and Ruback (1991). These studies, however, concentrated on targeted share repurchases.

Dann and DeAngelo focused on standstill agreements, which are voluntary contracts between the corporation and a major shareholder. Standstill agreements limit the shareholder's ownership of voting shares for a number of years and are frequently accompanied by a repurchase of a block of shares from the major shareholder at a large premium (higher than 16 percent, on average) that is not offered to other shareholders. Dann and DeAngelo reported a negative excess return of about 2.5 percent around the announcement of a premium-negotiated repurchase, and a negative excess return of 2 percent if the premium-negotiated repurchase was not accompanied by a standstill agreement. Their results support the management entrenchment hypothesis; that is, managers attempt to prevent takeovers at the expense of shareholders, whose wealth is decreased.

Bradley and Wakeman examined block repurchases in cases where a merger bid was involved and compared the results to cases where no merger bid existed. They reported that, when a merger was involved, a negative excess return of 12.5 percent was experienced from the day before the announcement to thirty days after the announcement. They attributed the price drop to the reduced possibility of a merger. In contrast, when a merger was not involved in the block repurchase, they were unable to find any material wealth effect for a comparable period around the event.

Klein and Rosenfeld examined the association between targeted block repurchase on favorable terms (also known as *greenmail*) and subsequent changes in top management. They found that firms involved in greenmail subsequently had above-average top management turnover. This observation supports the management entrenchment hypothesis and the existence of internal monitoring mechanisms.

Mikkelson and Ruback found that the negative wealth effects of target share repurchases on the remaining shareholders are not a function of the premium paid to the large-block shareholder. Rather, they are a result of the reversal of positive market expectation associated with a potential takeover, unless a standstill agreement is negotiated, in which case the premium matters. They did not find, however, that a standstill agreement reduced the probability of a subsequent takeover.

10.6.4 Share Repurchase Interpretations

Table 10.2 summarizes the main results of the event studies on the various forms of share repurchases and includes the interpretations of the results by the researchers. The average premium for tender offer share repurchases generally is about 22 percent, the fraction sought of the firm's outstanding share is about 16 percent, and the remaining shares have excess returns of 12 to 18 percent upon the repurchase announcement. Most of the researchers interpreted these results as being consistent with the positive information content of tender-offer share repurchases or the signaling hypothesis.

Open-market repurchases are the most common form of share repurchases. The average fraction of firm's share sought is about 5 percent, which is substantially lower than tender-offer buybacks. The wealth impact on the remaining shares is also lower (about 3 percent) and, obviously, no premium is paid on the repurchased shares. As previously noted, open-market repurchases provide a weaker signal than do tender offers. Nevertheless, the authors of studies that analyzed open-market repurchases claim that firms tend to engage in such repurchase programs when their shares are undervalued, thereby giving a positive signal to market participants.

Dutch auctions are a new form of share repurchases. Companies that use this method seek to repurchase about 15 percent of the outstanding shares, which is comparable to tender offers. However, the

Table 10.2 Summary of Main Results and Interpretation of Event Studies of Share Repurchases

Author(s) of Study	Type of Repurchase	Sample Size	Average Premium Paid (percentage)	Average Fraction of Firm's Shares Sought (percentage)	Wealth Impact on Outstanding Remaining Shares, Days −3 to +30[a] (percentage)	Hypothesis Supported by the Result (Researcher's Interpretation)
Masulis (1980)	Tender offers	199	23	16	18.2	Tax benefits and wealth transfers
Dann (1981)	Tender offers	143	22.46	15.3	18.5	Positive information content (signaling)
Vermaelen (1981)	Tender offers	131	22.76	15.0	13.6	Signaling
Lakonishok and Vermaelen (1990)	Tender offers	221	21.8	17.0	12.54	Information for small firms' defense against takeover by large firms
Hertzel and Jain (1991)	Tender offers	127[b]	16.7	14.8	10.1	Information about the level and risk of future earnings
Dann, Masulis, and Mayers (1991)	Tender offers	122	24	16	17.68	Information about the level and risk of future earnings
Comment and Jarrell (1991)	Tender offers	59	20.6	18.8	12	Signaling
Vermaelen (1981)	Open market	243	—	5.0	3.3	Signaling
Bartov (1991)	Open market	185	—	5.28	2.96	Information about the level and risk of future earnings
Comment and Jarrell (1991)	Open market	1,157	—	7[c]	2.3	Signaling
Comment and Jarrell (1991)	Dutch auction	63	12.8	15.6	8.3	Signaling

Author(s) of Study	Type of Repurchase	Sample Size	Average Premium Paid (percentage)	Average Fraction of Firm's Shares Sought (percentage)	Wealth Impact on Outstanding Remaining Shares, Days −3 to +30[a] (percentage)	Hypothesis Supported by the Result (Researcher's Interpretation)
Bagwell (1992)	Dutch auction	31	13.4	15.3	6.7	Heterogeneous valuation (higher valuation for new marginal investor)
Dann and DeAngelo (1983)	Targeted block repurchases[d]	41	16.4	11.0	−6.7	Management entrenchment
Bradley and Wakeman (1983)	Targeted block repurchases	61	9.8	11.1	−3.5	Management entrenchment
Mikkelson and Ruback (1991)	Targeted block repurchases	99	19.5	12.9	−4.82	Revision of expectations about the outcome of the block holding
Denis (1990)	Defensive repurchases	40	N/A	28[e]	−3.68	Management entrenchment
Bradley and Wakeman (1983)	Small holdings targeted	15	10	Negligible	1.6	Servicing cost reduction

[a] Several of the studies reported shorter periods around the events.

[b] Firms followed by *Value Line.*

[c] Not reported, estimated from reported results.

[d] Negotiated repurchases at a premium.

[e] Estimated from Table 6 in Denis (1990).

auction nature of the repurchase allows firms to pay a lower premium—about 13 percent. Excess returns range between 6 and 8 percent, which are also lower than tender-offer repurchases. Again, one interpretation of the results is in the context of the signaling hypothesis. A different interpretation is that the remaining shareholders have a higher reservation price for their shares, causing a rise in share prices.

Finally, studies that examined targeted block share repurchases are the only ones that consistently reported negative excess returns of 4 to 6 percent around the repurchase announcements. The authors of most of these studies viewed this form of repurchase as a defensive mechanism against a hostile takeover and concluded that the results are consistent with the management entrenchment hypothesis.

10.7 Conclusions

A common share repurchase program is an alternative to paying dividends, which firms may use to distribute cash to shareholders. The disproportionate nature of stock repurchases (i.e., selective participation) differentiates the declaration of a cash dividend from a share repurchase decision. The tax treatment of share repurchases also is different from that of dividends. Theory suggests three main motives for a firm to use a share repurchase: (1) a tax motive, (2) a signaling motive, or, (3) a takeover deterrent motive.

Overall, in earlier periods most repurchase programs seemed to be motivated by the desire of corporate management to convey positive information to market participants. Management felt that market perception of the value of the firm's shares was biased or that its shares were undervalued. A share repurchase is an effective tool to change these perceptions. Although this motivation seems to persist in the studies we summarized, especially by small firms, many of the more recent repurchase programs appeared to be defensive maneuvers in corporate control contests.

The market reaction to a share repurchase announcement is often strong and depends on the form of the repurchase selected by the firm and the reasons for choosing share repurchase rather than a cash dividend. The recent popularity of share repurchases suggests that they are a viable alternative to dividends and should be considered by a firm when making its payout decision. The popular press adds a word of caution, however:

> Investors automatically cheer buybacks, due to the mistaken premise that they necessarily contribute to a self-fulfilling circle of higher

share prices. They would do better to think about who is paying for the so-called reward: namely, everyone who continues to own the stock.[26]

We add an additional caveat. In spite of the impressive amount of research that has been done on dividends and common stock repurchases, we still do not have all the answers regarding why managers choose one method of cash disbursement over the other. Moreover, in practice the repurchase can substitute for a dividend, as in the case of Quaker State Corporation, which halved its dividend at the same time it announced a buyback plan. At the same time, however, more often the repurchase is complementary to the dividend. Such cases include actions by General Motors Corporation, General Electric Company, and RJR Nabisco Holdings Corporation in recent years to boost their dividends and launch a big share repurchase at the same time. Developing a model that accurately and completely describes the dividend versus stock repurchase choice remains a fertile ground for further research.

---

[26] *Wall Street Journal*, September 26, 1996, p. C1.

Chapter **11**

Management Implications and Conclusions

In the preceding ten chapters we demonstrated that academic researchers cannot specify a theoretical optimal dividend policy that simultaneously fits all firms (a macro-level policy). Because of the complexities involved, we are skeptical that a one-size-fits-all theory of dividend policy will ever gain acceptance. Over the years researchers have proposed numerous theories on how imperfections—various market frictions—might influence dividend policy. These researchers have "tortured" the data, imploring a confession to support or reject the various theories. However, to a very large degree, the data have resisted providing definitive answers.

We believe that the lack of empirical support for a particular dividend policy theory is the result of problems in quantitatively measuring market frictions and the statistical complications in dealing with the myriad interactive imperfections that likely affect individual firms differentially. In other words, since each firm faces a combination of potentially different market frictions with varying levels of relevance, the optimal dividend policy for each firm *may* be unique. If each firm has a uniquely optimal dividend policy, we should not be surprised that significant statistical generalizations still elude researchers. Current models of the impact of dividend policy on firms' values cannot fully reflect the complexity of the market environment. Following this line of reasoning, we provide scenarios in Sections 11.5.1 and 11.5.2 of firms tailoring their dividend policy as a function of the market imperfections they face. Our goal is to provide general guidelines to assist managers in making dividend policy decisions.

11.1 What Do Managers Think about Dividend Policy?

As an illustration that managers are attuned to the importance of market imperfections when it comes to setting dividend policy, we provide the following passage from Abrutyn and Turner (1990):

> Chief executive officers were surveyed in an attempt to determine why they paid dividends to shareholders prior to the Tax Reform Act of 1986, before which there appeared to be a large tax penalty for shareholders if dividends were paid. Completed surveys that detailed dividend payout ratios, shareholder demographics, and other factors were received from CEOs of 163 of the top 1,000 U.S. corporations. . . . The results show that 63 percent of the firms ranked a signaling explanation either first or second as a possible reason for their dividend payout ratio, whereas 44 percent gave a high rank to an agency cost explanation, and 36 percent highly ranked a view that is consistent with the "new" view of taxes and dividends. (p. 491)

Note from these survey results that the "big three" imperfections—signaling (asymmetric information), agency costs, and taxes—influenced the dividend decisions of these managers.

A summary of a 1998 study of corporate decision makers entitled "A Study of Dividend Policies Among Chief Financial Officers of S&P 500 Companies" was reported by Lazo (1999). This research was conducted by Insights & Directions, a market-research firm in New York City. The survey was commissioned by San Francisco–based Spare, Kaplan, Bishcel & Associates. One hundred and ten of the 500 S&P firms responded. Lazo quoted the research report as follows:

> The fact remains, however, that, in overwhelming numbers, the boards of directors and the senior management of large corporations understand the importance of dividends, even if some investors have temporarily lost sight of the information value dividend payments provide. . . . Dividends don't lie although sometimes reported earnings do.
>
> [S]enior financial officers rank dividends as a high-priority use of cash flow. Corporations view dividends as more than simply a form of distribution of excess cash flow to shareholders. Quite clearly, dividend policy should matter to institutional and individual investors. Those investors who pay attention to corporate dividend policy

derive valuable insight into the valuation attractiveness of those companies' stocks.

We have a good idea about how financial managers make their dividend decisions. As illustrated in Chapters 1 and 8, managers have been consistent in their management of dividend policy for decades. A significant factor influencing our position on dividend policy is the respect that we hold for financial practitioners; we cannot simply dismiss as irrelevant a decision that they view as so important. The policy of carefully managing dividend policy has persisted, and practices with such strong survival properties may have merits that have escaped theoretical modeling and empirical detection.

11.2 What Do We Think about Dividend Policy?

- Where do we come down on the issue of dividend policy relevance?

- What prescriptions can we provide practicing financial managers on how to establish dividend policies for their firms?

As we have emphasized, we believe that any advice we offer managers on how to set their dividend policies must be made at the firm-specific, or micro level. Financial managers must examine how the various market frictions affect their firms, as well as their current claimholders, to arrive at "reasonable" dividend policies for their firms.

11.2.1 The "Balance Scale" of Dividend Relevance

To set the stage for our answers to those two questions, let's plant ourselves firmly in the real world, complete with numerous and significant market imperfections. As a way of describing our position regarding dividend policy relevance, think of a balance scale on which we are weighing the merits of dividend policy relevance on the right-hand side against dividend policy irrelevance on the left-hand side, as illustrated in Figure 11.1. Panel (a) reflects our view of dividend policy relevance in a world of perfect capital markets, in which the scale strongly tips toward the irrelevance of dividend policy. In Panel (b) we portray the scale in a world beset with market imperfections. Here we believe that the forces of market frictions tip the scale toward

Figure 11.1 The Balance Scale of Dividend Policy Relevance

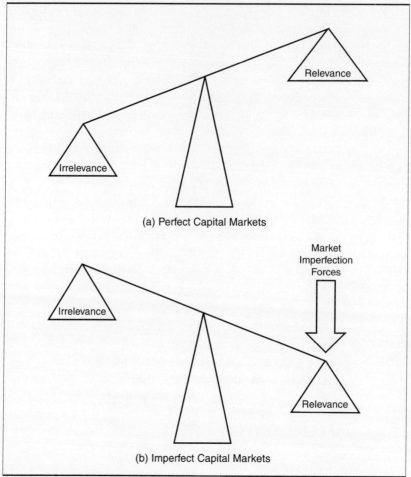

(a) Perfect Capital Markets

Market
Imperfection
Forces

(b) Imperfect Capital Markets

the relevance of dividend policy. For certain firms, specific frictions will have a large influence; for other firms these same market imperfections may be insignificant. In other words, the weights on the market frictions will differ from firm to firm.

We believe that dividend policy is relevant, but we must add candidly that we also do not believe that dividend policy ranks in importance with investment policy, for example, in determining a firm's value. Nonetheless, we believe that dividend policy can influence shareholder wealth and, accordingly, is worthy of serious management attention.

11.2.2 The Competing Frictions Model

As an example of our position, let's say that management of a firm believes that three market frictions are relevant to their firm—taxes, asymmetric information, and agency costs. This competing frictions framework, or schematic model, is shown in Figure 11.2. The firm's managers evaluate the impact on a dividend decision of each market friction in isolation and then consider the potentially complex interaction of the three imperfections before formulating a reasonable dividend policy.

11.3 Individual Market Imperfections

In this section we focus on how imperfections individually can influence a dividend decision and offer our interpretation on how financial managers should incorporate these imperfections into their decision making. We discuss the big three imperfections first because we know the most about them. Then we turn to the impact of transaction costs, flotation expenses, and behavioral considerations, or the little three frictions.

11.3.1 Taxes

Firms should have a reasonable idea of the identity of their main categories of shareholders; they have access to lists of shareholders

Figure 11.2 Competing Frictions Model

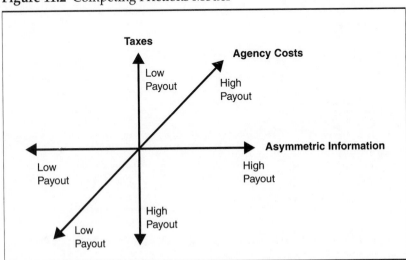

used to mail proxy statements and dividend checks to these owners. Proxy solicitation firms can tell management a great deal about the attributes of its shareholders, who generally can be classified as

- investors who prefer capital gains,
- investors who prefer dividend income, and
- investors who are tax-neutral.

Evidence supporting the existence of tax-induced dividend clienteles of shareholders is limited. However, we believe that investors have a tendency to self-select into investing in firms that have dividend payouts that best match their tax circumstances.

Individual investors with high tax rates, all else being equal, should prefer firms with no or low dividend payouts. The top current tax rate on dividend income for these investors is 39.6 percent versus 20 percent for long-term capital gains. Note that this effective capital gains rate drops dramatically if the capital gains are postponed into the future. If a low-payout firm with high-tax stockholders has an occasional large residual free cash flow, these investors should prefer a share-repurchase program rather than a large dividend payout. A share repurchase gives the investor the opportunity, but not the obligation, to participate, whereas a dividend payment is received by all shareholders on a pro rata basis.

Corporate investors, who pay taxes on only 30 percent of dividend income received, should, all else being equal, prefer dividend income over capital gains. With a current corporate tax rate of 35 percent on ordinary income, the effective rate on dividends is only 10.5 percent, or 35×30 percent.

Of course, if corporate investors know that they will be deferring the realization of capital gains long enough, the effective capital gains rate could drop below 10.5 percent. Accordingly, the corporation's horizon of the investment will determine whether dividends or capital gains are advantageous in terms of taxes.

For tax-neutral investors—investors that pay no taxes (e.g., public or private pension funds, trusts, charitable foundations, etc.)—taxes alone should not dictate a preference for the dividend policy of a specific firm.[1] However, some tax-neutral investors may be restricted to

---

[1] Including transaction costs with taxes may change a tax-neutral investor's preferences. Here, however, we are considering taxes in isolation.

consume from income (e.g., dividends) and not allowed to sell securities to generate income. Institutions under these restrictions may prefer to invest in firms with predictable dividend patterns. In addition, some institutions are prohibited from investing in stocks that don't have a long history of uninterrupted dividends. Accordingly, these institutions also will be concerned about a firm's dividend consistency.

In the long-run, one tax-induced dividend clientele should be as good as another. Accordingly, why should the firm design its dividend policy to serve the tax preferences of its existing shareholders? The answer may be the adverse one-shot investor tax consequences of a dividend policy shift and the costs associated with realigning the firm's ownership base. For example, what if a low-dividend firm suddenly switches to a high-dividend policy? Assuming that high-tax investors comprise the ownership of this firm, they must either pay taxes on the unwanted dividends or sell their shares and reinvest in other low-dividend firms. Accordingly, this migration of high-tax shareholders may result in unanticipated taxes and/or transaction costs, along with considerable inconvenience. Share price, at least in the short-run, undoubtedly will fall. Further, investors that actually prefer the new high-dividend policy, may wait for signs that the new high-dividend policy is credible. Overall, the dividend policy shift can create considerable tax-induced disruptions for existing shareholders.

The problems with a one-shot shift in dividend policy obviously are magnified by a firm adopting a totally residual policy. Under this policy, dividend prediction is unusually difficult; investors with any tax or consumption concerns are likely to stay away from firms that have such erratic dividend payouts.[2]

Because of the potential importance of tax considerations in making the dividend policy decision, financial managers should keep a close eye on changes in the tax code. Substantial changes may dictate a shift in dividend policy. The dual moral of our discussion is, Know Both Thy Investors and Tax Code! The tax situation of investors is the logical first place to look for clues about a firm's appropriate dividend policy. Evidence suggests that managers do pay attention to changes in the tax code. In the United Kingdom, for example, where the tax code changes frequently, firms adjust their payout policies in the direction of the tax changes (see Chapter 9).

---

[2] However, considering investors that hold well-diversified portfolios of stocks, erratic dividend payouts by any individual firm may lessen the volatility of the portfolio dividend yield.

11.3.2 Agency Costs

Firms should adopt a dividend policy that allows implementation of an investment policy that maximizes market value. In general, firms should not underpay dividends. Retained funds should be invested in projects that pass the NPV Rule. Having too much cash lying around is an ill-advised investment.[3] Consistent with this observation is research that illustrates that the market responds positively to the announcement of increases in capital expenditures.[4]

In short, excessive cash balances increase managers' degree of investment flexibility, which may be to the detriment of shareholders. After all, managers experience a normal set of human temptations. On the one hand, if management compensation and/or prestige is based on firm size or sales, the temptation exists to overinvest in projects or to acquire other firms that may not be strategically advisable nor value enhancing.

On the other hand, overpayment of dividends and underinvestment in positive NPV projects also are potential problems. These problems can be overcome by bond covenants that restrict dividend payouts.

As we have discussed, when managers negotiate dividend constraints with lenders, they attempt to obtain the optimal trade-off between future dividend flexibility and debt-holder protection, which influences the required interest rates. Managers should keep in mind the consequences of these dividend constraints with respect to their future options.

In general, high-growth firms can afford to write strict or tight dividend constraints that severely limit their ability to pay future dividends. Why? These firms are not plagued by overinvestment concerns given the abundance of good investment projects. These firms are likely to need outside financing regularly and therefore are subject to the discipline of frequent capital market scrutiny. Further, these firms have less need for future dividend flexibility because of their need to finance investment. High-growth firms have little need for dividend slack, or retaining dividend reserve-paying capacity under the con-

---

[3] See the discussion on Kerkorian versus Chrysler in Chapter 6, for example. Of course, flotation costs may make a temporary buildup of cash desirable if it is needed in subsequent periods. Again, however, this conclusion relies on an additional imperfection—flotation costs. Here, we are considering only agency-induced imperfections.

[4] See, for instance, the evidence in McConnell and Muscarella (1985). They found positive stock price reactions for announcement of capital expenditure increases for firms in industries that did not have established patterns of overinvestment.

straints, to ensure maintenance of an existing dividend payout in the future should tough economic times occur. Moreover, dividends are less important to investors in high-growth firms who seek out these firms in the expectation of receiving little, if any, dividend income. Dividend slack decreases the protection of debt holders and results in an interest rate that is too high relative to the risk of the debt.

For the opposite reasons, low-growth firms should negotiate looser dividend constraints. With a scarcity of future positive NPV investments, these firms are likely to generate large free cash flows that should be paid to shareholders. Without the dividend payout commitment, overinvestment may be a temptation. Dividend slack under the constraints is desirable in case of future economic setbacks and the desire to maintain a high dividend payout level.

Highly leveraged firms can write strict dividend policy constraints. Heavy debt service obligations limit these firms' ability to overinvest, and frequent refinancing provides capital market discipline. These firms also do not need to maintain dividend slack since it reduces the risk of the debt relative to the negotiated interest rate. Indeed, empirical research indicates that growth firms and firms with higher leverage, all else being equal, choose tighter dividend constraints and pay fewer dividends (see Kalay 1979). Thus, the evidence suggests that many financial practitioners share our views.

Low-leveraged firms also should negotiate looser dividend constraints relative to firms with high debt levels to provide future flexibility. Low debt service obligations mean less debt refinancing and discipline imposed by capital markets. Accordingly, dividends and dividend slack are relatively more important. Moreover, since debt levels are low anyway, wealth transfers to bondholders by maintaining slack is not a significant concern.

For high-growth firms with low leverage and broad ownership, dividends are relatively more important in controlling potential agency conflicts between managers and shareholders. All else being equal, dividend payments force a firm—especially a high-growth firm—to the capital markets more regularly. The scrutiny provided by the capital markets limits the extent of managements' self-serving behavior.

But, if managers own a significant percentage of outstanding shares, their interests are more closely aligned with shareholders than if they own few shares. Accordingly, we expect the optimal dividend payout to be a function of the level of management ownership. From an agency perspective, high management ownership suggests that a lower dividend payout may be appropriate, and vice versa.

As we have discussed, share repurchase is an alternative to dividend payments. In Chapter 10 we noted that share repurchase levels have increased rapidly since the mid 1980s. However, since repurchases are not proportional, they can be used to adjust the ownership base, which *may not* be in the remaining shareholders' best interest. In particular, repurchases can be used to thwart takeovers. In short, shareholders should be aware of consequences of repurchases versus dividends. From an agency cost perspective, the two methods of distributing cash to shareholders are quite different; share repurchases may amplify agency conflicts, whereas dividends may lessen them.

11.3.3 Asymmetric Information

Research consistently has shown that dividend changes convey significant information to the market. One of the most compelling pieces of empirical evidence regarding dividends is the announcement effect of dividend changes on share prices. Several empirical studies have documented significant increases in share prices when firms initiate payment of dividends for the first time or after a hiatus of at least five years. Several studies also have documented share-price increases on announcement of dividend increases versus dramatic share-price decreases when firms reduce dividends. Hence managers must be aware of documented market reactions before they make dividend policy decisions.

The collective wisdom of the literature suggests that, when a firm is underpriced relative to the private information held by managers, managers may be able to use dividends to establish a market value for the stock that is more in line with their private information. Since the payment of dividends has costs to management, managers have to evaluate the importance and urgency of establishing an appropriate market value. For example, if the firm or its shareholders are planning to sell securities, or if the firm is a potential takeover target, establishing the proper value of the firm—a value that incorporates favorable private information—is important. The extent of undervaluation by the market and the size of the required equity sale may be determinants of the dividend payout. For example, utility firms that issue equity periodically, often are advised by consultants to increase their dividend payout in anticipation of equity issues.

The empirical evidence also documents that the market infers different messages with respect to different dividend types. For instance, the market reacts more strongly to regular dividend increases relative to specially designated dividends, or dividends labeled *extra* or *special*.

Tender-offer share repurchases also are viewed as a more favorable signal versus open market repurchases, or Dutch-auction repurchases. This viewpoint suggests that temporary free cash flow increases are better distributed as special dividends and that regular dividends should be raised only when a permanent increase in free cash flow is anticipated.

Decreases in free cash flows should not be accompanied by dividend cuts, unless the reduced levels of free cash flow are expected to continue into the future. Investors interpret dividend cuts as especially bad news, and share prices decline dramatically when dividend cuts are announced.

Similarly, managers should be cautious about large increases in dividends, again to avoid the possibility of subsequent dividend decreases. If increases in free cash flows occur and are expected to persist, the dividend increases should be made gradually over time. Alternatively, or simultaneously with the increase in dividends, a firm should declare some of the distribution as a specially designated dividend or engage in some share repurchases, along with smaller dividend increases. This approach avoids making implicit (optimistic) statements that later may have to be reversed.

Again, while the market's interpretation of the underlying cause of dividend changes is not well understood, we do know that such changes are met with significant market reactions. This observation supports an effort to smooth dividends in relation to expected free cash flows over time.

Managers, by law, must not trade on inside information. In particular, managers should not trade in advance of imminent dividend change announcements to avoid the appearance of impropriety. Similarly, with respect to share repurchases as a substitute for dividends, insiders should avoid trading in their firm's shares prior to a share repurchase. Restrictions on managers' participation in share repurchases seems beneficial to shareholders, since insider trading influences the market's interpretation of the share-repurchase announcement.

11.3.4 Transaction Costs

Considered in isolation, the existence of transaction costs favors a managed dividend policy. If firms have a consistent and stable dividend policy—whether the policy is high, low, or no distribution—investors can select the policy that best matches their consumption and tax profiles.

Accordingly, based on this imperfection, managers should attempt to forecast the level of free cash flows over a reasonable time horizon. They should then attempt to tailor and stabilize their dividend payout level in accordance with anticipated free cash flows. Such a policy will minimize the transaction costs incurred by investors.[5]

For a growing company, where investment needs are high and the volatility of operating cash flows may be large, residual cash flows are likely to be low or even negative and erratic. Such firms are best advised to delay any dividend payments until a level of payout can be sustained comfortably. This payout gradually can be increased as growth rate and investment requirements moderate. For the mature company, the payout levels should be more generous, but again stabilized and targeted around the expected residuals.

11.3.5 Flotation Costs

Considered in isolation, flotation costs favor a residual policy. As we pointed out in Chapter 4, flotation costs can be substantial, especially for small firms and small equity issues. Accordingly, small firms should pay out cash only if operating cash flows exceed expected capital expenditure levels. Managing dividends will, almost without doubt, result in a higher level of flotation costs.

Use of a residual dividend policy, however, assumes that firms cannot forecast free cash flows. If a firm can forecast that free cash flows are positive this period, but that they will be negative in subsequent periods, they may wish to bank some of this excess to minimize future flotation costs. This decision can be viewed as a basic capital budgeting decision—choose the option of paying out or retaining free cash flow that has the most positive valuation impact.

11.3.6 Behavioral Considerations

To paraphrase Abraham Lincoln, you can fool all of the investors some of the time, some of the investors all of the time, but you can never fool all of the investors all of the time. Undoubtedly, some investors are seldom rational. However, only a few rational and

---

[5] Of course, diversified investors will achieve some stability of dividends by virtue of the portfolio effect relative to an investment in only a single firm that does not smooth dividends. In other words, the variability of the aggregate dividend in a portfolio of stocks, even if all stocks follow a residual dividend policy, should be less than the dividends for a single firm following a residual policy. This diversification effect will likely reduce the importance investors place on a stable dividend policy for a single firm.

well-endowed investors can call into question the notion that investor irrationality determines the relevance of dividend policy.

Imagine that irrational investors bid up the price of a firm having a "better" dividend policy relative to an otherwise identical firm (as measured by risk and future free cash flows) having a policy that is not preferred because of consumption and investment goals. If this pricing disequilibrium occurs, an arbitrage opportunity exists for investors that are neutral to dividend policy. These dividend-neutral investors will buy the low-priced firm and sell the high-priced firm until valuation differentials disappear. While in general we can subscribe to the potential influence of most market imperfections on the impact of dividend policy on firm valuation, the lack of investor rationality causes us the most difficulty. Accordingly, we have trouble including investor irrationality on the managers' list of dividend policy concerns.

11.4 Interactions of Market Imperfections

To this point we have discussed how individual market imperfections might influence dividend policy when viewed in isolation. However, in the real world, imperfections affect firms interactively, and managers should consider these interactions when making dividend policy decisions.

The number of permutations of the six market imperfections discussed is large. For instance, we could consider a market setting that includes (1) taxes and agency costs, (2) taxes and asymmetric information, (3) taxes plus transaction and floatation costs, (4) agency costs plus floatation costs, or (5) asymmetric information, taxes, transactions costs, and flotation costs. Even this partial list of interactions shows clearly that dealing with the numerous combinations comprehensively soon becomes mind-numbing; we begin to lose sight of the forest for the trees. Accordingly, we resist the temptation to discuss these interactions exhaustively.

11.5 Strategies in Dealing with Market Imperfections

Dealing strategically with market imperfections can be diagrammed on multidimensional axes in a *competing frictions* model, as illustrated in Figure 11.2, wherein the frictions (imperfections) are weighted by management's assessment of importance. As a starting point, we suggest the following strategy. Managers should qualitatively mark each market imperfection having an impact on their firm on a continuum reflecting their assessed level of importance. A few imperfections may loom large. Others may be dropped as inconsequential. Then the managers can sequentially analyze the dividend policy implications of the relevant imperfections. Decisions on the trade-offs among imperfections must be made in the context of their relative importance.

For example, let's say that management believes that three market imperfections—taxes, asymmetric information, and agency costs—are relevant to the dividend decision for their firm. Further, they believe that these imperfections affect their dividend decision in this same order of importance. Refer again to Figure 11.2. Within this framework, the managers consider each imperfection in isolation and then in combination to arrive at their choice of dividend policy.

11.5.1 An Example of Competing Frictions Resolution

Assume that the following characteristics are true of a certain firm.

- The firm is mature and has modest growth opportunities and large free cash flows.

- The firm has a moderate level of debt relative to others in its industry.

- The firm's majority owners are financial institutions and other corporations.

- The firm's management owns a modest equity stake.

These firm/owner characteristics suggest that a generous dividend payout level is appropriate. The majority owners do not suffer stiff taxes on an ample dividend payout since, with a current 70 percent dividend exclusion, only 30 percent of the dividends are taxed at 35 percent—an effective tax rate of only 10.5 percent. The high free cash flows give rise to potentially high agency costs. The moderate debt levels and low management ownership do not lessen these potential agency problems, but the generous dividend policy does reduce the overinvestment temptation. When management forecasts sustainable increases in the free cash flow, dividends are increased to reflect this positive asymmetric information. When management forecasts a temporary or intermittent increase in free cash flows, management engages in open market share repurchases.[6] The flexibility afforded by share repurchases allows management to keep payout low and avoid the need to reduce dividends when free cash flows later decrease. Under these conditions, transaction costs are not an issue because owners have selected this high-payout situation, and selling shares back to the corporation during a share repurchase is optional. Flotation costs are not an issue since the firm is generating cash flows in excess of investment needs.

11.5.2 A Dividend Life Cycle Example

Table 11.1 illustrates how a firm's dividend payout policy changes as a function of its life cycle. In this example, a promising start-up firm is initiated by a small group of entrepreneurs using their own capital, perhaps supplemented by funds from family members and/or venture capitalists. Outsiders understand little about the firm and its prospects. Management believes that growth prospects are outstanding but, to finance this growth, capital requirements will be large. However, access to the capital markets on any reasonable terms is not possible. Accordingly, at this early stage of the firm's life cycle, no dividends are practical. If we assume that the principals have high marginal tax rates, dividends would result in excessive personal taxes, capital requirements to finance growth are large, agency costs are nonexistent since agents and owners are the same, and, although asymmetric information is large, the firm has little need to signal its immediate prospects.

After a period of sales and asset increases, along with favorable earnings growth, the firm undertakes an initial public offering. At this point the underwriter, as well as the disclosure mandated by SEC filing requirements, serve as the signaling device for the market. However, ownership is still heavily concentrated among insiders and capital requirements are large. In order to issue debt financing on reasonable terms, the firm writes tight dividend constraints. Again, through this period of the firm's life cycle, a zero payout is best.

During a rapid growth phase with favorable earnings increases, the firm begins to tap the capital markets with debt issues and seasoned equity sales, although most of the investment is still financed with internally generated funds. Ownership concentration begins to fall as new equity investors are added. Some institutional investors

---

[6] Specially designated dividends might also be considered in lieu of share repurchases during periods of temporary free cash flow increases.

Table 11.1 Dividend Life Cycle

Firm Life-Cycle/ Market Frictions	Start-Up[a]	IPO[b]	Rapid Growth[c]	Maturity[d]	Decline[e]
Taxes to Equity Holders	High	High to majority owners	Declining with the addition of new equity owners	Declining with growing institutional ownership	Declining with institutional and corporate ownership
Agency Costs	Low	Low	Growing	High	Very high
Asymmetric Information	Extremely high	Very high	Moderating	Falling	Modest
Floatation Costs	High	High	Moderating	Low	Low
Transaction Costs	High	High	Moderating	Falling	Low
Implied Dividend Policy	No dividends	No dividends	Low-dividend payout policy	Growing dividend payout policy	Generous dividend payout policy

[a] Assumes abundant positive NPV investment opportunities, concentrated ownership among principals, and low leverage.

[b] Assumes abundant positive NPV investment opportunities, concentrated ownership, and low leverage.

[c] Assumes abundant positive NPV investment opportunities, frequent stock sales, decreasing ownership concentration, and growing leverage.

[d] Assumes declining positive NPV investment opportunities, growing institutional ownership, and stable leverage.

[e] Assumes scarce positive NPV investment opportunities, growing free cash flows, large institutional/corporate ownership, and declining leverage.

begin to take positions in the firm, lessening the average adverse impact of taxes on dividend payments. With frequent tapping of the capital markets, disclosure increases and the level of asymmetric information begins to fall.

Even though the firm has heavy investment needs, it may begin to pay a modest dividend to establish a dividend track record and appeal to a broader group of institutional investors. Competition begins to challenge the firm's dominant market position. The dividend constraint in the new debt issues is reduced, and the firm starts to build its capacity for dividend payments, or its reservoir of payable funds, for periods in which it will face declining investment opportunities.

The now-mature firm attracts growing institutional ownership, and the ownership level of officers and directors shrinks. Periodic external financing and continuous following by analysts reduces asymmetric information. However, positive NPV projects are harder to discover and sales growth slows. Potential agency costs begin to develop as the classic problem of the separation of ownership and control arise. Although leverage ratios remain at levels consistent with the firm's basic business risk, the firm may gradually increase its dividend payout in a sustainable manner based on forecasts of free cash flows.

Finally, further market erosion and new technology began to supplant the firm's basic markets. Operating cash flows far exceed investment requirements. Potential agency problems become increasingly large. The firm can begin to self-liquidate through extremely high dividend payout levels.

11.6 Conclusions

In Chapters 1–3 we demonstrated the irrelevance of dividend policy under the assumptions of perfect capital markets (PCM). In Chapters 4–7 we relaxed the individual PCM assumptions, one by one, to establish which, if any, market imperfections cause us to conclude that dividend policy is relevant. We then examined the theories regarding these market imperfections and summarized the empirical tests that relate to these theories. In Chapter 8 we documented the long-term consistency of management behavior in setting dividend payouts. In Chapter 9 we examined dividend policies around the world for insights into how various market imperfections—influenced by different laws and regulations in various countries—might be used to support or disprove various theories. Finally, in Chapter 10 we examined share repurchase as an alternative to dividend policy.

In conclusion we believe that dividend policy *can* have an impact on shareholder wealth because of various market imperfections. Accordingly, managers must design dividend policies around the market imperfections that most significantly affect their firms. Considering the imperfections in isolation (e.g., taxes) is not a trivial task. However, an even more challenging task for managers is evaluating the interaction of the permutations and combinations of market imperfections that may have an impact on the firm and its shareholders.

We believe that managers can assign weights to the imperfections that affect their firms and make reasonable assessments of the interactions of these imperfections. Once this task has been completed, managers can arrive at a "reasonable" dividend policy. Since the various imperfections affect firms differently, dividend policies naturally vary significantly from firm to firm.

Once a well-reasoned dividend policy has been articulated to the market, we are convinced that the market can be trusted to interpret the signal in a rational valuation process. Correct valuation is, after all, a major contribution of the capital markets.

References

Abrutyn, S., and R. Turner. "Taxes and Firms' Dividend Policies: Survey Results." *National Tax Journal* 43 (1990): 491–496.

Agrawal, A., and N. Jayaraman. "The Dividend Policies of All-Equity Firms: A Direct Test of the Free Cash Flow Theory." *Managerial Decision Economics* 15 (1994): 139–148.

Aharony, J., and I. Swary. "Quarterly Dividend and Earnings Announcement and Stockholders' Returns: An Empirical Analysis." *Journal of Finance* 35 (1980): 1–12.

Ambarish, R., K. John, and J. Williams. "Efficient Signaling with Dividends and Investments." *Journal of Finance* 42 (1987): 321–344.

Amihud, Y., and M. Murgia. "Dividends, Taxes, and Signaling: Evidence from Germany." *Journal of Finance* 52 (1997): 397–408.

Ang, J., D. Blackwell, and W. Megginson. "The Effect of Taxes on the Relative Valuation of Dividends and Capital Gains: Evidence from Dual-Class British Investment Trusts." *Journal of Finance* 46 (1991): 383–399.

Asquith, P., and D. Mullins, Jr. "The Impact of Initiating Dividend Payments on Shareholder's Wealth." *Journal of Finance* 56 (1983): 77–96.

———. "Signaling with Dividends, Stock Repurchase, and Equity Issues." *Financial Management* 18 (1986): 27–44.

Bagnoli, M., R. Gordon, and B. Lipman. "Stock Repurchase as a Takeover Defense." *Review of Financial Studies* 2 (1989): 423–443.

Bagwell, L. "Dutch Auction Repurchases: An Analysis of Shareholder Heterogeneity." *Journal of Finance* 47 no. 1 (1992): 71–105.

Bagwell, L., and J. Shoven. "Cash Distributions to Shareholders." *Journal of Economic Perspectives* 3, (1989): 129–140.

Bailey, W. "Canada's Dual Class Shares: Further Evidence on the Market Value of Cash Dividends." *Journal of Finance* 43 (1988): 1143–1160.

Baker, K., G. Farrelly, and R. Edelman. "A Survey of Management Views on Dividend Policy." *Financial Management* 14 (1985): 78–84.

Barclay, M. "Dividends, Taxes, and Common Stock Prices: The Ex-Dividend Day Behavior of Common Stock Prices before the Income Tax." *Journal of Financial Economics* 19 no. 1 (1987): 31–44.

Barclay, M., and C. Smith, Jr. "Corporate Payout Policy: Cash Dividends versus Open-Market Repurchases." *Journal of Financial Economics* 22 no. 1 (1988): 61–82.

Barker, C. "Price Changes of Stock-Dividend Shares at Ex-Dividend Dates." *Journal of Finance* 14 (1959): 373–378.

Bartholdy, J., and K. Brown. "Ex-Dividend Pricing and Personal Taxation in New Zealand 1982–1987." Working paper, University of Otago, Otago, New Zealand, 1994.

Bartov, E. "Open-Market Stock Repurchases as Signals for Earnings and Risk Changes." *Journal of Accounting and Economics* 14 (1991): 275–294.

Behm, U., and H. Zimmermann. "The Empirical Relationship Between Dividends and Earnings in Germany." *Zeitschrift fuer Wirtschafts und Sozialwissenschaften* 113 (1993): 225–254.

Benartzi, S., R. Michaely, and R. Thaler. "Do Changes in Dividends Signal the Future or the Past?" *Journal of Finance* 52 (1997): 1007–1034.

Bhattacharya, S. "Imperfect Information, Dividend Policy, and 'The Bird in the Hand Fallacy'" *Bell Journal of Economics* 10 (1979): 259–270.

Black, F. "The Dividend Puzzle." *Journal of Portfolio Management* 2 (1976): 5–8.

Black, F., and M. Scholes. "The Effects of Dividend Yield and Dividend Policy on Common Stock Prices and Returns." *Journal of Financial Economics* 1 (1974): 1–22.

Blume, M. "Stock Return and Dividend Yield: Some More Evidence." *Review of Economics and Statistics* 62 (1980): 567–577.

Blumenstein, Rebecca. "GM Directors Are Expected to Boost Dividend, Launch Stock Buy-Back." *The Wall Street Journal*, January 24, 1997, A3.

Booth, L. "The Dividend Tax Credit and Canadian Ownership Objectives." *Canadian Journal of Economics* 2 (1987): 321–339.

Booth, L., and D. Johnston. "The Ex-Dividend Day Behavior of Canadian Stock Prices: Tax Changes and Clientele Effects." *Journal of Finance* 39 (1984): 457–476.

Bradley, M., and L. Wakeman. "The Wealth Effects of Targeted Share Repurchases." *Journal of Financial Economics* 11 (1983): 301–328.

Brennan, M. "Taxes, Market Valuation and Financial Policy." *National Tax Journal* 23 (1970): 417–429.

Brennan, M., and A. Thakor. "Shareholder Preferences and Dividend Policy." *Journal of Finance* 45 no. 4 (1990): 993–1019.

Brickley, J. "Shareholder Wealth, Information Signaling, and the Specially Designated Dividend: An Empirical Study." *Journal of Financial Economics* 12 (1983): 187–210.

Brittain, J. "The Tax Structure and Corporate Dividend Policy." *American Economic Review* 54 no. 3 (1964): 272–287.

———. *Corporate Dividend Policy.* Washington, D.C.: The Brookings Institution, 1966.

Brook, Y., W. Charlton, Jr., and R. Hendershott. "Do Firms Use Dividends to Signal Large Future Cash Flow Increases?" *Financial Management* 27 (1998): 46–57.

Brown, D., and M. Ryngaert. "The Determinants of Tendering Rates in Interfirm and Self-Tender Offers." *Journal of Business* 65 (1992): 529–556.

Brown, P., and T. Walter. "Ex-Dividend Day Behavior of Australian Share Prices." *Australian Journal of Management* 11 (1986): 140–152.

Campbell, J., and W. Beranek. "Stock Price Behavior on Ex-Dividend Dates." *Journal of Finance* 10 no. 4 (1955): 425–429.

Capitelli, R. "The Dividend Puzzle: Some Empirical Evidence on the Swiss Stock Market." *Finanzmarkt und Portfolio Management* 3 (1989): 263–270.

Chaplinski, S., and N. Seyhun. "Dividends and Taxes: Evidence on Tax Reduction Strategies." *Journal of Business* 63 (1990): 239–260.

Chowdhry, B., and V. Nanda. "Repurchase Premia as a Reason for Dividends: A Dynamic Model of Corporate Payout Policies." *Review of Financial Studies* 7 no. 2 (1994): 321–350.

Comment, R., and G. Jarrell. "The Relative Signaling Power of Dutch-Auction and Fixed-Price Self-Tender Offers and Open-Market Share Repurchases." *Journal of Finance* 46 no. 4 (1991): 1243–1271.

Constantinides, G. "Capital Market Equilibrium with Personal Taxes." *Econometrica* 51 (1983): 611–636.

———. "Optimal Stock Trading with Personal Taxes." *Journal of Financial Economics* 13 (1984): 65–89.

Constantinides, G., and B. Grundy. "Optimal Investment with Stock Repurchase and Financing as Signals." *Review of Financial Studies* 2 (1989): 445–465.

Dammon, R., and R. Green. "Tax Arbitrage and the Existence of Equilibrium Prices of Financial Assets." *Journal of Finance* 42 (1987): 1143–1166.

Dann, L. "Common Stock Repurchases: An Analysis of Returns to Bondholders and Stockholders." *Journal of Financial Economics* 9 (1981): 113–138.

Dann, L., and H. DeAngelo. "Standstill Agreements, Privately Negotiated Stock Repurchases, and the Market for Corporate Control." *Journal of Financial Economics* 11 (1983): 275–300.

Dann, L., R. Masulis, and D. Mayers. "Repurchase Tender Offers and Earnings Information." *Journal of Accounting and Economics* 14 (1991): 217–251.

Denis, D. "Defensive Changes in Corporate Payout Policy: Share Repurchase and Special Dividends." *Journal of Finance* 45 (1990): 1433–1456.

Dewenter, K., and V. Warther. "Dividends, Asymmetric Information and Agency Conflicts: Evidence from a Comparison of Dividend Policies of Japanese and U.S. Firms." *Journal of Finance* 53 (1998): 879–904.

Dhillon, U., and H. Johnson. "The Effect of Dividend Changes on Stock and Bond Prices." *Journal of Finance* 49 (1994): 281–289.

Dorfman, J. "The Power of Dow Dividends." *The Wall Street Journal*, 11 November, 1996, C1.

Dunsby, A. "Share Repurchases, Dividends, and Corporate Distribution Policy." Working paper, Wharton School of Business, Philadelphia, 1994.

Durand, D., and A. May. "The Ex-Dividend Behavior of American Telephone and Telegraph Stock." *Journal of Finance* 15 no. 1 (1960): 19–31.

Dybvig, P., and S. Ross. "Tax Clientele and Asset Pricing." *Journal of Finance* 41 (1986): 751–771.

Dyl, E., and R. Weigand. "The Information Content of Dividend Initiations: Additional Evidence." *Financial Management* 27 (1998): 27–35.

Eades, K., P. Hess, and E. Kim. "On Interpreting Security Returns During the Ex-Dividend Period." *Journal of Financial Economics* 13 no. 1 (1984): 3–34.

———. "Time-Series Variation in Dividend Pricing." *Journal of Finance* 49 no. 5 (1994): 1617–1638.

Easterbrook, F. "Two Agency-Cost Explanations of Dividends." *American Economic Review* 74 (1984): 650–659.

Eckbo, E., and S. Verma. "Managerial Shareownership, Voting Power, and Cash Dividend Policy." *Journal of Corporate Finance* 1 (1994): 33–62.

Elton, E., and M. Gruber. "Marginal Stockholders' Tax Rates and the Clientele Effect." *Review of Economics and Statistics* 52 (1970): 68–74.

Fama, E. "The Empirical Relationship Between the Dividend and Investment Decisions of Firms." *American Economic Review* 64 (1974): 304–318.

Fama, E., and H. Babiak. "Dividend Policy: An Empirical Analysis." *Journal of the American Statistical Association* 63 no. 324 (1968): 1132–1161.

Frankfurter, G., and R. Wood, Jr. "The Evolution of Corporate Dividend Policy." *Journal of Financial Education* 23 (1997): 16–33.

Gay, G., J. Kale, and T. Noe. "Share Repurchases Mechanisms: A Comparative Analysis of Efficacy, Shareholder Wealth, and Corporate Control Effects." *Financial Management* 20 (1991): 44–59.

Gn, H. "Corporate Dividend Dynamics in Singapore: A Two-Step Approach." Working paper, National University of Singapore, 1994.

Gonedes, N. "Corporate Signaling, External Accounting, and Capital Market Equilibrium: Evidence on Dividends, Income, and Extraordinary Items." *Journal of Accounting Research* 16 (1978): 26–79.

Gordon, M. "Dividends, Earnings, and Stock Prices." *Review of Economics and Statistics* (1959): 99–105.

Gordon, R., and D. Bradford. "Taxation and the Stock Market Valuation of Capital Gains and Dividends: Theory and Empirical Results." *Journal of Public Economics* 14 (1980): 109–136.

Graham, B., D. Dodd, and S. Cottle. *Security Analysis.* Homewood, Ill.: Irwin, 1961.

Guthart, L. "More Companies Are Buying Back Their Stocks." *Harvard Business Review* 43 no. 2 (1965): 40–54.

Handjinicolaou, G., and A. Kalay. "Wealth Redistributions or Changes in Firm Value: An Analysis of Returns to Bondholders and the Stockholders around Dividend Announcements." *Journal of Financial Economics* 13 no. 1 (1984): 35–63.

Hausch, D., and J. Seward. "Signaling with Dividends and Share Repurchases: A Choice between Deterministic and Stochastic Cash Disbursements." *Review of Financial Studies* 6 (1993): 121–154.

Hayashi, F., and R. Jagannathan. "Ex-Day Behavior of Japanese Stock Prices: New Insights from New Methodology." *Journal of the Japanese and International Economies* 4 (1990): 401–427.

Healy, P., and K. Palepu. "Earnings Information Conveyed by Dividend Initiations and Omissions." *Journal of Financial Economics* 21 no. 2 (1988): 149–176.

Heath, D., and R. Jarrow. "Ex-Dividend Stock Price Behavior and Arbitrage Opportunities." *Journal of Business* 61 no. 1 (1988): 95–108.

Hertzel, M., and P. Jain. "Earnings and Risk Changes around Stock Repurchase Tender Offers." *Journal of Accounting and Economics* 14 (1991): 253–274.

Hietala, P. "Equity Markets and Personal Taxation: The Ex-Dividend Day Behavior of Finnish Stock Prices." *Journal of Banking and Finance* 14 (1990): 327–350.

Hubbard, J., and R. Michaely. "Do Investors Ignore Dividend Taxation? A Reexamination of the Citizen Utilities Case." Working paper, Cornell University, Ithaca, N.Y., 1996.

Ibbotson Associates. *Stocks, Bonds, Bills, and Inflation.* Chicago: Ibbotson Associates, 1998.

Ikenberry, D., J. Lakonishok, and T. Vermaelen. "Market Underaction to Open Market Repurchases." *Journal of Financial Economics* 39 (1995): 181–208.

Jayaraman, N., and K. Shastri. "The Valuation Impacts of Specially Designated Dividends." *Journal of Financial and Quantitative Analysis* 23 (1988): 301–312.

Jensen, G., D. Solberg, and T. Zorn. "Simultaneous Determination of Insider Ownership, Debt, and Dividend Policies." *Journal of Financial and Quantitative Analysis* 27 (1992): 247–264.

Jensen, M. "Agency Costs of Free Cash Flow, Corporate Finance, and Takeover." *American Economic Review* 76 (1986): 323–329.

Jensen, M., and C. Smith, Jr. "Stockholder, Manager and Credit Interests: Application of Agency Theory." In *Recent Advances in Corporate Finance*, edited by E. Altman and M. Subrahmanyam, 93–131. Homewood, Ill.: Irwin, 1985.

John, K., and A. Kalay. "Costly Contracting and Optimal Payout Constraints." *Journal of Finance*, 37 no. 2 (1982): 457–470.

John, K., and L. Lang. "Strategic Insider Trading around Dividend Announcements: Theory and Evidence." Working paper, New York University, 1991.

John, K., and B. Mishra. "Investment Announcements, Insider Trading and Market Response: Theory." *Journal of Finance* 45 (1990): 835–855.

John, K., and D. C. Nachman. "On the Optimality of Intertemporal Smoothing of Dividends." Working paper, New York University, 1986.

John, K., and J. Williams. "Dividends, Dilution, and Taxes: A Signaling Equilibrium." *Journal of Finance* 40 (1985): 1053–1070.

Kalay, A. "Dividend Policy: A Collection of Related Essays." Ph.D. diss., University of Rochester, 1979.

———. "The Ex-Dividend Day Behavior of Stock Prices: A Re-examination of the Clientele Effect." *Journal of Finance* 37 (1982a): 1059–1070.

———. "Stockholders–Bondholder Conflict and Dividend Constraints." *Journal of Financial Economics* 10 (1982b): 211–233.

———. "The Ex-Dividend Day Behavior of Stock Prices: A Re-examination of the Clientele Effect: A Reply." *Journal of Finance* 39 (1984): 557–561.

Kalay, A., and U. Loewenstein. "The Information Content of the Timing of Dividend Announcements." *Journal of Financial Economics* 16 (1986): 373–388.

Kalay, A., and R. Michaely. "Dividends and Taxes: A Reexamination." Working paper, University of Utah, Salt Lake City, Utah, 1993.

Kale, J., T. Noe, and G. Gay. "Share Repurchase through Transferable Put Rights: Theory and Case Study." *Journal of Financial Economics* 25 (1989): 141–160.

Kamma, S., G. Kanatas, and S. Raymar. "Dutch Auction versus Fixed-Price Self-Tender Offers for Common Stock." *Journal of Financial Intermediation* 2 (1992): 277–307.

Kaplanis, C. "Options, Taxes, and Ex-Dividend Day Behavior." *Journal of Finance* 41 (1986): 411–424.

Karpoff, J., and R. Walking. "Short Term Trading around Ex-Dividend Days: Additional Evidence." *Journal of Financial Economics* 21 (1988): 291–298.

Kato, K., and U. Loewenstein. "The Ex-Dividend-Day Behavior of Stock Prices: The Case of Japan." *Review of Financial Studies* 8 (1995): 817–847.

Kato, K., U. Loewenstein, and W. Tsay. "Voluntary Dividend Announcements in Japan." *Pacific-Basin Finance Journal* (forthcoming).

Klein, A., and J. Rosenfeld. "Targeted Share Repurchases and Top Management Changes." *Journal of Financial Economics* 20 (1988): 493–506.

Kumar, P. "Shareholder–Manager Conflict and the Information Content of Dividends." *Review of Financial Studies* 1 no. 2 (1988): 111–136.

Lakonishok, J., and T. Vermaelen. "Tax Reform and Ex-Dividend Day Behavior." *Journal of Finance* 38 (1983): 1157–1179.

———. "Tax Induced Trading around Ex-Dividend Dates." *Journal of Financial Economics* 16 (1986): 287–319.

———. "Anomalous Price Behavior around Repurchase Tender Offers." *Journal of Finance* 45 no. 2 (1990): 455–477.

Lambert, R., W. Lanen, and D. Larcker. "Executive Stock Option Plans and Corporate Dividend Policy." *Journal of Financial and Quantitative Analysis* 24 (1989): 409–426.

Lang, L., and R. Litzenberger. "Dividend Announcements: Cash Flow Signaling vs. Free Cash Flow Hypothesis." *Journal of Financial Economics* 24 (1989): 137–154.

La Porta, R., F. Lopez-de-Silanes, A. Shleifer, and R. Vishny. "Agency Problems and Dividend Policies around the World." Working paper, Harvard University, Cambridge, Mass., 1997.

Lasfer, M. "Ex-Day Behavior: Tax or Short-Term Trading Effects." *Journal of Finance* 50 (1995): 875–898.

Lazo, S. "Speaking of Dividends, How Do Corporate Leaders See Payouts?" *Barron's Online* (1999). Copyright 1999 Dow Jones & Company.

Leithner, S., and H. Zimmermann. "Market Value and Aggregate Dividends: A Reappraisal of Recent Tests, and Evidence from European Markets." *Swiss Journal of Economics and Statistics* 129 (1993): 99–119.

Lewellen, W., K. Stanley, R. Lease, and G. Schlarbaum. "Some Direct Evidence on the Dividend Clientele Phenomenon." *Journal of Finance* 33 no. 5 (1978): 1385–1399.

Lintner, J. "Distribution of Incomes of Corporations among Dividends, Retained Earnings, and Taxes." *American Economic Review*, 46 no. 2 (1956): 97–113.

Lipson, M., C. Maquieira, and W. Megginson. "Dividend Initiations and Earnings Surprises." *Financial Management* 27 (1998): 36–45.

Litzenberger, R., and K. Ramaswamy. "The Effects of Personal Taxes and Dividends on Capital Asset Prices: Theory and Empirical Evidence." *Journal of Financial Economics* 7 (1979): 163–195.

———. "Dividends, Short Selling Restrictions, Tax-Induced Investor Clientele and Market Equilibrium." *Journal of Finance* 35 (1980): 469–482.

———. "The Effects of Dividends on Common Stock Prices: Tax Effects or Information Effects?" *Journal of Finance* 37 (1982): 429–443.

Loderer, C. "The Residual Decision: Dividend Payments or Outside Financing." *Finanzmarkt und Portfolio Management* 3 (1989): 301–312.

Loewenstein, U., and J. Wang. "Strategic Tendering in Dutch Auction Share Repurchases." Working paper, University of Utah, Salt Lake City, 1997.

Long, J. "The Market Valuation of Cash Dividends: A Case to Consider." *Journal of Financial Economics* 6 (1978): 235–264.

Masulis, R. "Stock Repurchase by Tender Offer: An Analysis of the Causes of Common Stock Price Changes." *Journal of Finance* 35 no. 2 (1980): 305–321.

McConnell, J., and C. Muscarella. "Corporate Capital Expenditure Decisions and the Market Value of the Firm." *Journal of Financial Economics* 14 no. 3 (1985): 399–422.

McDonald, J., B. Jacquillat, and M. Nussenbaum. "Dividend, Investment and Financing Decisions: Empirical Evidence on French Firms." *Journal of Financial and Quantitative Analysis* 10 (1975): 741–755.

Michaely, R. "Ex-Dividend Day Stock Price Behavior: The Case of the 1986 Tax Reform Act." *Journal of Finance* 46 (1991): 845–860.

Michaely, R., and M. Murgia. "The Effects of Tax Heterogeneity on Prices and Volume around the Ex-Dividend Day: Evidence from the Milan Stock Exchange." *Review of Financial Studies* 8 (1995): 369–399.

Michaely, R., R. Thaler, and K. Womack. "Price Reactions to Dividend Initiations and Omissions: Overreaction or Drift?" *Journal of Finance* 50 (1995): 573–608.

Michaely, R., and J. Vila. "Equilibrium Determination of Stock Prices around the Ex-Dividend Day." *Journal of Financial and Quantitative Analysis* 30 no. 2 (1995): 171–198.

Mikkelson, W., and R. Ruback. "Targeted Repurchases and Common Stock Returns." *Rand Journal of Economics* 22 (1991): 544–561.

Miller, J. M., and J. J. McConnell. "Open-Market Share Repurchase Programs and Bid-Ask Spreads on the NYSE: Implications for Corporate Payout Policy." *Journal of Financial and Quantitative Analysis* 30 no. 3 (1995): 365–382.

Miller, M. "Debt and Taxes." *Journal of Finance* 32 no. 2 (1977): 261–275.

———. "The M–M Proposition after Thirty Years." *Journal of Economic Perspective* 2 no. 4 (1988): 99–120.

Miller, M., and F. Modigliani. "Dividend Policy, Growth and the Valuation of Shares." *Journal of Business* 34 no. 4 (1961): 411–433.

Miller, M., and K. Rock. "Dividend Policy under Asymmetric Information." *Journal of Finance* 40 (1985): 1031–1051.

Miller, M., and M. Scholes. "Dividends and Taxes." *Journal of Financial Economics* 6 (1978): 333–364.

———. "Dividends and Taxes: Empirical Evidence." *Journal of Political Economy* 90 (1982): 1118–1141.

Morgan, I. "Dividends and Capital Asset Prices." *Journal of Finance* 37 (1982): 1071–1086.

Ofer, A., and D. Siegel. "Corporate Financial Policy, Information, and Market Expectations: An Empirical Investigation of Dividends." *Journal of Finance* 42 (1987): 889–911.

Ofer, A., and A. Thakor. "A Theory of Stock Price Responses to Alternative Corporate Cash Disbursement Methods: Stock Repurchases and Dividends." *Journal of Finance* 42 (1987): 365–394.

Peterson, P., D. Peterson, and J. Ang. "Direct Evidence on the Marginal Rate of Taxation on Dividend Income." *Journal of Financial Economics* 14 (1985): 267–282.

Pettit, R. "Dividend Announcements, Security Performance, and Capital Market Efficiency." *Journal of Finance* 27 (1972): 993–1008.

Poterba, J. "The Market Valuation of Cash Dividends: The Citizens Utilities Case Reconsidered." *Journal of Financial Economics* 15 (1986): 395–406.

Poterba, J., and L. Summers. "The Economic Effects of Dividend Taxation." In *Recent Advances in Corporate Finance* edited by E. Altman and M. Subrahmanyam. Homewood, Ill.: Irwin, 1985.

———. "New Evidence That Taxes Affect the Valuation of Dividends." *Journal of Finance* 39 (1984): 1397–1415.

Procianoy, J., and H. Snider. "Tax Changes and Dividend Payout: Is Shareholders' Wealth Maximized in Brazil?" Working paper, New York University, 1994.

Rosenberg, B., and V. Marathe. "Tests of Capital Asset Pricing Hypotheses." *Research in Finance* 1 (1979): 115–224.

Ross, S., R. Westerfield, and J. Jaffe. *Corporate Finance*. Chicago: Irwin, 1996.

———. *Corporate Finance*. Chicago: Irwin, 1999.

Shefrin, H., and M. Statman. "Explaining Investor Preferences for Cash Dividends." *Journal of Financial Economics* 13 (1984): 253–282.

Shoven, J. "The Tax Consequences of Share Repurchases and Other Nondividend Cash Payments to Equity Owners." In *Tax Policy and the Economy Vol. I*, edited by L. Summers, 29–54. Cambridge, Mass: NBER and MIT Press, 1986.

Singh, A., M. Zaman, and C. Krishnamurti. "Liquidity Changes Associated with Open Market Repurchases." *Financial Management* 23 (1994): 47–55.

Sinha, S. "Share Repurchase as a Takeover Defense." *Journal of Financial and Quantitative Analysis* 26 (1991): 233–244.

Smith, C., Jr. "Alternative Methods for Raising Capital: Rights versus Underwritten Offerings." *Journal of Financial Economics* 5 no. 3 (1977): 273–307.

Smith, C., Jr., and R. Watts. "The Investment Opportunity Set and Corporate Financing, Dividend, and Compensation Policies." *Journal of Financial Economics* 32 no. 3 (1992): 263–292.

Thaler, R., and H. Shefrin. "An Economic Theory of Self-Control." *Journal of Political Economy* 89 no. 2 (1981): 392–406.

Vermaelen, T. "Common Stock Repurchases and Market Signaling: An Empirical Study." *Journal of Financial Economics* 9 (1981): 139–183.

———. "Repurchase Tender Offers, Signaling, and Managerial Incentives." *Journal of Financial and Quantitative Analysis* 19 (1984): 163–181.

Wansley, J., W. Lane, and S. Sarkar. "Managements' View on Share Repurchase and Tender Offer Premiums." *Financial Management* 18 (1989): 97–110.

Watts, R. "The Information Content of Dividends." *Journal of Business* 46 no. 2 (1973): 191–211.

Williams, J. "Efficient Signaling with Dividends, Investment, and Stock Repurchases." *Journal of Finance* 43 (1988): 737–747.

"Windmere-Durable Holidays, Inc. to Omit Dividend for Reinvestment Purposes." PR Newswire Association, Inc. (August 28, 1997).

Woods, D., and E. Brigham. "Stockholder Distribution Decisions: Share Repurchases or Dividends?" *Journal of Financial and Quantitative Analysis* 1 (1966): 15–25.

Woolridge, J., and C. Ghosh. "Dividend Cuts: Do They Always Signal Bad News?" *Midland Corporate Finance Journal* 3 (1985): 20–32.

Credits

F. Black. "The Dividend Puzzle" from *Journal of Portfolio Management* 2, 1976. Copyright © 1976 by Institutional Investors' Journals. Reprinted by permission.

R. Blumenstein. "GM Directors Are Expected to Boost Dividend, Launch Big Stock Buy-Back" from *The Wall Street Journal*, January 24, 1997. Copyright © 1997 by Dow Jones & Company, Inc. Reprinted by permission of Dow Jones, Inc., via Copyright Clearance Center, Inc. All rights reserved worldwide.

K. Bradsher. "Chrysler Lifts Dividend and Splits Its Stock" from *The New York Times*, May 17, 1996. Copyright © 1996 by the New York Times Co. Reprinted by permission.

"Dividend Dilemmas" from *The Economist*, August 15, 1992. Copyright © 1992 by The Economist Newspaper Group, Inc. Reprinted by permission. Further reproduction prohibited (www.economist.com).

J. R. Dorfman. "The Power of Dow Dividends" from *The Wall Street Journal*, November 11, 1996. Copyright c 1996 by Dow Jones & Company, Inc. All rights reserved worldwide. Reprinted by permission of Dow Jones, Inc., via Copyright Clearance Center, Inc. All rights reserved worldwide.

K. Eades, P. Hess, and E. Kim. "Time-Series Variation in Dividend Pricing" from *Journal of Finance* 49:5, 1994. Copyright © 1994 by Journal of Finance. Reprinted by permission of Blackwell Publishers.

"Financial Indicators" from *The Economist*, June 4, 1994. Copyright © 1994 by The Economist Newspaper Group, Inc. Reprinted by permission. Further reproduction prohibited (www.economist.com).

R. Forsyth. "MOF Beckons Japanese Capital Homeward" from *Barron's*, March 2, 1992. Copyright © 1994 by Dow Jones & Company, Inc. Reprinted by permission of Dow Jones, Inc., via Copyright Clearance Center, Inc. All rights reserved worldwide.

G. Frankfurter and R. Wood, Jr. "The Evolution of Corporate Dividend Policy" from *Journal of Financial Education* 23, 1997. Copyright © 1997 by Journal of Financial Education. Reprinted by permission.

"German Corporate Governance: Stirring Things Up" from *The Economist*, December 18, 1993. Copyright © 1993 by The Economist Newspaper Group, Inc. Reprinted by permission. Further reproduction prohibited (www.economist.com).

R. D. Hylton. "How to Ride Along When the Board Tries to Boost the Stock" from *Fortune*, February 20, 1995. Copyright © 1995 by Time Inc. All rights reserved.

S. McGee. "Universe of Attractive Stocks Is Shrinking" from *The Wall Street Journal*, October 22, 1997. Copyright © 1997 by Dow Jones & Company, Inc. Reprinted by permission of Dow Jones, Inc., via Copyright Clearance Center, Inc. All rights reserved worldwide.

"Muddle About Dividends" from *The Economist*, June 4, 1994. Copyright © 1994 by The Economist Newspaper Group, Inc. Reprinted by permission. Further reproduction prohibited (www.economist.com).

R. Narsetti and G. Anders. "IBM Plans $3.5 Billion Repurchase" from *The Wall Street Journal*, October 29, 1997. Copyright © 1997 by Dow Jones & Company, Inc. Reprinted by permission of Dow Jones, Inc., via Copyright Clearance Center, Inc. All rights reserved worldwide.

S. Neumeier. "Finding the High-Yielding Stocks of Tomorrow" from *Fortune*, August 22, 1994. Copyright © 1994 by Time Inc. All rights reserved.

F. Norris. "Dividends Rise, But Not as Fast as Stocks" from *The New York Times*, January 3, 1997. Copyright © 1997 by the New York Times Co. Reprinted by permission.

"Reebok to Buy Back 17 Million Shares for $612.7 Million" from *The Wall Street Journal*, August 30, 1996. Copyright © 1996 by Dow Jones & Company, Inc. Reprinted by permission of Dow Jones, Inc., via Copyright Clearance Center, Inc. All rights reserved worldwide.

"U.S. Firms Buy Back Stock at a Record-Setting Pace" from *Los Angeles Times*, March 23, 1996. Copyright © 1996 by Los Angeles Times Syndicate. Reprinted by permission.

T. T. Vogel, Jr. "Global Trades Proving to Be Taxing Issue" from *The Wall Street Journal*, November 16, 1994. Copyright © 1994 by Dow Jones & Company, Inc. Reprinted by permission of Dow Jones, Inc., via Copyright Clearance Center, Inc. All rights reserved worldwide.

W. T. Wilson. "Investor's Memo: Market Often Takes Cue from Dividends" from *The Detroit News*, August 5, 1996. Copyright © 1996 by The Detroit News. Approved by Mark Silverman, Publisher and Editor. Reprinted by permission of The Detroit News.

"Windmere-Durable Holdings, Inc., to Omit Dividend for Reinvestment Purposes" from *PR Newswire*, August 28, 1997. Copyright © 1997 by PR Newswire Association, Inc. Reprinted by permission of Windmere-Durable Holding, Inc.

Index